W.B. YEATS

Vain, Glorious, Lout

A Maker of Modern Ireland

[handwritten signature]

04/06/03

Bought in Kenny's, Galway.

ANTHONY J. JORDAN

WESTPORT BOOKS 2003

ACKNOWLEDGEMENTS

I would like to thank the following for assistance and permission to use material:

The Pembroke and Ringsend Public Libraries of Dublin City Council, Mary Kelligher and Gerard Whelan of the Royal Dublin Society Library, National Library of Ireland particularly Noel Kissane and his successor Gerry Lyons, St Patrick's College, Drumcondra Library, National Archives, Trinity College Archives, UCD Archives, Yeats Society Sligo, Abbey Theatre, Allen Library, National Gallery Ireland, Hugh Lane Municipal Gallery, AP Watt on behalf of Michael Yeats, Royal Irish Academy, Anna MacBride White for her great generosity, Brian Mooney, Donal O'Donnell, Donal McCracken, Una Higgins O'Malley, Mary Jordan, Fiona Jordan, Tom Delanty, Kevin Kiely, Gerard MacAtasney, Jonathan Williams, Fr. Aidan Lehane, Michael McCann, Michael O'Connor, Donal O'Connor, Eamonn McGoldrick, Eamonn Scully, and David Lowe.

Designed and Printed by the Central Remedial Clinic.

THIS BOOK IS DEDICATED TO:

MARY

JOAN

PAT

SINEAD

TERRY

and

MR. MICHAEL MURPHY,

whom I love, despite or may be because of, his affinity with Robert Browning's *Last Duchess,* which so annoyed the Duke.

CONTENTS

Introduction 6

Ch. 1 A Betrayal of Lady Gregory 12

Ch. 2 Son and Sibling 25

Ch. 3 Patrons of the Artist 46

Ch. 4 Machiavelli at the Abbey 62

Ch. 5 Sectarian Snob 80

Ch. 6 John O'Leary's Grave 88

Ch. 7 *An Old Bellows, full of angry wind?* 98

Ch. 8 Glorious Willie Yeats 115

Ch. 9 Assassinating John MacBride 129

Ch. 10 Nation Builder 153

Ch. 11 A Fanatic Heart 168

Notes 178

Select Bibliography 190

Index 191

INTRODUCTION

The Yeats family had a background as ministers in the Church of Ireland. WB Yeats' great-grandfather was Rector at Drumcliff in Sligo. His grandfather retired from his ministry in County Down to live in Sandymount in Dublin, beside his rich cousins, the Corbets of Sandymount Castle. William's father, John Butler Yeats, was a non-believer with artistic pretensions, who disapproved of religious practices. He attended Trinity College in Dublin and became a lawyer. He devilled for Isaac Butt at the Four Courts and qualified as a barrister in 1866.

The Pollexfens of Sligo, William's mother's family, were successful shipping merchants. They had married into the Middleton family, and both became synonymous with the commercial life of Sligo for over a century.[1] They were known as hard-nosed business people.

John Yeats, the poet's father, went to school at the Atholl Academy on the Isle of Man. George Pollexfen of Sligo was a fellow student there. He was a dour youth, interested in séances and astrology. These unusual interests made him a magnet for his peers, especially John Yeats. Their friendship led to John becoming acquainted with Susan Pollexfen, George's beautiful sister. Without knowing each other very well, apart from much letter writing, they married in St. John's Church in Sligo on 10 September 1863.

George's Villas, Sandymount.

7

It was reasonable to suppose, as the Pollexfen family did, that Susan had prospects of a comfortable middle class life with a professional man, who had Sligo connections. The couple moved into a house at George's Villas, on Sandymount Avenue, and John continued his legal studies. He had a small income from his father's estate. Their first child, William, was born less than two years after the marriage, on 13 June 1865. John was called to the Bar six months later.

Susan was lonely in the city, away from her large family and without servants. She had the Pollexfen characteristic of being dour and unemotional. During their brief courtship, John had regularly drawn little pictures on his letters to Susan. At the Four Courts, as long legal arguments developed, he passed the time by continually drawing sketches of Court figures. When a London magazine praised one of these, John decided that the law was not for him. He would go to London, train to be a portrait painter and become rich and famous. To the consternation of the Pollexfens and his wife, this is what he did. Encumbered with two infants, to be quickly followed by four more, John took his family to live, in poverty, in a variety of rented accommodation in London. He proved to be a hopeless, feckless husband and father, interested only in pursuing his own bohemian lifestyle, a great conversationalist, but never able to make ends meet.

The Pollexfens, though having their own domestic and business problems, did the best they could for Susan and her children. They gave them long summer holidays in Sligo, keeping them there continually from July 1872 to October 1874. When Jack, the youngest child, was born, his grandparents insisted, for the most part, in raising him in Sligo. Merville, the Pollexfen house, and Sligo were excitement, family, recognition, position, freedom, for the children and Susan.

When John Yeats visited, there was tension. He sought to establish an especially close relationship with his eldest son, called Willie by family and friends. Willie was sensitive, nervous and exceptionally poor at reading, and his father blamed it on the Pollexfen influence. This caused grievance to Susan, who began to see Willie as quite like his father. She grew to detest Willie, always blaming him as a child for anything that went amiss. He and the next-born child, Lily, became close confidants with their father. During one visit to Merville, John insisted on Willie returning with him to London to escape the Pollexfen influence.

Susan's hopes for any improvement in family life were constantly shattered.

The early death of two of her children made her depressed. Lily and Willie heard her cry out, *my little son, my little son*, as Robert was taken away from Merville to die. She hated London and each return journey drove her to more and more despair. Her health suffered badly and the family unit became more dysfunctional.

For the young poet this unhappy childhood, and the rejection by his mother, was to leave a permanent scar that he never came to terms with. The closest he dealt with it was possibly in his 1891 autobiographical novel, *John Sherman*, as he writes tenderly of Sligo and his mother. At the Godolphin School in London from 1877 to 1881, he is remembered as exhibiting sensitive and artistic tendencies.

In the autumn of 1881, a collapse in the already precarious family finance forced the family back to Dublin. They lived in the port town of Howth first, where Susan recovered some of her old self. John took a studio in Harcourt Street, and Willie enrolled in the Erasmus Smith School. Father and son travelled by train together into the city each day, with John endeavouring to influence his son's literary tastes by reading Shelley to him. The family later moved to Terenure, and Willie and his two sisters enrolled at the Metropolitan School of Art. Willie feared that he would fail the matriculation examination for Trinity College, and did not follow in the family tradition there.

During these years, Willie began to write poetry and meet people who would influence his future career, including, George Russell, Ellen and John O'Leary, Charles Johnston, Katherine Tynan, Sara Purser, TW Rolleston, Charles Oldham, Edward Dowden and Douglas Hyde. The single most important of these was John O'Leary, whom he met at the Contemporary Club and the Young Ireland Society. O'Leary inspired Willie and provided him with the books to educate himself in the ancient culture of Ireland, which hitherto had been alien to him.

After spending six years in Dublin, the family moved back to London again in 1887. London was horrid for the two sisters, but they made the best of it. Jack, because of his more normal upbringing by his grandparents in Sligo, was a happy-go-lucky, pleasing individual, who gradually developed a successful career as an illustrator and painter. John continued in his normal routine, forever the optimist.

Willie, who had fashioned his own lifework with Ireland, developed sufficient contacts there to commute regularly between Ireland and London.

His introduction to Maud Gonne led to further reasons for him to become closely involved in matters Irish. All the time, he was raising his profile as a poet of stature who would greatly influence the Irish Revival.

Maud Gonne had a profound influence on Willie Yeats from 1889 to at least 1917, only beginning to diminish after his marriage. Maud, his muse, regarded his poetry as their children, the result of their spiritual marriage. They collaborated on many projects and, though he continually lusted after her, he would never compromise his artistic principles to assuage her more advanced form of nationalism. In the text, I have been able, through extensive usage of her letters to him, to illustrate their long and intense interaction. Their unique friendship survived many differences of fundamental opinion over the years. After her marriage to Major John MacBride in 1903, Willie's interest in Irish nationalism waned somewhat. He would not blame Maud for abandoning him, but deflected all his hatred on to the person of her husband.

Willie was attractive to many women and he used this to good effect in a variety of ways during his lifetime. Edward Martyn wrote of him: *he has, above all a weird appearance, which is triumphant with middle-aged masculine women, and a dictatorial manner which is irresistable with the considerable bevy of female and male mediocrities interested in intellectual things.*[2] Willie was Victorian in his attitude to women, and most existed to be used and could not be regarded as equal to men.

His first lecture tour in America in 1903, organised by John Quinn, was of enormous importance to him. It liberated him from the narrow sectarianism of Dublin. The lionisation he received in America reassured him in his political and aesthetic attitudes, and reinforced his new Nietzschean philosophy of the superman. Willie's new attitude of superiority was applied to all he came in contact with, except the very very few he felt shared his exalted stature of 'artist'. His close collaborators in the Abbey Theatre enterprise bore the brunt of this exalted status, save for JM Synge alone. He became even more insufferable to his family. He put on a mask for the rest of his life, and became a 'hero', a 'superman'. He was aware of how important he and his role in the Irish Revival was, and would be viewed in history. He became very careful of how his work and actions would appear to others, seeking to have his version available and accepted. It may be in this context that Denis Donoghue argued in *The Hard Case of Yeats* in 1977 that the ideal critical study would deal with virtually everything, but *never take his [Yeats'] word for anything, or mistake the intention for the achievement.*[3]

Eventually all of the Yeats family returned to live and work in Ireland. After living for a few years in Dublin with his daughters, John Yeats went on a holiday to New York, and remained there for the rest of his life. Jack lived in Devon after his marriage, but in 1910 returned to live permanently in Ireland. Willie continued his peripatetic existence between England and Ireland for several more years.

The advent of the quest for Home Rule, but especially the Easter Rising of 1916, with its tragic aftermath, re-ignited Willie's earlier advanced nationalist feelings. While some may argue that his great canonical poem, *Easter 1916,* was equivocal, *Sixteen Dead Men* and *The Rose Tree,* together form a powerful statement of an Irish national identity separate from England.

The refusal of his proposal of marriage by the widowed Maud Gonne, and by her daughter Iseult Millevoye, brought Willie to his senses, as he quickly married Georgie Hyde Lees in 1917. A family life, the arrival of children, the return to live in Ireland, and the War of Independence and the Civil War, all gave the poet a new lease of creative energy.

The new State was very happy to welcome and honour the poet. He became a friend of Government Ministers and was appointed to the second House of Parliament, the Senate. International recognition quickly followed, as he won the Nobel Prize for Literature in 1923. This brought a welcome monetary reward. He played a formidable role in the development of the new State, particularly in the field of civil liberties. He became disillusioned as he saw the hated Catholic clerical class dominate.

1932 was a watershed year in Ireland as De Valera came to power in peaceful circumstances. Lady Gregory died and Coole Park was no more for Yeats. His friend from youth, though more recently a severe critic, George Russell, left Ireland, disillusioned by political developments and the power of the Church. He wrote to WB Yeats in language which he may have intended as a commentary on the recipient himself, *Dublin is depressing these days. Ireland seems to be in my age like a lout I knew in boyhood who had become a hero and then subsided into being a lout again.*

The advent of Fascism in Europe gave Yeats the opportunity to dally with a pseudo - Irish version The Blueshirts. His innate conservative and aristocratic elitist tendencies rose as he dabbled with the notion of a pure noble race, so beloved of Nietzsche, and adopted by the Nazis.

Ill-health and impending old age beckoned and he repaired more and more to the warmth of the continent. He had a minor operation that renewed him physically and psychologically. His poetry flourished with his renewal of sexual energy.

Willie Yeats was a great poet and thinker, and a great Irishman, though not without faults.

The treatment in the text is of a thematic nature, resulting in some repetition.

CHAPTER 1

A BETRAYAL OF LADY GREGORY

Lady Augusta Gregory was born to the large evangelical Persse family in County Galway in 1852. Unlike her older siblings she was quiet and bookish, and despite her mother's efforts remained unmarried at the age of twenty-seven. Her eldest brother, Richard, fell seriously ill, and a warm climate was recommended for him. His mother took him to Nice. Augusta went with them to help with the nursing. There, they met a near neighbour of theirs, Sir William Gregory of Coole Park. He had recently retired from the governorship of Ceylon, aged sixty-three. Sir William naturally paid attention to the Persses and, to everyone's surprise, was quite at ease in the company of the shy Augusta. When they moved on to Rome, Sir William followed. He discovered that Augusta was interested in literature, but her home at Roxborough had no library. When they all returned to Galway, Sir William invited Augusta to select any six books from his fine library at Coole. They married the following year of 1880. They also had a house in London. Her son Robert was born there in 1881, with questions raised about his paternity. Some of the locals believed that a blacksmith named Seánín Farrell was the father. He later emigrated to America, with passage paid.[1]

The married couple spent much time travelling in Europe and the Middle East and, while in Egypt, they met and became close friends with Wilfred Scawen Blunt and his wife. Blunt was a poet and well- known philanderer, who took up the cause of Egyptian nationalism and later Irish Home Rule. Lady Gregory fell in love with him and they had a passionate affair. Blunt, a Catholic, described Lady Gregory in his *'Secret Memories',* which were never published and form part of his papers in the Fitzwilliam Museum, as a *quiet little woman of perhaps five and twenty, rather plain than pretty, but still attractive, with much good sense and a fair share of Irish wit. It was a consummation neither of us, I think, foresaw and was a quite new experience in her quiet life…the passionate element in our intercourse at this time proved* a *source of inspiration and of strength. It was under its influence that I was able to carry on that hardest battle of my life, the rescuing of Arabi from the vengeance of his enemies - she working with me and advising and encouraging.* Lady Gregory described the affair as *the joy I was so late to understand.* She wrote several sonnets celebrating the affair.

Lady Gregory by J.B. Yeats 1903.
(Courtesy of National Gallery of Ireland)

I kiss the ground
On which the feet of him I love have trod,
And bow before his voice whose least sweet sound
Speaks louder to me than the voice of God.

Elizabeth Longford's biography of Blunt, *A Pilgrimage of Passion,* makes it clear that Blunt's wife knew of the affair with Gregory[2]. It is less certain that Gregory's husband also knew. Longford writes that Blunt and Lady Gregory remained life-long friends. He assisted her and Willie Yeats obtain a patent for the Abbey, through his cousin, George Wyndham, the Irish Secretary. He contributed to the *Cuchulain* Cycle of plays produced the Abbey, with his, *Fand of the Fair Cheek.*[3]

After her husband's death in 1892, Lady Gregory spent more of her time at Coole, but kept the family home in London. She developed an interest in the Irish language and Irish folklore.

Though Lady Gregory had seen WB Yeats in the spring of 1894 in London,[3a] it was some two years later before their fateful meeting, at Tulira Castle, in county Galway, occurred. Yeats, nearly thirty years old, soon began a custom that was to last for twenty years of spending long summers at Coole Park. Gregory and Coole replaced the Pollexfens and Sligo for him.

In the beginning, she was quite interested in having an affair or even possibly marrying Yeats, though she was thirteen years his senior. She found him an attractive, amusing and entertaining genius. Gregory made her intentions clear when she presented herself to Maud Gonne at the Nassau Hotel, demanding to know what Gonne's 'intentions' were, to Mr. Yeats.[3b] Maud thought her most relieved when informed that there was no question that she would marry Mr Yeats. He had told Gregory almost at the start of their relationship of his love for Maud and his unavailability to other women. He made a point of always addressing her in the formal way as 'Lady Gregory', though she addressed him as 'Willie'. The local people would sometimes refer to him mockingly as *Lady Yeats.* Gregory and Yeats developed a close collaborative personal working relationship for the next forty years.

She appealed to him as a higher class Protestant, and a generous benefactor.

Their first collaborative exercise consisted of a survey on local fairy tales and folklore. While they both visited the local cottages, she, knowing the language, carried out the work. He, dressed all in black, appeared like a proselytiser to the people. Yeats wrote up the survey, which was published under his name alone. Under the influence of Gonne, and others, Willie was moving towards a form of nationalism, while Gregory was disembarking from traditional unionism.

Coole Park proved a sanctuary and an inspiration for Yeats. The paths, woods, lake, the walled garden, rare trees, and the long driveway up to the Georgian house, were what he imagined his own rightful inheritance should have been. In the evenings, after hours of tortuous composing, he emerged to regale Gregory and her guests, often including George Russell, Edward Martyn, JM Synge, over dinner with captivating conversation and monologue. For Yeats, Coole Park was like a compass point, which attracted artists, the last romantics, for a period. Fortified by Lady Gregory's powerful character, and the intellectual sweetness of the dreaming air, they flew away, certain of their mission. Everything at Coole was organised to facilitate the great man's comfort and provided an ambience for work. It was there that the idea of an Irish theatre was first mooted, which Yeats envisaged being a French-style playwrights' theatre, rather than an English-style actors' theatre.

Lady Gregory involved herself with the three Yeats menfolk. She championed Jack's painting, buying some of his early work and organising an exhibition for him in Dublin. She tried to set up an exhibition for John Yeats. When Willie was ill in London, she looked after him at Woburn Buildings. She bought him a large leather chair, a new suit, and decorated his rooms. There was no element of his health that she did not involve herself in. In London, too, she was able to introduce him to an upper stratum of society that alone he could only dream about. She was instrumental in lobbying the Government to grant licences to theatres whose aims were , with both the Royal and the Gaiety booked out by English touring companies, for the most profitable periods of each year.

One of the longest and personally disagreeable services Gregory had to minister to Willie concerned his love for Maud Gonne. In spite of her own feelings for him, she acted as his agony aunt, counsellor and nurse, on interminable occasions, as his hopes were raised and dashed and raised again. To make matters worse, Gregory could not abide Gonne, about whom she wrote, 'God is unjust if she dies a quiet death'.[3c] Gregory must have felt Willie a fool to be taken in so readily and so long by his adherence to his spiritual marriage with Gonne. Despite her acceptance of a proprietorial responsibility towards Willie, she accepted all his faults and failings. She

16

was adamant that together they would produce a revolution of theatrical culture that would survive them all.

The early plays of Yeats were in fact collaborative works with Gregory. She appears, moreover, to have been the main author of his Cathleen ni hUalachain,[4] which, featuring Gonne in the leading role, had such an effect on nationalist Ireland. In their early years working together, Gregory purported to be content with oblique acknowledgement.[5] He was willing enough to acknowledge her material involvement, but not her creative input, which might challenge his authorial primacy. She later complained of his tendency to treat one as a 'tag', whether in collecting peasant folklore for him, or in producing peasant speech for his plays, while he retained complete 'authorship' and she has to be satisfied with a mention as an anonymous helper.[6]

Maud Gonne realised the literary importance of Lady Gregory. She also realised that Willie did not quite appreciate it. After reading Gregory's play, *The White Cockade* in December 1905, Gonne wrote to Willie in December 1905, saying:

I have just read the 'White Cockade'. Indeed you did not say too much about it! It is wonderful to read, & must be wonderful to see acted.

Lady Gregory knows the soul of our people & expresses it as no one else does. Through the surface of triviality, of selfish avarice, of folly which often jars on one, she never ceases to see & express in her writing that deep passion which only heroic action or thought is able to arouse in them, & when once aroused makes them capable of sacrifice for ideals as no other people on earth are. It is a play that will live & I know I shall often have the opportunity of seeing it, which consoles me little for missing its first production. It is a play that will be popular – don't look contemptuous – such plays are needed for your work & for the public.

Maud and Lady Gregory had a strained relationship. They were competitors. Maud was concerned at the amount of Willie's time taken up by theatrical affairs. She believed that Willie was essentially a poet and that she was his muse. On occasion she became annoyed that he spent so much time on the Abbey. She wrote him in extraordinary terms:

Our children were your poems, of which I was the Father sowing the unrest & storm which made them possible & you the mother who brought them forth in suffering & in the highest beauty & our children had wings.

Despite this, Maud did realise the importance of his work in the theatre. She had no hesitation in acknowledging the comparable role of Lady Gregory there, and so informed Willie, on 15 September 1911:

You & Lady Gregory have a child also, the theatre company & Lady Gregory is the Father who holds you to your duty of motherhood in true marriage style. That child requires much feeding & looking after. I am sometimes jealous for my children.

As late as January 1914, Maud was most careful to let Yeats know how highly she regarded Lady Gregory's writings. She was, however, critical of a new book by Lady Gregory on the history of the Abbey Theatre, but added a postscript to a letter to Willie, explaining:

I have opened my letter this morning to add this. I don't want you to think that because I don't care much for Lady Gregory's book on the theatre, I underrate her work – I think she has done great work & has shown great courage & staying power – her perseverance under difficulties has been wonderful – I also think her books on Cuchulain & Finn most valuable & most charming. I have read & reread them many times & always with delight.

At the age of sixty, Lady Gregory had a passionate affair with John Quinn during an Abbey tour of America. She confessed to him how she felt that Willie had been terribly unfair to her, in failing to attribute any major collaborative recognition to her.[7] Indeed as late as 1925 Gregory was complaining that Willie never gave her credit for *Caithin ni hUalachain*[8].

Willie's nationalist credentials became so prominent that he was offered a Directorship of the *United Irishman*. He did not accept it, lest it send out the wrong message to his increasing circle of English and Unionist friends. *Caithlin ni hUalachain* proved the high point of Willie's flirtation with advanced nationalism, being, in some part, an attempt to please Maud Gonne. But that lady was soon to devastate him with her conversion to the hated Catholicism and marriage to Major John MacBride of Boer War fame. It was, as usual, to Lady Gregory he turned for solace, and she took him to recuperate and write at Coole.

Yeats went on a lecture tour to America in November of that fateful year of 1903, remaining there for five months. Writing to Gregory, he recounted hearing rumours that Gonne's husband was drinking. Both Yeats and Gregory spent the rest of 1904 in preparation for the triumphal first season of the National Theatre Society. The Abbey featured their plays in the December opening. But almost immediately afterwards, Gonne re-entered their lives again as her marriage collapsed. She turned to Willie for practical advice and emotional support. He in turn depended on Gregory to supply advice and support to him. The subsequent divorce action took some years to play out, in the Parisian courts. All the while, Willie was Maud's second and Gregory his own nursemaid. When it was all over, Willie hoped for a carnal relationship with Maud, but apart from one successful incursion, he was again fobbed off by a renewal of their spiritual marriage.

Maud wrote,

Dearest,

That struggle is over & I have found peace. I think today I could let you marry another without losing it – for I know the spiritual union between us will outlive this life, even if we never see each other in this world again[9].

Gregory, who was an annual visitor to Italy, decided that it was opportune for Willie to accompany herself and her son there. Though it was but a sight-seeing trip for her guest's benefit, the visit made a lasting impression on him, not least the walled town of Urbino, from where the idea of living in a Tower came.

Later in that same year of 1907, Robert Gregory married Margaret Parry. Robert had become the legal owner of Coole Park since he had attained majority. The presence of an almost semi-permanent guest installed in the master bedroom, had mattered little previously. As the newly-married couple set up home at Coole and began to raise their family, it became an irksome encumbrance. Gradually, husband and wife came to resent Yeats and his free-loading ways. In deference to Lady Gregory, they sought to mask their growing enmity, though Willie was latterly advised by Lady Gregory to bring his own wine with him.

The financial burden of running the Abbey took a toll on its three directors. JM Synge was seriously ill in a Dublin hospital with Hodgkin's disease. Willie was sick in Dublin and wrote begging Lady Gregory to leave Coole for the Abbey. Unknown to him, she had suffered a stroke and nearly died. Robert Gregory told Yeats in no uncertain terms that the Abbey would have to be looked after without his mother. Willie was shocked by the notion that Gregory might have died. His reaction to that news advances the theory that Lady Gregory was, in a very real way, a mother figure for him. At first, in his disturbed state, he thought that it was his mother who was ill. Later he remembered that his real mother was long since dead, and that Gregory was indeed even more important to him than family.[10] He realised that his life, his work, revolved about and depended on her. He captured this most beautifully in the poem, *A Friend's Illness,* which he sent to Coole, before travelling there himself. When she was fit enough again, Lady Gregory went to Venice to recuperate.

The death of Synge brought Yeats and Gregory even closer together. The latter, knowing how much Willie had admired Synge's work, told him that he had done more for Synge than anyone else. He had given him the means of expressing himself, just as Willie had done for her. Gregory, who had demurred from praising *The Playboy of the Western World,* had not liked its author either. She recalled his many deficiencies to Willie, ungraciousness to fellow-workers, authors and actors, ready to accept praise but parsimonious in giving it.

That same summer Willie repaired to Coole to write, leaving Gregory in Dublin working at the Abbey. With his writing completed he was forced, through a lack of funds, to remain on at Coole, waiting in expectation. Eventually a royalty cheque arrived and he travelled to Dublin, taking rooms there for a short period. He went on to London, where the Abbey Company later played a very successful season at the Court Theatre, attracting many moneyed upper-class power-brokers.

During the year of 1910, Willie's continuing penury led to establishment moves, in London and in Dublin, to reward his well-recognised cultural status. The first formal step in this direction saw him become a founding member of the Academic Committee of English Letters. It was composed of prominent academics and writers. Yeats was the sole Irish invitee and played a full part in its deliberations. Laurence Binyon, Joseph Conrad, Rudyard Kipling and Arthur Balfour were also members. Gregory said that it would make Yeats' name recognised by the 'stupid public', and allow him to mix with his peers in a distinguished body.

The Academy was the brainchild of Edmund Gosse, an English poet, biographer and literary critic, and an establishment manipulator par excellence. He was Librarian at the House of Lords. Willie spoke to Gosse about the possibility of Lady Gregory becoming a member of the new body. Gosse replied with a chauvinistic remark about the wife of one of his friends. Yeats comforted Gregory as best he could by talking about too many old men on the Committee.[11]

Willie had cultivated the friendship of Gosse since sending him a copy of his *Poems,* in 1895. Gosse had acted as a fundraiser for the Abbey, and was also a direct financial contributor to Willie. He intended to secure a State pension for Willie, by placing him on the Government Civil List. He first mentioned the matter to Willie in December 1909. The latter first thought it impossible, as it would limit his political freedom as an Irishman. He had been upset when *The Leader* took him, the author of Caithlin ni hUalachain, to task for being present at a *God Save the King dinner.* He explained to the *Leader* that, while he had long ceased to be an active politician, he was anxious to follow with all loyalty, the general principles laid down by Parnell and never to be renounced by any Nationalist party.[12]

Lady Gregory was enthusiastic about the idea of a pension and collaborated with Gosse on the elaborate political manoeuvrings involved. While achieving a State pension would be very desirable for Willie, it would also have dangers attached. He was Irish, a Home Ruler at least, managing the Abbey. He could not afford, despite his great need, to be seen 'to take the Queen's shilling'. Gregory assured him that there were no inherent contradictions involved. She told him that Standish O'Grady, a major Irish literary figure who was often called 'father of the Irish literary revival', and one who had a major influence on Willie, had the pension. She urged him to talk to O'Grady for advice. Willie was reassured.

Gregory organised a petition on Willie's behalf, in Ireland, to be presented to the Chief Secretary Augustine Birrell, with whom she was very friendly. Gosse realised that Birrell's support would be very important. Then, a very strange thing happened, as Gregory asked Gosse to assist her Irish petition. He resented this and a major difference on the matter developed between them. Gregory felt that Gosse's draft petition, which he had sent to her on 22 July, placed too much store on Willie's loyalty to the establishment and not enough on his poetic prowess. Gosse on the other hand wanted Gregory's petition to Birrell to place greater emphasis on Willie's poverty. Gosse was notoriously a very prickly character. Henry James, in particular, instanced his way of dealing with the prickly Gosse, writing: *I answered in mildness, in meekness, and I await him with the other cheek turned.*[12a]

A contest between the two people, Gosse and Gregory, who both felt a proprietorial interest in Yeats, came to a climax. Gosse, feeling far superior to Gregory and resenting what he perceived as her interfering in his high level machinations, wrote an astonishingly insulting letter to her on 25 July:

Dear Madam,

I cannot express my surprise at the tone of your letter. If this is your attitude, I wish to have no more to do with the matter, and I am lost in wonder at what can have induced you to interfere in an affair when your opinion was not asked, and when you seem to intend neither to give and help nor to take any trouble.

It so happened that Yeats was staying at Coole Park when this letter arrived. At first he was reluctant to get involved. The stakes were very high for him. Both Gregory and her son Robert insisted that he must reply to Gosse. He agreed to do so, but wrote a very restrained letter. Gregory described it later to John Quinn as *a milk-and-water thing.* She was furious with his letter and *insisted on a stronger reply.* She reminded him that *if he hadn't any sense of dignity or self-respect he should remember he was her guest.* She demanded that he write a more forthright letter. Yeats' second reply to Gosse expressed his outrage at the insult offered to his best and oldest friend. He acknowledged that Gosse, as a far older man than himself, had tried to be of assistance to him, but the letter had put paid to all that. He told Gosse than an apology could not recover the situation but that, unless one was forthcoming, he could have no further contact with him, apart from a mere formality.

Gregory knew that Willie was in a desperate state as he handed over the letter to her for posting. She knew that he did not want her to post it. As she later told Quinn, *she would let him be unhappy, and she didn't tell him for over two weeks that she hadn't sent his letter to Gosse, and then she handed it back* to him. On July 29 Willie received a letter from Gosse saying that the Prime Minister had accepted his petition and would pass it on to the King. He emphasised to Willie that he should not do or say anything controversial. As material in the Berg Collection reads, Willie was to, *be absolutely passive.* Meantime, Gregory continued to collect signatures for her own petition to Birrell, telling him of the row with Gosse. An air of tension hung over Coole. Robert Gregory was furious with Willie, as was his mother. It was clear to them that Yeats did not wish to do anything that would endanger his chance of achieving a secure financial base.

In the meantime, Willie wrestled with his conscience. As James Pethica has written, his *resentments of Lady Gregory repeatedly surfaced…criticising her as morally and socially inflexible, they reach their climax in a slashing rejection of her as an artist.*[13] He refused to regard her as part of the *Artists World, being a writer of* mere *comedy,* and belonging essentially to the political or social world. He believed that as a writer of *tragic art,* this made him different and superior to the rest of mankind. He fell into rationalisation on his life long attempt to avoid vanity by giving into *instinctive indignation.* He filled his diary with pages of personal commiserations at what he was forced to do. He wrote an imaginary letter to Robert Gregory, explaining and defending his inaction. He purports to believe that his second letter to Gosse was posted. He ends by saying that Robert would believe that Willie was thinking of himself and that he would be right, but that self was not his own self-interest. He assured Robert that he never feared quarrelling with Gosse or losing the pension. Willie meandered on, seeking self-justification through his role and attitude as artist wearing a mask, where words are not a method for action, rather than a way of investigation. He regarded reason as almost blasphemous, the stopping of the pendulum, a kind of death, as people are limited social beings, half-artificial. Life is a constant injustice, he believed. He had no time for codes of conduct that made one course of action obvious and therefore necessary. He recognised that Lady Gregory and Robert were Jupitereans and code bound. He admitted that this had been a serious quarrel with Gregory, but being an artist with *irreconcilable attitudes towards life,* he felt constrained to avoid general standards and generalised thoughts, lest his talent fade.

On 6 August a letter arrived at 18 Worburn Buildings addressed to William Butler Yeats Esq. The envelope was marked *Confidential* at the top, with the words *Prime Minister* printed on the bottom. The letter read:

Confidential

> *10 Downing St.*
> *Whitehall SW*
> *5th August 1910.*

Dear Sir,

I am desired by the Prime Minister to inform you that, on his recommendation, the King has been graciously pleased to award you a Civil List Pension of £150 a year in recognition of your distinguished literary attainments and of your eminence as a poet.

The pension will be paid to you by the Paymaster General, Whitehall, London, to whom I would ask you to communicate as soon as possible the address to which it should be sent.

The pension will date from 1ˢᵗ April 1910.

I am, at the same time, to request that you will keep this information confidential until it is announced to Parliament in June next year.

Yours faithfully

R. S. Micklejohn

William B. Yeats Esq.

This letter was readdressed *c/o Lady Gregory, Coole Park, Co. Galway, Gort. Ireland,* and posted on 8ᵗʰ of August at 8. p.m. The speed of postal delivery then has to be admired, as this redirected letter, reached its destination the very next day. The atmosphere must have been very strained at Coole when the above letter arrived to Lady Gregory. Did she hand it over personally to her guest? In any event, Willie wasted no time in responding, as requested in the letter. He replied immediately. On 11ᵗʰ August a letter was posted to him at Coole Park, Gort, Co. Galway, from the Paymaster's Office in Whitehall. It read;

Sir,

> *I am directed by the Paymaster General to acknowledge the receipt of your letter of 9ᵗʰ instant, relative to your Civil List Pension, and to inform you that it shall receive attention.*

I am to add that the first payment becomes due on the 1st of October next.

I am, Sir,

Your obedient servant,

M. J. Maude

C. S. Davies.

Mr. W. B. Yeats.[14]

Willie subsequently thanked Chief Secretary, Birrell, for *a service that set me free from anxiety and from the need of doing less than the best I can.*[15]

The Chief Secretary replied;

The Prime Minister was as eager as I was. I know you don't much care about Dr. Johnson, but I always think his pension was the money best spent in England during the whole of my beloved 18th century. It is well that the 20th century should follow suit.[16]

The American publication, *The Register*, carried the following report in its issue of 29 April 1911:

Yeats is Pensioned

According to a report given publicly in the columns of The Booklover, WB Yeats, the Irish poet, has been accorded a pension of $750 per annum by the government in recognition of his many services to the cause of literature. The news will be welcomed by Irishmen the world over as Mr. Yeats is recognised as one of the greatest and most brilliant of living Irish writers. His efforts on behalf of Irish literature have been untiring and spread over a period of several years. His work has had the effect of bringing about a more widespread study of the ancient poets and singers of his native land.

His own work stands out pre-eminent among that of many clever craftsmen. Recently his plays have been presented with considerable success both in Dublin and in London. His poems have an appeal to a much wider public than that of his own people, and lovers of verse everywhere have expressed keen appreciation of his work.

CHAPTER 2

SON AND SIBLING

Declan Kiberd, writing in the Irish Times of 20 January 2001, on the subject of the cultural role of the family in the creation of the State said: *a happy family, like a contented nation, is unlikely to have hair-raising adventures. The great works of literature tend to begin with a frustrated character that feels compelled to break out of a social structure. In that sense many of our cultural narratives focus on some sort of dysfunctional family...* "*Wherever there is Ireland there is the family*" remarked GK Chesterton with something like envy, "*and it counts for a great deal*". He made the comment after a visit to the artistic family of John Butler Yeats, in London. The portrait painter and his poet son, Willie, had so often raised their voices during their conversation that their neighbours on Blenheim Road concluded the two were close to coming to blows. One of the Yeats girls patiently explained that this was simply "*the Irish way*", at home and overseas.

Willie Yeats was the eldest of six children, born to Susan Pollexfen and John Butler Yeats between 1865 and 1875. He was born at Sandymount in Dublin, Lily at Enniscrone in Co. Sligo, Lollie, Robert, Jack and Jane in London. Robert and Jane both died in infancy. Willie's relationship with all the members of his family was problematical, though especially so with his sister Lollie. He was closer to Lily and they played together as children. She was quieter, gentler, less emotional, and less ambitious than Lollie. Willie and Lily were friends, while Willie and Lollie were adversaries. John Yeats, their eccentric and self-absorbed father, blamed the Pollexfen side of the family for Willie's excitability and Lollie's grumpiness. Both children detested criticism. One might have thought that since both encountered teasing, they might have become allies. But their mutual experience only heightened their quarrels. The father sided with his son, seeking to protect him, leaving his daughter to protect herself. Living in London, Willie attended the Godolphin School in Hammersmith for four years, while Lily was also sent to school locally. Lollie, though, remained at home to look after the house and family. Jack Yeats did not figure in the family dynamics, largely because he spent his childhood years happily, living in Sligo with his grandparents. When eventually he did join the others in London, he had developed a pleasing disposition that proved a tonic to each of the other members of his family.

When the family returned to live in Dublin in 1882, and went to live in Terenure, their house was quite small. At that stage Willie was making a name for himself composing poetry. In doing so, his technique was to act out his verse by chanting it aloud and at great length. In *Reveries Over Childhood* he claimed that he did this unconsciously.[1] This grated on Lollie's nerves in particular, and was another cause for quarrelling between them. The three siblings soon enrolled at the same Metropolitan School of Art in Kildare St. There they learned design. Both Willie and John liked to deride the girls' efforts. At that time Willie had met Katherine Tynan and had begun to visit her farmhouse home in Clondalkin. Katherine encouraged him to bring his sisters with him. At first he only brought Lily but later Lollie came. Both sisters became good friends with Tynan, and with Sara Purser, who also frequented Clondalkin. Tynan, like his sisters, found Willie's behaviour challenging. She wrote, *He is an extremely bothering visitor. He thinks all the rest of the world created to minister to him and there is no rebuffing of him possible. I did nothing while he was here, nor should I, if he was here a twelve month.*[2]

In 1887, unfortunately for the family, John decided that he would return to London to pursue his unsuccessful career as a portrait painter. Their first house was at Eardley Crescent, which they all hated. The constant poverty and hopelessness of her husband caused the mother of the family, Susan Mary Yeats (nee Pollexfen), to have a stroke. When she had married, Susan and her family expected that her husband would remain in the law and establish a comfortable family home in the manner that she had been reared in Sligo. Instead, the marriage turned out to be a nightmare for her, her children and the Pollexfen family, who were constantly trying to make up for their son-in-law's deficiencies. At this time too, Lily fell seriously ill. Both she and her mother repaired to Yorkshire to recover.

The absence of mother and sister afforded Lollie unusual freedom. With six other ladies she formed a cultural group called 'The Pleiades'. They discussed all sorts of topics. Lollie decided that the group should produce a magazine, called *Ye Pleiades* which ran to three issues. In the issue of January 1888, Lollie published one of her own stories. Her father liked it and wrote to Willie praising it. Willie read it and was quite impressed. So much so that he wrote in praise of it to his mentor John O'Leary, though in a somewhat superior manner. He added that Lollie *lives on the right sort of mental plane for that sort of work.* However, significantly, he did not make any mention of his opinion to Lollie herself. She would have been so pleased, that the writer in the family admired her own effort. The production quality of the magazine was of an extremely high standard, all done by hand, embroidered with gold satin stitches. For the last issue, Lollie got contributions from her two brothers, and Katherine Tynan. Her father produced a portrait of Lollie for the issue. She described Jack as an honorary member of 'The Pleiades', though Willie, who at the time was the sole breadwinner for the family, did not get that honour.

Lollie Yeats

William Murphy in *Family Secrets,*[3] writes rather harshly of Lollie, and I suspect, misses the dynamics of the interplay between the siblings. He says; *It is no wonder that Lollie and her older brother did not hit it off. One of her problems with him sprang from her stout refusal to accept the notion that her brother was her superior in any way … she was angry that her talents were not recognised as the equal of his … Naturally Willie would not accept Lollie's self serving evaluation, especially from one he regarded as irrational and 'silly' … To have Willie and Lollie together made for an explosive combination.*

The two sisters, like their mother before them, expected that they would marry and thus ensure their futures. They had no training to earn a living, and their father could offer them nothing. They were well aware that unmarried women merited little respect from society.

The family moved house to Bedford Park in 1888, while Lily and her mother were still away. All the work attached therefore fell to Lollie and restricted her time greatly. This did not change or improve significantly when her mother and sister came home, particularly as Susan had another stroke. Jack Yeats felt that a specialist should have been hired to examine his mother earlier. With his first earnings, he arranged this but to no avail. He continued to treat her as if she was in full control of her faculties. Susan remained an invalid and became totally reclusive.[4]

The Bedford Park house location provided many opportunities for the sisters to educate themselves and develop their social circle, as there was a vibrant cultural life within the district. Their brother, the poet, was usually the first point of contact for a variety of visitors which included Katherine Tynan, Sara Purser, Louis Purser, John O'Leary and famously in January 1889, Maud Gonne.[5]

In 1888 a group of socialists began to learn French in order to prepare for a tour of France. Willie was one of the group. He mentioned this at home one evening and the sisters expressed an interest in joining the class. He did not want them there and put them off. But they continued to exert pressure until he relented. It soon became clear why he had not wanted his sisters in the class. His attempts at speaking French caused much amusement to the teacher and the almost entire male class. After the arrival of his sisters, he soon abandoned the class. It was there that the sisters first encountered May Morris, who had an influence on their futures.

Morris & Company Embroideries needed staff. May offered a job to Lily and in December 1888 Lily returned home proudly, having earned the sum of ten shillings. Willie was not enamoured of this development. He felt it was socially unacceptable for his sister to go out to work. In his dealing with friends, he sought to explain it as helping out a family friend, and emphasised the artistic element of the operation. In fact there was none of the latter involved. She spent six years there, but never got to work in design, though she did learn about fabric, threads, dye, colours and the current fashion favourites. Both Lily and Willie were attracted by William Morris' socialism, though Willie doubted that he would become a socialist.[6]

Lollie's role continued to be the homemaker, particularly keeping the accounts of an impecunious family. She was ambitious and continued to write. *The Vegetarian* accepted one of her stories. Her brother Jack did the accompanying illustrations. In 1889 she was invited to join a Froebel teacher named Miss Jones, who ran a private school. If she proved adaptable, she could sit preliminary examinations for enrolment in a Teacher Training College. She was unpaid for her school- work. This annoyed Willie who berated her. He told Katherine Tynan that higher education for women was not a good idea. He felt that education provided women with no peace and generally upset their minds making them into "loud chatterers". Lollie passed a preliminary examination and, with the formal test approaching, she became extremely nervous. She sat the first formal entrance test successfully and was very proud of herself. However, she failed the second part and became very upset. The family employed a servant, to allow Lollie time to study for the repeat examination. This time, she passed the Higher Certificate in Education.

At this same time Lily was finding her work at Morris's quite boring. Willie was, as usual, sympathetic to her. She was able to tolerate Willie's unusual behaviour in constantly seeking to draw attention to himself, both at home and in public. She played up to his interests in the occult, his visions, his public trances. For him she was the ideal type of woman, with a preference for home life, accepting and not ambitious. Years later, in a letter to John Quinn in 1921, as she was sending him a sketch of Willie by her father, Lily recalled a pleasant occasion during this period. She, Willie and John sat around the fire in Blenheim Road. It was some Bank holiday at Easter, she remembered: *Anyway I had a day of freedom from May Morris and was at home and had got myself into a happy state of mind by reading "The Prisoner of Zenda". I sat on one side of the fire, Papa the other and Willy between us. The talk was pleasant. We all had a holiday feeling and Papa did this beautiful sketch of Willie ...* [6a]

Willie and Lollie were quite alike in temperament and traits; both were outspoken. In his *Journal,* Willie wrote that he always doubted but that there was some inherited nervous deficit in himself and Lollie.[7] They competed. Lollie would not play up to Willie. He continued to belittle her, and her attempts to become independent. Yet despite herself, Lollie usually depended on Willie for her contacts, as when he founded the Irish Literary Society in Bedford Park in 1891 and brought many visitors to the house.

The family accounts received a boost when William Pollexfen died, leaving £50 a year to Susan. Lily finally ceased working for Morris', having quarrelled with May Morris. John was thrilled to have Lily at home again. She then got involved in preparing work for the First Exhibition of the Arts and Crafts Society in Dublin.

All the siblings were forced to take stock in 1894, as their youngest member, Jack, aged 23, married. Their friend Katherine Tynan had married the previous year. Willie was nearly thirty, Lily twenty-eight and Lollie twenty-seven. Jack was a favourite with each of the family, having little of his brother's character. He had avoided the hardship of growing up in poverty in London, and was the better for it. When he had returned to live there with the family, aged seventeen, he studied art. He then worked as a professional illustrator for a variety of publications. He later turned to painting in oils, mostly on Irish themes. He regarded painting as greater than writing:

Painting is direct vision and direct communication Three years after his marriage Jack removed himself again from the family ambience, as he and his wife, Mary Cottenham White (Cottie), went to live in Devon. She had a private income. They lived permanently in Ireland from 1910. John Quinn described him thus in 1904: *He is one of the most simple and unaffected kind-hearted genuine and sincere men I have ever met and I like him more than I can tell.*

Lollie's hard work was rewarded when her first book, called *Brushwork,* on the teaching of painting, was published. Harold Laurence the publisher, who also published Willie, informed him that it was a fine book. Despite the lack of acknowledgement or support from Willie, Lollie spread her earnings generously throughout the whole family.

Around that time, Willie decided to move out of the family home and take rooms, first at the Temple and later at Woburn Buildings, to progress his relationship with Olivia Shakeaspeare. Lollie, who had borne the brunt of keeping the family home functioning by continuous penny-pinching, took his departure as a rejection of the family. Lily, though, approved of Willie's move. She too was about to leave as she had got a post as a governess in France. After Willie moved out, in a rare show of consideration, he invited Lollie to Woburn Buildings for lunch.

A description of Willie and his Woburn Buildings apartment, dated 20 October 1900, reads:

Down a side street, long narrow door, next to a cobbler's shop, tiny brass plate, WB Yeats inscribed ... squeaking creaking staircase ... shake his long bony hand deliberately, dressed in black, topmost story; large room, hung about with Blake's engravings of Dante, a Rossetti, Beardsleys; wondrous view over roof tops: long white cadaverous clean-shaven face, topped by a lock of blue black hair, enthusiastic nose, broad at the root, pointed at the tip; strange mouth, long neck, black brown eyes behind the glasses, which he must wear.

Such is Mr. Yeats in "the outer", which together with all his strange contradictions and narrowness, his fiery independence, as opposed to a strange obedience in occultism- passes away and in spirit you see a beautiful soul hungry after a perfect happiness, that the world in which its lot is cast, can never give.[7a]

Lollie had always been shown great consideration by Louis Purser, Sara's brother. Louis now moved to London and became a regular caller to Bedford Park. Lollie and the rest of the family felt it was only a matter of time before Louis proposed marriage. Much to Lollie's disappointment and frustration, this never happened. When Lily returned home a year later, she was very ill and unable to consider going out to work again. Lily became the centre of attention at home, with Lollie still having to manage the finances. They decided to invite a distant cousin, Susan Mitchell, to come and live with them as a paying guest. John liked her greatly, as he liked Lily, thus causing Lollie to feel further isolated and taken for granted by the family.

Willie had recently met Lady Augusta Gregory and she came to visit Bedford Park. For the sisters, her visit was a rerun of the earlier visit by Maud Gonne, as Gregory devoted her entire attention to John and his two sons, ignoring Lily and Lollie. They were amazed at the influence the visitor appeared to have on Willie. His focus of attention on Ireland increased apace, and that of the sisters naturally followed. They became regular attendees at the Irish Literary Society, which was chaired by the biographer of Parnell, Barry O'Brien, with Evelyn Gleeson as secretary. Gleeson, who was a well-off suffragette, was familiar with Willie's work She was interested in art and embroidery, and knew that Lily had worked in the latter and that Lollie had published a book on the teaching of painting.

Willie's play, *The Countess Kathleen,* written for and dedicated to Maud Gonne, was to be performed at the Antient Concert Rooms in Dublin in May 1899. Lollie decided to support her brother and travelled to Dublin to attend the play. She enjoyed it, and though he showed no interest in her work, she was very proud of him. She found Dublin an exciting and interesting place. The advent of and the agitation surrounding the Boer War, combined with the solidarity of the entire family in opposition to the war, led the sisters to realise all the more that they were Irish, and living in an alien country.

The death of Susan Yeats on 3 January 1900 hardly caused a ripple effect in the family, except for Jack. Willie, who was at home when she died, wrote to Lady Gregory on 4 January. He told her that it was a very long time since his mother was able to properly recognise any members of the family. He feared the effect it would have on Jack, saying *he was devoted to his mother.* Jack could not work for six months after her burial at Acton Rural Cemetery on 6 January.[8] He later organised the erection of a plaque to her memory at St. John's Church in her native Sligo. Willie reluctantly agreed to be a party to the cost of erecting the plaque.

Sara Purser organised an exhibition of John Yeats' paintings in Dublin. Though he was a good painter, John's problem was in finishing his commissioned work on time. He was never satisfied that a painting was complete. He did not return home to London. He remained on in Dublin, counting on the generosity of friends to offer him bed and board.

Evelyn Gleeson resigned as secretary of the Irish Literary Society in London. Barry O'Brien invited Lollie to replace her. This was a great honour and recognition of Lollie's capabilities. But she had received another proposal from Evelyn Gleeson. She was moving to Dublin to set up an arts and crafts business and offered a partnership to Lily and Lollie. After much discussion, and with the approval of John and Jack, and together with Lollie's idea of setting up a printing press as part of the partnership, the sisters decided to return to Dublin. Dr. Augustine Henry, a mutual friend of the Yeats sisters and Miss Gleeson, drew up articles of association. He provided a capital loan, and also guaranteed an annual income for the sisters until the business became profitable. John wrote to Lollie telling her that she was as intelligent as Willie, but lacked his ethereal self-confidence. When Lollie informed Willie of her plans for a printing press, he too became interested. He agreed to become literary editor and find books for publication. Lollie did a crash course on the business and practicalities of running a printing press before she left London. The cost of transferring the family was borne by Willie in a loan to his father.

Evelyn Gleeson leased a house in Dundrum for the business. It was called Dun Emer. Only females were to be employed there. Lily, through a friend of Willie's, got an early order to make banners for the new cathedral at Loughrea in Co. Galway, for which Sara Purser was designing the stained glass windows. The first book that Lollie produced was, *In The* Seven *Woods,* by Willie. It was an expensive, high quality, hand-made production. The difficulties that would arise between Lollie and her literary editor became apparent during this first production. Willie dithered over the inclusion of his play, *On Baile's Strand,* in the book. The responsibility for the production and succeeding stages of the operation rested with Lollie, but the entire operation was stalled until Willie could make up his mind. Then he wanted to change the pressmark, the publisher's name, the colour of the paper and the cover design. Though admitting he knew nothing about printing, he thought the whole process quite simple. Finally in July 1903, the book appeared. Three hundred and twenty-five copies were printed, at ten shillings and sixpence each. They sold out by September.

The family home in Churchtown, Gurteen Dhas, together with the sisters and John, became part of the local cultural scene. Regular visitors included their famous brothers, George Russell, Susan Mitchell, Willy and Frank Fay, John Quinn, Maire nic Shiubhlaigh, who also worked at Dun Emer. Lily and Lollie became members of the National Theatre Society and played their part in supporting their brother in that arena of ongoing difficulties.

The sisters, whose business efforts were constantly in dire financial trouble, had the added burden of keeping their father, John, who rarely earned any income. George Russell, who was a family friend, and also a long-time associate of Willie's, had the temerity to castigate the latter for this situation. Willie was furious with Russell for suggesting that he bore some responsibility for his father, as well as interfering in family affairs. Of course, Willie blamed his sisters for informing Russell and was extremely angry with them.

In Dun Emer Industries, Evelyn Gleeson, Lily and Lollie, each pursued their separate and independent business interests. But Gleeson had assumed overall financial responsibility for the company, and became increasingly unhappy with that position. Lollie and Gleeson began to quarrel over finance. Willie, though he had no official link with Lily's business, quarrelled with her over the banners that Jack was to design. He even commissioned new designs without informing her. This led to a row between Lily and Gleeson over the finance involved. An arbitrator was called into the company and a three-way split on expenses and rent was agreed. Lily had no immediate finance and wrote to Willie for assistance. He was then on an American lecture tour and prevaricated, writing to Lady Gregory for advice. Lily was very annoyed with him. However, her immediate problem was solved as she received a large order from Liberty's in London. Lollie, too, met success with a certificate for printing from an exhibition held in Antwerp. On his return from America, Willie visited Dun Emer, criticising everything he saw. He could recognise that Lollie was a strong business-like person. However, she did want his approval for the books she published. Now, he appeared arrogant. John told Willie that Dun Emer was vital for both sisters and begged him to be more careful, with Lollie in particular, who became ill after her brother's recent tirade.

Willie was not adverse in seeking to direct his younger brother Jack. He usually sought to do this through their father. Lily chided John for saying too much to Jack. She reminded John that Jack was much younger than Willie, and still at the beginning of his career. She added, with great prescience, that in future years Jack's paintings would command great prices.

At that stage, Louis Purser was back in Dublin, too. His friendship with Lollie continued as previously, but with no marriage proposal. She began to feel the emotional strain and could not relax. Both Lily and John tried to avoid her as much as possible. The latter refused to walk into the city in her company, purporting to prefer a different though longer route to her. John again blamed the instability in his wife's Pollexfen family for Lollie's difficulty, as he had earlier done when he feared for Willie's mental stability.

When the National Theatre *Society* received a patent to run a theatre in Dublin, it helped the Yeats family finances. Willie succeeded in getting the Englishwoman, Annie Horniman, to finance the theatre. He commissioned portraits from his father and large embroidered drapes from Lily. At that time, the shrewd Irish American John Quinn visited Dublin, and he too gave commissions to John and Jack. He bought manuscripts from Willie and visited Gurteen Dhas, showing great interest in Lollie. But she realised that Quinn was only interested in having affairs, and was not the marrying kind, and so she declined his advances. The sisters also became friends with JM Synge. Much to Lily's disappointment, in particular, he fell in love with an eighteen-year-old Abbey actress named Molly Allgood.

Willie embroiled the sisters in the acrimonious takeover of the Abbey. He had insisted that they vote in support of his plans. One of the actors, Máire nic Shiubhlaigh, a friend and employee of Lily's, on accepting an Abbey contract had to cease working at Dun Eme*r*. Later, when she discovered that Sara Allgood had got more money and higher status that herself, she complained to Willie. He reacted furiously. Maire was so shocked that she fled for safety to the sisters at Gurteen Dhas. The latter had become, paradoxically, a meeting point for those who opposed Willie. Lollie knew that he could only see his own side of anything, and that there was no point in trying to reason with him. When he was opposed, he became rude and overbearing. Willie confronted Maire at Gurteen Dhas in front of Lollie, who wrote that:

His manner was sneery & offensive & Máire would discuss nothing. Willie kept on telling her that she was a 'beginner' & had much to learn & so on, & at the same time spoke the whole time of Mr. Fay & Miss Allgood & the others as if they were finished actors & actresses ... I know what harm he would have done here if he could have baulked us in our own work. He does not understand practical life, Since he was a small boy he was always too easily led to make a good leader himself & instead of learning to control a naturally disagreeable temper, of late years, he has indulged himself in fits of temper. I have indeed heard Miss Horniman speak of his bad temper as if it were a feather in his cap. Just as stupid people would speak of a child of two, showing self will by kicking and screaming for what he wanted.[9]

Máire nic Shiubhlaigh later joined her brother in the rival company, Theatre of Ireland. When it claimed the right to use the name, National Theatre of Ireland, Willie threatened to sue her for breach of contract. Despite their difficulties with him and their friendship with ni Shiubhlaigh, both sisters supported Willie.

Dire financial problems continued in the sisters' businesses. One fundamental problem was that they had no showroom or location in which to market their produce. Lollie felt that Willie, as a director, had a duty to procure more books for publication. When George Russell offered her a volume of his own poetry, she accepted it eagerly. On hearing of this, Willie was furious. He and Russell had been on totally different sides in the Abbey takeover, and Willie felt that Russell was using his poetry volume just to get at him. Of course, it was Lollie who bore the brunt of her brother's fury. He told her in no uncertain terms that he was editor and adviser, and that his reputation was on the line. He ordered Lollie not to publish Russell's work She refused. Willie replied in fury. John, who had a vital interest in the success of the business, defended Lollie. He said that Dun Emer was merely a hobby for Willie; it was vital for his sisters. He also said that Lollie was just as intelligent and stubborn as Willie. He added that Willie should be an adviser only, or resign. He did resign. Lollie published Russell's poetry. She decided to publish a volume of Katherine Tynan's next, which caused Willie more angst.

John Quinn had not given up on seducing Lollie. Dun Emer Industries was invited to show its products in New York. Quinn sent a personal invitation to Lollie, including a travel ticket. Willie was furious, as he resented another member of the family getting involved with his patron. Lollie decided to involve Quinn in the selection of the poems for the Katherine Tynan collection. Willie sought to get Tynan to insist that he alone should select the poems. When Lily backed Lollie in the row, Willie became more pliable. He wrote to Lollie, still in New York with Quinn, proposing his return as editor, on certain terms. Quinn advised her to work out the terms herself. Lollie, who essentially wanted her brother's affection and recognition, wrote a very friendly letter to Willie, avoiding mention of the previous rows, asking him to select the Tynan poems.

Lollie departed New York very suddenly, raising suspicion that Quinn may have made unwelcome advances towards her. Back in Dublin she met George Russell. They discussed Willie's return as editor and together drew up a contract, which Willie duly signed, though the tension between himself and Lollie continued.

In December 1907, Lily accepted what was to be a financially-rewarding invitation from John Quinn to visit New York, and display her embroideries there at an Irish exhibition. Evelyn Gleeson also attended in competition. Hugh Lane had earlier raised funds to send John Yeats on a holiday to Italy. However, the latter decided instead to use the money to travel to New York with his daughter. Once there, he was reluctant to return home. Lily had to delay her return home as John refused to agree a date for their departure. He loved America and its constant possibilities and openness. He relied on John Quinn for contacts at first. But then, his own personality had endeared him to many that he entered a bohemian lifestyle, getting by on very little. Eventually Lily realised that John was not going to return home with her and she travelled alone in June of 1908.

All the time Lily was away, Lollie was being pressurised by Evelyn Gleeson that Dun Emer Industries could not continue. Willie and his adviser, Lady Gregory, told Lollie to leave Dun Emer and get her own premises. She knew this was too costly. On Lily's return they called in an arbitrator. Gleeson was to retain the *Dun Emer* name, which she continued to run until the 1930's. She wrote off the bad debts owed by Lily and Lollie to the company. Though income from printing and embroidery had increased, trading was still at a loss. The sisters then formed their own Cuala Industries, with Embroidery, managed by Lily, and Hand-Press managed by Lollie. Her first book was *Poetry and Ireland* by Willie. Máire nic Shiubhlaigh continued to work for Evelyn Gleeson.

The controversy surrounding the first production of JM Synge's *The Playboy of the Western World* at the Abbey in 1907 was particularly upsetting for the Yeats family, when Susan Mitchell wrote a review containing personal criticism of Willie. Both sisters supported their brother against Susan. The premature death of Synge in 1909 also upset the entire Yeats family. Lily wrote to John Yeats on 28 March 1909:

I spent the evening after the funeral with Willy. He asked me to go in [to the Nassau Hotel] He wanted to talk. He feels it deeply and says now he has no friend left... Lily then writes of consoling Synge's fiancée, Molly Allgood, at the Abbey, and helping her write letters of acknowledgement. She wrote that the Synges were a strange, rigid people, who did not appear to realise the genius of JM. She told how Willie had sought the family permission to take a death mask of JM, but was refused. She also mentions how she and JM were so close. She ended by again referring to how Willie, *talked and talked on Friday to me of everything and anything ...*[9a]

The absence of John in New York meant that the two sisters were now alone, and dependent on each other like never before. Lily began to find Lollie's moodiness insufferable. The only consolation she could find was in letters to her father and his considerate, though unhelpful replies. He wrote Lily that Lollie had the Pollexfen curse, just like her mother and Willie, and that she would never be cured. He said that all of that family liked to be alone. This was untrue and unhelpful to the menopausal Lollie, who continued without sympathy from any quarter in her aloneness. Lily even ventured the opinion that one of the reasons John did not return home with her was the thought of having to live again with Lollie. Willie on the other hand continued to be minded by Lady Gregory in all his personal and public crises.

In the meantime Cuala was already £500 in debt, and another major row between Lollie and Willie was imminent. Lollie agreed to publish the poetry of the late Edward Dowden, Professor of English Literature at Trinity College. He had been a friend of John's and Cuala desperately needed the work. Lollie knew that Willie would object, as Dowden was no friend of his, either politically or artistically. She took care not to inform her brother until the book was typeset. When he did hear of it, he was absolutely furious and attacked Lollie in an insulting and demeaning fashion. He was further dismayed when he read the poems. It had only been a short time previously, when Dowden fell ill and was expected to die, that Willie was put forward as a possible successor at Trinity. Willie did not have a high regard for the College, but the prospect of rooms within Trinity and £600 per annum were enough to enable him to forget about past events. Having done the necessary canvassing, it appeared that the position was about to be offered to him. He was foolish enough to tell several friends, including Maud Gonne, that the position was his. She wrote in April 1913, advising him to take it, though she wished it had been in *the other university. You would have made things LIVE there.* Dowden did not die and thwarted his proposed successor, ridiculing

38

him as a non-scholar, who would have to climb the academic ladder like any other candidate.

Willie ordered Lollie not to publish the poems. She refused, telling her brother that she had to make a living, and he was not bringing in any books. Willie insisted that the publication should not be in the regular Cuala series, as selected and approved by him. John got involved in the row and backed Willie, telling Lollie that Cuala was dependent on Willie's name as editor. Though Willie's main interest was in the literary merit of the publications, he was critical of Cuala's continued losses. The following year of 1914, Lollie complied with Willie's demand as the Cuala prospectus indicated that Dowden's book was not linked to WB Yeats. This episode did serve to bring it home to Willie that he had to bring more books to Cuala. He recommended that Lollie should publish a collection of John's letters. Since he went to New York, John had become an inveterate letter-writer to Willie and the rest of the family.

Another row ensued when Cuala published Willie's book, *Responsibilities,* in 1914. As usual, he dithered over his selection and over some individual word placements. Eventually, Lollie had to begin printing. When Willie wanted more changes, she could not comply. He tried to insist that an erratum slip go with each volume blaming the printers for errors. She did include the slip, but it stated that the errors were due to late changes by the author. At that time Willie was writing his *Autobiographies.* He cooperated closely with Lily on this project, insisting that she did not inform Lollie of the work in progress. In the first section, called *Reveries over Childhood and Youth,* he indulges himself with recollections that differed from his earlier reminiscences and writings. For instance he recalls very positive memories of his mother, admitting that she was responsible for making Sligo, its people and places and stories, magical to him. *"I can see now"* he wrote, *"that she had great depth of feeling, that she was her father's daughter".* He acknowledges that she suffered greatly in her poverty-stricken, child-rearing life. Lily featured quite prominently in the text, with little mention of Lollie. This led to Lily becoming a sought-after source for material on her brother. This was especially so for Joseph Hone's book, *The Poet in Contemporary Society.*

The next row with Cuala concerned Willie's attempts to get Lollie to publish his friend Ezra Pound's *Noh Plays.* She objected on the grounds that Cuala only published Irish writers and doubted that it would be a commercially successful publication. Willie overcame this objection by writing an introduction to the plays, which would guarantee their sales. She had almost as much trouble with Pound over printing, than she was accustomed to with her brother. Then, to add to her difficulties, Willie nominated Pound to select and edit the collection of John's letters for publication. Lollie was most concerned with Pound's esoteric editing and many errors. She objected in particular to Pound having the names of many of John's friends in capital letters. She told her brother that Pound's *Noh Plays* were selling poorly. Willie backed Pound until Lily, too, objected to Pound's text. Lollie got Louis Purser to proof-read the text and he corrected many mistakes, but Pound overrode this and insisted the 'mistakes' be printed. The book was eventually published in 1917 to critical and commercial acclaim. At last Lollie received some praise from the family, and was pleased to be able to send a royalty cheque to the grateful John.

At the suggestion of Robert Gregory, Willie bought Thoor Ballylee, a rundown cottage and tower, close to Coole Park in 1917. While John was particularly pleased that Willie had bought some property, his sisters wondered if Willie was thinking of marriage and to whom. Willie did indeed marry later that year in London. He gave so little information on the wedding that his sisters had no time to make travel arrangements. Ezra Pound was the best man.

The tragic death of Robert Gregory in 1918 brought Willie and his bride, Georgie, to Ireland. They stayed in the Royal Hibernian Hotel in Dawson St. A family reunion took place at Gurteen Dhas with Willie and Georgie, Jack and Cottie as well as Joseph Hone and his wife. Both sisters found Georgie intelligent and not too talkative. They could detect an improvement in Willie's disposition. Georgie treated both sisters with respect and interest. She visited Lily's embroidery shop and took Lollie on a shopping expedition for Ballylee. Lollie produced a volume of John's journalism to great success and much family pride. Georgie became pregnant and Willie was insistent that the baby be born in Ireland. The baptism of baby Anne took place in St. Mary's, Donnybrook, literally a few hundred yards from where Willie had been born on Sandymount Avenue. Lily gave the baby an embroidered christening cloak. Lollie gave a decorated cradle, which drew such praise from Willie that Lollie based a new line for Cuala Industries on her gift. The newly-married couple continued to travel between Ireland and England, while Ballylee was being renovated.

Willie then began writing *Four Years* of his *Autobiography,* covering the years 1887-1891. This caused much grief to his father, particularly the description of the family as *enraged,* and the description of Susan as '*my Sligo born mother whose actions were unreasoning and habitual like the seasons'.*[10] John felt his daughters were maligned, and wrote to Willie, defending both sisters, and reminding him that at that period they were keeping the family going by working, housekeeping and looking after Susan. He pointed out that it was totally unfair that he should look down on his sisters for such efforts. John also wrote directly to Lollie, trying to ameliorate the matter by suggesting that her brother was not being intentionally malevolent. John's strictures had no effect on Willie, who continued to quarrel with Lollie over every book of his that Cuala produced. Furthermore, when Michael Yeats was born, Lollie was ignored in her expectation to be the godmother.

The death of John in New York in 1922 was a sad and shocking occasion for the family, especially for Lily and Lollie, who were then, aged 55 and 53 respectively. News of the death on 3 February (the same date *Ulysses* was published) came in a telegram from Quinn to the two sisters, saying:

"*Regret your father passed away today … If resting place to be in Ireland temporary vault can be arranged here until Spring* [11] All of John's letters and memoirs were returned to Gurteen Dhas. I wrote in an earlier book that: "*Willie now expressed the view to Lily that it was best that their father had been spared a long illness. His two daughters, who had not seen their father for thirteen years, were very sad that he had died so far away from home and alone in a cheap boarding house. One of the last letters he wrote was to John Quinn thanking him for $30. He told Quinn that he was badly in need of underwear and socks. John's daughters could not afford to travel to America or have his remains brought home. When boxes of John's letters arrived to Gurteen Dhas later in the year, it became clear that he had been well aware of the failures in his own life. He commented that if he had remained practising at the Bar, his daughters would most likely have had happily married lives. But he doubted that his two artistic sons would then have achieved their potential. He had remained on, living in poor circumstances in America, rather than coming home to confront his failures. John Quinn, who knew him well, wrote of him as an amalgam of quicksilver and iron, his iron determination to have his own way, to do as he pleased, never to think of other people's worries or cares or efforts".*[12]

Quinn might well have been describing Willie, who had on occasion paid a subvention towards John's living expenses. John also, at last, acknowledged that his wife's problems had been caused by poverty. While recognising that

41

he had enjoyed Willie's great successes and fame, he also knew that he had never won his son's respect, nor, he admitted, had he any self-respect, as his own life had been such a failure. He once wrote to Quinn saying, *there is a good deal of his mother in Willie. I often said to her these words "You know I have to take your affection for granted" for I never saw the slightest sign of it.*[13]

Mrs Jeanne Robert Foster, who had nursed John in his last illness, organised the funeral in New York. At twenty-fou hours notice, two hundred and fifty people attended. She had the casket initially placed in a vault in Westchester. The following June she had it transferred to a plot of her own in Chesterton, in the lower Adirondacks, in Warren County in New York State. A white marble monument was erected there, paid for by John Quinn. It reads, *In Memory of John B. Yeats of Dublin, Ireland. Painter and Writer.* As late as 1958 Mrs Foster asked the Irish Government, unsuccessfully, to repatriate the remains to Ireland. She then took steps to have it cared for as a shrine for seventy-five years.[14]

Lily wrote to Mrs Foster on 25 February about the death of her *Papa: ... He was my very beloved father and also my closest friend, I feel lonely, sad and suddenly old ... His going has slammed a great door between me and so much...*[14a]

Lily, whose health continued to be delicate, got tuberculosis. Willie and Georgie sent her to a London nursing home. John Quinn wanted her sent to Switzerland. Cuala Industries moved into the basement of Willie's new family home on Dublin's Merrion Square. The first book printed from there, in 1923, was Oliver Gogarty's *An Offering of Swans and Other Poems,* with a preface by Willie. This was important, as it marked the 'outing' of Gogarty as a writer. He had earlier used the pseudonym "Gideon Ousley". Georgie had by then become the go-between with her husband and Lollie, as rows continued. Later that year Willie won the Nobel Prize for Literature, travelling to Sweden to receive the valuable prize.

Lily remained ill in London, becoming virulently critical of the effect Lollie had on her life. She believed that her ill-health was due to Lollie, whom she believed was losing her mind and who was gradually killing her by suspicion and jealousy. She wanted a complete separation from Lollie, demanding that Cuala should be sold and Lollie paid off. Lily wished to remain at Merrion Square with her embroidery business. Lily wanted her freedom. She did not get it entirely, returning again to live at Gurteen Dhas.

The family patron, John Quinn, died in 1924, and in 1925 Cuala finally acquired its own premises in the city at 133 Lower Baggot St. There they proudly displayed a portrait of Willie. The first book produced there was Willie's *The Bounty of Sweden*. It contained impressions of his visit, and was a gesture of gratitude to the Swedish Academy, and his admiration for the royal ritual and protocol. The money from the Prize paid off the debts of Cuala Industries. Lily had little energy to do much work, and often worked from home so as to avoid her sister's company. But Lollie expanded the business and printed a variety of greeting and novelty cards, prints, and produced books privately for clients. She tried to avoid taking on books that could lead to rows with Willie and generally deferred to him as Editor. She also continued teaching painting to girls. Though the Cuala Press was very successful, with its books becoming collector's items, it continued to need subventions. Both ladies exhibited their work in Birmingham in 1928 and stayed with the Quaker family, the Cadburys, at Bournville. Lily's poor health soon saw her finish with the embroidery business. Anne Yeats began taking painting lessons from her aunt Lollie. She proved an apt pupil and produced paintings which won prizes at the Royal Dublin Society competitions. Her father was sceptical about the matter when Anne could not produce such good work without the tutoring of Lollie. He believed that Lollie was producing the material for Anne, and banned any further entries to the Royal Dublin Society competitions. When her parents began to find Anne's personality rather difficult, they chided her with the warning, that, if she did not learn to behave, she would turn out to be like her aunt. This stricture ruined the hitherto good relationship Anne had with Lollie, furthering Lollie's aloneness.

The year of 1932 was a traumatic one for the family members. Willie lost Lady Gregory, and Louis Purser, who had remained friendly with Lollie, also died. Their long-standing friend George Russell decided to leave Dublin. He wrote to Willie saying:

Dublin is depressing these days. Ireland seems to be in my age like a lout I knew in boyhood, who had become a hero and then subsided into being a lout again.[15]

Even in his final few years, Willie caused much grief to Lollie at Cuala. Because he was abroad so much, he decided that Cuala required reorganisation with a board of directors. This consisted of Willie, Georgie, Lollie and F.R.Higgins. The latter was Willie's nominee and a guard on Lollie. He was a poet, whom Willie also appointed to the board of the Abbey

43

Theatre. Lollie found the board a hindrance. The bankers regarded Willie as the boss and refused to deal with her. The tradition of only employing female staff was ended.

During Willie's last period in Ireland, Frank O'Connor met Lollie. He described her as, *a woman of great beauty, who had what in America would be recognised as the gift of calculated indiscretion.* Lollie asked O'Connor directly, *Why don't you go and see W.B.? When you do call, he always talks about it. He's very lonely, you know.*[16]

On his final journey to France, Willie told Lady Dorothy Wellsely that he and his sister had quarrelled around the cradle and were continuing to the edge of the grave.

He and Georgie were staying at the Hotel Ideal Sejour in Cap Martin in the south of France. Several good friends, including Lady Wellesley, Miss Hilda Matheson, the Misses Heald, Dermod O'Brien (President of the United Arts Club Dublin 1919-1945), and Mrs O'Brien, were staying in the immediate area. It was obvious that Willie was unwell, as his appearance and strength began to fluctuate widely, though he continued to work and entertain visitors. He spent Christmas Day of 1938 at Lady Wellesley's villa above Beaulieu, where he entertained the other guests with his story-telling. He continued writing, completing *The Death of Cuchulainn* and giving corrections for *Under Ben Bulben* shortly before he died. The end came on Saturday 28 January 1939. Georgie Yeats asked Mrs Mabel O'Brien to write to

Grave at Drumcliffe.

44

Lily Yeats, her husband's favourite sister, and tell her what happened. This she did the day after the death. The letter reads:

My Dear Miss Yeats,

Mrs Yeats has asked me to write to you something about the last few days, for Dermod is a very old friend of your family's and I count myself a friend too and we are now staying quite close to Cap Martin.

Last Sunday afternoon Dermod and I went to call at the Ideal Sejour. Mrs Yeats was out but Dr. Yeats invited us into his room where he was in bed, but did not seem to be suffering or to feel ill. He struck us both as being in very good spirits. He was full of chat and told he was feeling so happy that he had given up reading detective novels and that he was writing lots of poetry. He did not seem in the least like an invalid, rather a delightful and endearing host.

Then on Saturday afternoon Dermod was called to the telephone and came back to tell me that the end had come. Mrs Yeats wanted Dermod to make some arrangements about the funeral service, so in the evening we got a car and went to Canon Tupper Carey's house in Monte Carlo and took him with us to the Ideal Sejour, where Mrs Yeats told us that Dr. Yeats had said at some time that he would like to be buried either in Sligo or at Roquebrune – the cemetery is by one of those little rock-built towns of which there are so many about here, but Roquebrune is one of the most picturesque and looks down on Cap Martin. He is to be taken to the little Chapel on the hill tomorrow (Monday) morning early, and to lie there till 3 o'clock, when there is to be a simple graveside service.

She took us in to see him, looking very beautiful and dignified, and the Canon repeated some of the church prayers when we knelt in the quiet room.

We were told that he had a bad turn at about 5 o'clock on Saturday morning and the doctor said there was no hope. He had one or two bouts of pain and breathlessness and was of course given morphia. Then he sank into unconsciousness and passed away quite peacefully at 2 p.m. Miss Matheson is staying there now and I think some other friends but I am not sure of their names.

You will understand that, besides our own feelings of loss, Dermod and I have very real sympathy with you and your sister and of course for Ann and Michael. It is a terrible blow for those two young things.[17]

45

Lily wrote to Mrs Jeanne Robert Foster on 8 March about her brother's death. She wrote:

... He and I were very close friends all our lives and I feel very lonely now – he was a fine man and went with his fine intellect undimmed ... Willy will finally lie at Drumcliff Co. Sligo where my great grand father, Rev. John Yeats was rector over one hundred years ago - there is a fine old Celtic cross set up by the church – which is at the foot of Ben Bulben and he had left his wishes and written his epitaph ... Elizabeth and I have written over two hundred letters between us...[17a]

Lollie died some few months after Willie in 1939. Cuala ceased publishing in 1945. Lily died in 1949 and was buried with her sister at the graveyard of St. Nahi's Church in Dundrum, Dublin.

Grave of Lollie and Lily
Dundrum, Dublin.

CHAPTER 3

PATRONS OF THE ARTIST

John Quinn, the Irish American lawyer and patron of artists, was one of the few people who had the will to call Willie Yeats to account for unacceptable behaviour. Willie, with his loose bawdy tongue, had insulted the honour of Quinn's mistress, Dorothy Coates.[1]

Quinn, both of whose parents were Irish-born, was a native of Ohio, who became a wealthy lawyer in New York City. He was a forceful man who combined a shrewd investment sense with a connoisseur's eye for good paintings and valuable literary manuscripts. Though he was familiar with the early poetry of WB Yeats, it was Jack Yeats that he first made contact with, on a visit to London and Dublin in the summer of 1902. He bought a number of Jack's paintings, and ordered a series of portraits of his Irish heroes, Douglas Hyde, George Russell, John O'Leary, from John Yeats. The agreed price, on delivery, was to be twenty pounds per painting.[2]

Quinn's vacations were always brief, due to business commitments. He managed to meet all the figures of the Irish revival within one week, including Douglas Hyde, George Moore, Edward Martyn, Lady Gregory, TW Rolleston, the Yeats sisters. He was a guest at Coole Park. While there, he sought to put an end to the current row between Willie and George Moore over the fruits of their mutual collaboration. Willie used the resulting material to write the pla, *Where There is Nothing.* On his return to New York, Quinn arranged to have the play published, to ensure the copyright for Willie. During that process, Quinn felt confident enough to suggest improvements in the text to the author. The main result of Willie's brief interaction with Quinn, according to himself, was an introduction to the philosophy of the German, Friedrich Nietzsche, which was to have a profound impact on the poet.

When Willie was about sixteen years old, his father gave him a copy of Shelley's poetry. This early introduction evoked an enduring reverence for Shelley. He later wrote that the first attempt at serious poetry he made was when he was about seventeen and much under the influence of Shelley.[2a] He later read Shelley's essay, *A Defence of Poetry,* whose ideas he made his own. Shelley believed that poets were in direct touch with the ultimate reality, the realm of ideas. Poets participated in the eternal, the infinite and the one; a poem is the creation of action according to the unchangeable forms of human nature as existing in the mind of the creator, which is itself the image of all other minds. He also noted that in earlier epochs poets were legislators or prophets. A poet is a nightingale who *sits in darkness and sings to cheer its own solitude with sweets sounds.*[3]

Another significant influence on Willie was William Blake. Blake was a poet and visionary who lived from 1753-1827. His eccentric writings and behaviour, and frustration at a lack of contemporary acceptance, often had him regarded as a madman. Yeats insisted in believing that Blake, having a mother named O'Neill, was part-Irish. He saw him as being of the Irish Bardic Tradition. According to Yeats, his poetry had an Irish flavour, a *lofty extravagance of invention and epithet recalling the Tain Bo Cuailgne and other old Irish epics, and his mythology brings often to mind the tumultuous vastness of the ancient tales of god and demon that have come down to us from the dawn of mystic tradition in what may be fairly called his fatherland.*[4] Blake claimed that he was the visionary artist who could lead the soul of man back to God and help recover Paradise through his art. He held that art and artists are spiritual, and laugh at mortal contingencies.

Willie was so taken with Blake that in 1889 he and an older friend of John Yeats, Edwin Ellis, embarked on a five year study of Blake's writings, producing a three volume edition in 1893 entitled, *The Works of William Blake, Poetic, Symbolic and Critical.*[5] Willie also edited *The Poems of William Blake* in 1893. In January of that same year he was writing to Maud Gonne about Blake. She replied, *thank you so much for paper with the accounts of Blake; it must be very interesting I am so happy it is such a success.*[6] Again in 1896 Willie sent Maud copies of the *Savoy* magazine containing articles he had written on Blake. She wrote, still in the formal mode of:

My dear Mr. Yeats,

Thank you very much for the nos of the Savoy. The articles on Blake are most fascinating. I read them to my sister who was very much interested.[7]

Yeats named Blake as his main mystical source, in his 1915 poem, *An Acre of Grass,* writing,

> *Or that William Blake*
> *Who beat upon the wall*
> *Till Truth obeyed his call.*

Another poet who influenced Yeats had a very Irish name and was of Irish extraction, but his work did not show any Irish influence. That was Arthur O'Shaughnessy. Katherine Tynan wrote an article about him in *The Irish Fireside* in 1887, which Willie praised. Yeats had included O'Shaughnessy in his own, *A Book of Irish Verse,* in 1895. Willie wrote in admiration of O'Shaughnessy's most famous poem, *Ode,* in 1900[8]. It states what Blake, Shelley and Yeats claimed poets to be, music makers, power-brokers, prophets, dreamers, visionaries and ethereal renewers.

> *We are the music makers,*
> *And we are the dreamers of dreams...*
> *Yet we are the movers and shakers*
> *Of the world for ever, it seems.*

John Quinn spoke at length to Yeats about Nietzsche during his brief Irish visit of 1902. Upon his return to New York, he immediately sent Willie writings by Nietzsche. Quinn emphasised to Willie that he himself found abhorrent Nietzsche's *so-called philosophy ... of the exaltation of brutality.*[9]Willie immersed himself in an excited state, reading the new books. He neglected writing to Lady Gregory, later apologising, saying that his new friend had nearly come between them. He told her that Nietzsche completed Blake for him and had the same roots as him. He confessed that he had not enjoyed material like it for years. He admired its astringency in particular, but said that he could not *go, all the journey with him.* Willie told Quinn that he himself had come to the same conclusions on *several cardinal matters* as Nietzsche. He declared Nietzsche to be *exaggerated and violent,* but acknowledged that he had assisted *me greatly to build up in my mind an imagination of the heroic life.*[10]

Nietzsche (1844-1900) rejected Christianity and democracy. He proclaimed *the* survival of the mighty and the superiority of the aristocracy. He believed *the will to power* was the most essential human characteristic. He attempted a transevaluation of all values, arguing that the *superman* outside good and evil would prevail. His writings have a poetic grandeur. He went mad late in life.

Though Willie indicated to both Quinn and Lady Gregory that it was actually Quinn who had introduced him to Nietzsche's books, Roy Foster and Terence Brown both dispute this. Foster argues convincingly that Willie was very familiar with the *Savoy,* which had earlier carried material about Nietzsche.[11] Brown states that Yeats had probably been aware of

Nietzsche's, *narcotic, addictive philosophic and literary works since at least 1896 for in that year the 'Savoy' included the first series of Havelock Ellis's Friedrich Nietzsche's series alongside Yeats' ' Rosa Alchema'.*[12]

Yeats was ready psychologically for Nietzsche's *contempt for the herd* and his *glorification of the hero,* in Denis Donoghue's phrase.[13]

Otto Bohlmann in his study of *Yeats and Nietzsche*, cautions that *Nietzsche by no means single handedly altered the tenor of Yeats' work. We realise, for example that the poems completed in the early years of the century owe their burgeoning severity in some measure to events in Yeats life which preceded their composition.* Bohlmann lists some traumatic events in Willie's life, Maud's Gonne's marriage and the deaths of O'Leary and Synge.[13a] Nietzsche's writings fitted into the way Willie wanted to act in his social intercourse with the lesser beings in his life. That was a course of mastery and dominance, where by virtue of a hierarchical order, and the donning of a magic mask, he could enforce submission from his inferiors.

This superior being is clearly visible in the impassioned plea Willie wrote to Maud Gonne in January 1903. He begged her not to marry into a lower order. He told her that Irish people were aristocratic-minded and would never forgive her for surrendering leadership, which he saw as a great betrayal, a denial of God. He urged her to *take up again the proud haughty solitary life, which made you seem like one of the Golden Gods.*[14]

Soon after the trauma of her marriage, it became apparent to her that Nietzsche was influencing Willie's writings. When they met in the spring of 1903 at the Grosvenor Hotel in London, he read a *Celtic Rite* to her. Some weeks later she wrote to him rejecting Nietzsche as Celtic, and also rejecting Nietzsche's disavowal of God and recognising '*no other greater than himself*'. The letter, though written at a most difficult time for Maud, shows that she retained full confidence in her own philosophy and in her friendship with Willie. The letter, written on 7 May 1903, reads:

My Dear Willie,

I have been thinking over the Celtic rite you read to me & away from the glamour of the musical words I see some defects, which I think I should signal to you.

As I said at the time it is far too much influenced by Nietzsche, not only as to expression but as to fundamental thought, for Nietzsche is not Celtic, though his intense individualism & his rushing fiery paradox & his impatience & his contempt for the banality & smallness of the many useless ones, appeal to us – Nietzsche's central thought seems to be to do away with the Gods, & to reverence & to recognise nothing greater than himself, this is most contrary to Celtic thought.

The Celts have always worshipped & striven after an ideal purer, more spiritual than themselves & it is no abasement to them to kneel before such an ideal …

Willie's new 'brutal' mode soon made itself apparent to his colleagues. His rejection of James Cousins, who had played such an integral part in developing the Abbey Theatre, was an early example. When Máire nic Shiubhlaigh had the temerity of rejecting a contract at the *Abbey*, Willie reacted with such personal vitriol that she was forced to flee to his sisters' home for comfort and safety.

His abusive behaviour to his sister Lolly, over her management of her publishing business, became so outrageous that his father was forced to intervene. John Yeats realised exactly what was occurring. Publishing was Lolly's livelihood but Willie saw it as a hobby for himself. His father beseeched him to be gentle with Lolly, but without success. John Yeats knew that Willie had come under the malign influence of Nietzsche, and told his son, *the men whom Nietzsche's theory fits are only great men of a sort, a sort of Yahoo great men. The struggle is how to get rid of them, they belong to the clumsy and brutal side of things.*[15]

Even Annie Horniman realised that she could not compete with Willie's espousal of Nietzschean philosophy and practice. Though she loved and worked for him for so long, putting huge sums of money at his disposal for the theatre, she knew that he did not and would never treat her as any sort of equal. She wrote, still out of love, but in some desperation, on 8 July 1909:

I know that you hold the Nietzschean doctrine that you have no duties towards those who have neither Genius, Beauty,

Annie Horniman

51

Rank, race or family, nor distinction, that they are 'Slaves' & that I am one of them & that no arrangement or pact with me is of any importance. On my side I firmly hold that what I truly am_is_not_affected_by_your_opinion, & that you have as good a right to hold it as I have to resist it.

If you can get people to take my place with whom you can feel on terms of Nietzschean equality the position would be much simpler. They would have no delicacy (such as I feel) in insisting upon what they might think fit.

Perhaps you will see some good points in the 'despised' slave when you look back on the last six years when you are an old man.[16]

Of course, it would be inequitable to consider only the negative outcomes from the great man's adoption of his new philosophy. It did provide him with the strength and will-power to recognise, promote, and provide a theatre for the one other man of genius to emerge from this Irish revival, John Millington Synge. Willie brought him within the controlling group at the Abbey. Synge faced great odds in having his masterpieces produced. Willie was prepared to do whatever was necessary to bring that about. He even revelled in it, recognising that though his own plays might not have much of an impact, Synge's plays were the authentic voice of the genius of the theatre which he wanted to create. The controversy over Synge's greatest play, *The Playboy of the Western World,* gave Willie the opportunity he relished, to confront his many enemies for art's sake.

Though he missed the opening night of the play, he rushed to Dublin from Scotland on receipt of Lady Gregory's famous second telegram, *Audience broke up in disorder at the word shift.* She had sent a telegram after the first two acts saying, *Play great success.* On the second night he identified the troublemakers in the audience as *Griffithites.* He always courted publicity and defended the play vociferously, with a shattered Synge sitting beside him. On the third night the police were called in to eject those causing trouble. The newspapers blamed Willie for summoning the police and demanded that the play be taken off. He would have none of that, insisting that it complete its week's run. Disturbances continued, with Willie taking to the stage himself to defy the audience.

At the end of the week, against the advice of Lady Gregory and Synge, Willie organised a public debate. Willie asked Russell to chair the meeting. He refused and joined those criticising Willie. The journalist, PD Kenny, took the chair and tried, valiantly if unsuccessfully, to keep order. Willie, who was essentially defending artistic freedom against political interference, took full responsibility for the calling in of the police and railed against the *Sinn Féiners* opposing him.

When John Quinn returned to New York that autumn of 1902, he was full of enthusiasm for all things Irish. He set up a branch of the Irish Literary Society, envisaging it as a centre for people eager to keep in touch with matters Irish. The following year he organised a semi-professional production of three of Willie's plays at the Carnegie Lyceum. There was a good response with the takings at $500. But the expenses had been so great that he reported sadly to the playwright that there was nothing left to pay him.[17]

Willie was one of the Vice Presidents of the new Society. When it was realised that he was a Protestant and quite anti-clerical, another Vice President, Archbishop John Farley of New York, resigned. Quinn, who was anti-clerical, was furious. He wrote to Willie, *I would infinitely prefer you as one of the Vice-Presidents to six Archbishops. I don't care to have it*

understood that a literary society is dominated by churchmen, whether archbishops, or priests or laymen.[18] The Society soon ceased to function.

John Quinn paid another brief visit to Ireland during the summer of 1903. He attended a performance at the Abbey Theatre and donated fifty pounds, with the promise of more. He became a patron of Dun Emer Industries, ordering a large number of their embroideries and books for shipment to America. He bought several of George Russell's paintings and was introduced to Nathaniel Hone. He also went on a walking tour of the west with Jack Yeats.

Portrait of W.B. Yeats by Seán O'Sullivan in The Abbey Theatre.

53

Motivated by the prospect of bringing a most important Irishman to the attention of America and Irish-Americans, Quinn spoke to Willie about the possibility of organising a speaking tour of America for him, which he guaranteed would be successfull financially. Willie, who was quite comfortable as a public speaker, was most eager. On his return home, Quinn set about the complex task. He distributed much advance publicity material about Willie's achievements. He quickly received thirty confirmed bookings at seventy-five dollars each. Quinn put Willie up in his own extensive apartment, and entertained him liberally before the tour began. Quinn accompanied him to as many venues as he could. They went to Washington, after a lecture at the Catholic University, they were received by President Theodore Roosevelt. Willie spoke at Carnegie Hall on *The Intellectual Revival in Ireland,* with the famous Irish-American and relative of Winston Churchill, Bourke Cockran.[19] in the chair.

All the while Quinn was writing to his friends in Ireland, telling them how well Willie was doing. He described him to Lady Gregory as the most impressive visitor from Ireland since Parnell, and to Griffith as, *incomparably capable and winning.* For Quinn, Willie was the true artist. He wrote to Hyde saying that *compromise is the soul of politics, and the artist never compromises.* Back in Ireland, Willie, with over three thousand dollars in his pockets, wrote to Quinn, *I am facing the world with great hopes and strength and I owe it all to you and I thank you and I shall always be grateful.*

Quinn came to Ireland for another brief visit in October of 1904. In Dublin he extended his circle of friends, meeting Synge, Padraig Colum, John O'Leary, Standish O'Grady, Maud Gonne and Countess Marckiewicz.

Quinn was a keen businessman and soon established his own law firm. As a result of this, he was unable to visit Ireland again until 1909. By that time, he had become quite disenchanted with Ireland and the Irish. The row over the *Playboy of the Western World* had a bad effect on Quinn. He had been a great admirer of Synge. Quinn became embroiled in recriminations in New York over the play, seeking to have it considered for its literary value. He wrote to Willie, in utter frustration but with much validity, saying:

An Irishman can't ever be a sane critic. He can't criticise anything without thinking it fair to make it on the basis of a personal attack. The true critic dissects a thing lovingly and carefully. The Irish critic goes at the subject of dissection like a drunken sailor, and with a shillelagh and a sledgehammer batters the poor corpse all around the room ... They are not critics, they are only scavengers.[20]

Quinn could not resist attacking one of his favourite taboos, the Catholic Church, in particular the Irish Catholic Church, telling Willie that it was *the greatest curse in Ireland.* The factionalism and constant squabbling in Irish politics, and especially Irish-American politics, disgusted and repelled him. He had entertained the idea of going to live in Ireland at some stage, but that was past.

Lily Yeats was due to travel to New York in late 1907 to display her Dun Emer embroideries at an Irish Exhibition there. Quinn was a confirmed bachelor, and while having a long-term mistress, Dorothy Coates, indulged in regular affairs. He fancied both the Yeats sisters. At his personal invitation, Lollie had visited New York. Willie resented her going as Quinn's guest, fearing that in some way, it might lessen his relationship with Quinn.

In August of 1907, Hugh Lane, art collector and nephew of Lady Gregory, raised a fund to allow John Yeats to visit Italy. Having received the money, and against the wishes of the donors and the advice of family and John Quinn, he decided instead to travel to America with Lily on 29 December. He hoped that like his son he could make some money before returning home. But he never did either. Relying on the friendship of Quinn and the many friends he made himself, and his family, John Yeats eked out a bohemian lifestyle for the remaining fifteen years of his life. He loved America and the eternal possibility of becoming successful.

Early in 1908, while Lily was still in America, it was announced that *the National Theatre Company, with WB Yeats, who acts with the company in the leading role,* was arriving in New York. Quinn, Lily and John Yeats, though mystified, went to the port to greet the arrivals. They turned out to be a group which split from the Abbey, put together by William Fay. They put on Willie's *Pot of Broth* and were entertained by Quinn, who after contacting Willie in Dublin, realised what was happening. Quinn demanded from Fay that he make it clear they were not the Abbey Theatre. He also demanded royalties for Willie. Quinn became embroiled in this row for several months seeking to defend the reputation of Yeats and Abbey.

Quinn intended to assist John Yeats by organising commissions of famous people, beginning with President Roosevelt. Quinn commissioned a portrait of Dorothy Coates, which John completed and received payment for. Quinn was very pleased with it. But, as always, John was not quite satisfied with his work and preceded to make alterations. When Quinn saw these he was furious, because in his view the portrait had been ruined. It was only with great effort that he resisted the temptation to physically attack the artist. John was equally furious that Quinn would seek to interfere with his right to pursue his art, as he thought fit. This right he told Quinn was *inalienable* and *cannot be contracted out.* Despite this contretemps, Quinn and the older man remained firm friends, though Quinn was disabused of the idea of securing commissions of famous people.

During the spring of 1908 Dorothy Coates travelled to Europe. Quinn was unable to get away from his business. He wrote to Maud Gonne that Dorothy would be visiting Paris and that she might spend some time with her. Maud took her around the galleries and museums. She wrote to Willie on 8 April:

I had a letter from Mr. Quinn the other day introducing an American woman, Miss Coates. She is intelligent & rather psychic, but I don't like American women generally though for Mr. Quinn's sake I was very nice to her. She has wandered on to Italy now.

Willie himself met Miss Coates that same summer. According to John Yeats, she was quite open with Willie about being Quinn's mistress. Years later, John reported that she had told himself that she was a *bachelor girl.* He understood this to mean that she led a liberal sexual life[21]. Willie could not resist gossiping about her in Dublin. This was later reported back to Quinn, who raised the matter with Coates. She replied that Willie had, in fact, attempted to seduce her.

In August of 1909 Quinn again travelled to Europe. He met Maud Gonne in Paris and discussed the Coates-Yeats business. Maud realised the importance of the matter for Quinn, but especially for Willie. She felt it essential to inform him and give some advice. She wrote, marking her letter '*Private*':

My Dear Willie,

… I was in Paris two days ago & saw Mr. Quinn. Now, Willie there is something I am going to write, which I feel perhaps I ought not to write because it goes near to breaking confidence which of all things I hate doing, but it seems to me so important to you that I must say a few words, but I do beg you will be serious & not mention the subject of my letter to your hostess or to anyone. Things you have said to & about certain Ladies have been repeated probably exaggerated & caused harm. Mr. Quinn is very hurt about it & very angry with you, which if things are as he thinks he would have a

good right to be, but I am certain there has been misrepresentation & exaggeration & perhaps invention & I have asked him to speak to you quite frankly about the whole thing & give you the opportunity of explaining – otherwise your friendship with him is over & as I know you like him & value his friendship & it would be a great pity.

Remember if you talk to Lady Gregory or to anyone else about this you may make things worse, I write this to you so that you may not let anything prevent you meeting Mr. Quinn when he is in Ireland – I would prefer you not to tell Mr. Quinn that I have written, for though I gave no promise not to write it does seem a little like breaking confidence as he said he would see you himself...

Always your friend,

Maud

Willie understood the gravity of the situation, admitting in his *Memoirs*, *I know myself to be utterly indiscreet*. He replied immediately to Maud's letter. He sought more information from her and suggested that he believed that the difficulty arose from his own conversation with Miss Coates. Maud agreed with this, but reiterated to him that other people he had spoken to had repeated his words. She suspected that Quinn had only recently heard the gossip, possibly on his journey from America, and that he had investigated it thoroughly. She told Willie that Quinn only agreed to meet him, after she had said it would be unfair not to hear his version, as she felt certain Willie must have been misrepresented. Maud warned Willie that he should not tell anyone of his discussion with Quinn. She told him that Miss Coates was unwell, and that Quinn was in a highly sensitive state on the matter. She advised him to try and remember what he had said to Miss Coates, and if she had exaggerated, to say so but in a very gentle way. She said *nothing but your own personal influence and charm can make things right between you, but I trust much to that.*

The meeting in Dublin between the poet and his patron did not go well. It lasted ten minutes with voices raised. Quinn believed Miss Coates' version of what Willie had said to her in Paris. Unable to follow Maud's advice, and seeing high comedy in the exchange, Willie is believed to have remarked to Quinn, *If it had been your wife, yes, but your mistress – never.*[22] Quinn resolved not to have anything further to do with Willie. Despite an intervention by Maud Gonne, he held fast to that for the next five years, until he was persuaded to heal the rift by Dorothy Coates.

During these years Quinn continued with his close involvement with all his other Irish friends, including all the Yeats family, apart from Willie. He expanded his interest in art, becoming a collector of Post Impressionists in particular. He became a patron of Augustus John, guaranteeing him three hundred pounds a year for paintings.

Quinn decided to cease collecting books, and to buy manuscripts instead. Over a twelve-year period, he acquired nearly all the manuscripts of Joseph Conrad.

When Willie came to New York later, to do preliminary work for the forthcoming *Abbey* tour, he and Quinn did not see each other. Only when Lady Gregory replaced Willie, did Quinn play a major role in the tour. The controversy that had occurred in Dublin on the production of *The Playboy,* proved to be minor to what occurred in America. In Philadelphia the whole company was arrested and Quinn had to go there and get a *Habeas Corpus.* Through all the battles on behalf of the Abbey, Quinn had the consolation of having a passionate affair with Lady Gregory.

On one occasion Lady Gregory asked Quinn whether he would ever be friends again with Willie. She told Quinn that Willie recently said to her:

It is a strange thing that Quinn who knows me so well and I have lived with so much, should think me capable of what he does. Quinn replied; *When women get mixed up with things there are always quarrels,* and changed the subject immediately. Lady Gregory reported this conversation to Willie, adding, *I feel sure it is all right and that when you meet him again you can just talk as if nothing happened.*[23]

During the summer of 1913, Dorothy Coates fell seriously ill again with tuberculosis. Quinn, who had been unable to travel to Europe, went to the Adirondacks for a month. He was most concerned and upset by Dorothy's illness and wanted to be close to her at Saranac. He was able to visit her several times each week. Maud Gonne wrote from Paris to Quinn, reassuring him that tuberculosis was curable, as she had had it herself, and made a full recovery. Willie too was worried, and at one stage believed Dorothy was dying. He wrote her epitaph, showing it to her after her recovery[24]. Some time later, Dorothy asked Quinn to make up the quarrel with Willie. She was very conscious that she had been the focus of the row. Willie was then in America on a lecture tour. Quinn wrote to him on 9 February 1914:

My Dear Yeates, … I have always felt that apart from intellect you were always generous in your sympathies and full of humanity and that your heart was in the right place.

So if the suggestion appeals to you, I should be glad to shake hands with you and let by-gones be by-gones.[25]

Willie replied positively and within days was again staying in Quinn's apartment. The two disciples of Nietzsche put their difference behind them. On the night before Willie was due to sail home, Quinn laid on a dinner for thirty-eight guests in honour of the poet. Among the after dinner speakers were Augustus John, Bourke Cockran and Willie himself. All of their mutual friends were relieved, especially the members of the Yeats family.

As usual Quinn was full of ideas to assist the poet. Within a few months he put an idea of guaranteeing him a fixed income for his new manuscripts. He wrote on 28 April 1914:

... I will pay you so much a year for them, depending on the quantity and the different things, taking articles as they are or poems as they are. I would prefer them in separate cases, and I would pay you a reasonable price for them, more perhaps than you would get of any dealer, who would pay you only a small price and then shop them around at a high price.[26]

Willie was a shrewd businessman and declined any fixed annual amount. He professed that such an arrangement might put him under pressure to produce material. He did not want to risk Quinn feeling under pressure either. Instead he proposed that as manuscripts became available, he would send them to Quinn, who could pay him a fair price.[27] They agreed a price of £50 for the manuscript of the first part of Willie's memoirs, *Reveries*. Before that could be transmitted to Willie, his father had an accident with a motorcar.

Though John Yeates was not badly injured, the accident once again focussed Willie's mind on his father's upkeep. John earned small amounts spasmodically, but was never going to be able to make ends meet. He was getting old, and refused every overture to return home. Willie knew that, but for Quinn's generosity, his father would be a pauper in New York. He decided that Quinn should retain the £50 for expenses. Later he and Quinn decided to set up a trust fund to pay John's bills. Willie would contribute to the fund by way of manuscripts, or cash if he could afford it.

The quest for Home Rule raised Quinn's interest again in Ireland. He detested John Redmond's stance on encouraging Irishmen to join the British army. He became very friendly with Roger Casement and Patrick Pearse, both of whom he hosted in New York. The Great War made him very anti-German. He wrote to Gwen John, early in 1915, *Ten or fifteen years ago I was rather taken with Nietzsche and with the philosophy of the strong conquering man and with the notion that the conquering nations were the great nations. But I realise now that that is all wrong.*[28] He wrote similar thoughts to Willie in February of that same year. The loss of the *Lusitania*, with Lady Gregory's nephew, Hugh Lane, aboard, furthered increased his hatred of Germany.

Willie had assisted the struggling James Joyce as early as 1902. Quinn now began to buy all Joyce's major manuscripts after an intervention by Ezra Pound. Quinn demonstrated the same kind of enthusiasm for Joyce's artistic freedom, as he had earlier shown for JM Synge.

Quinn was somewhat sorry to hear of Willie's marriage. His bachelor status was one of the common factors that had endeared him to Quinn. The latter wrote to a male friend that he remained single, *by great foresight, courage and iron determination.*[29] Nevertheless he felt that *Yeats is a wise man and I doubt if he has made a mistake.* Willie wrote Quinn about his wife and sent a photograph, adding: *looks nearer to her twenty-five years than the photograph. She is a deep student in all my subjects, and is at present deep in the astrological works of Picodella Mirandola.*[30] Willie indeed made a wise move in marrying Georgie Hyde-Lees, as she played a significant role in the rest of his life.

Quinn experienced his first serious illness in 1918. He wrote to Willie in terms that the younger man could hardly understand:

My illness made me horribly sensitive and tender of suffering in others. Before, when I did kind or considerate things, they were perhaps mostly intellectually kind, kind without tenderness, except of course to my sisters and my parents and my brother when he lived. But tenderness must be felt. I never before realised what a power for good money could be if there were tenderness and love as well as intellect in its use.[31]

John Yeats was an inveterate writer of letters and Cuala Press published some of them successfully. Willie thought that if his father would write his autobiography, it would prove commercially successfully also. He and Quinn sought to interest the old man in this project. Willie proposed that Quinn offer John one pound for each one thousand words produced. Little manuscript was forthcoming.

In 1919 as John Yeats approached eighty years, he fell seriously ill, Quinn urged the family to pressurise him to return to Ireland. He feared that John would die in New York, and that he would have to organise things, adding to Willie, *all of which I shrink from horribly.* Quinn discovered in exasperation, that John owed nearly five hundred dollars at his boarding house. He offered to pay it if the family could get John to go home. Willie appeared non-plussed as he wrote to Quinn, *If we live long enough we shall all be trials,* though he did add, *When my father comes home he can be put into the University club where he can talk to the other atheists and my sister will give him the bodily comforts.* Willie sent a cheque of over two hundred pounds to Quinn to pay off John's debts. He also told Quinn that he would prefer to again separate fees for his manuscripts from his father's upkeep.

Willie went to America on a lecture tour in 1920, to make money to renovate his Ballylee Tower. He had not seen Quinn for six years and wanted to introduce his wife to him and his father. Willie and his wife spent the last month of their time in America staying with Quinn. Willie tried, unsuccessfully, to take his father back with him to Ireland. Ezra Pound felt that the tour was a success as he wrote to Quinn in June 1920: *Besides he'll have enough to buy a few shingles for his phallic symbol on the Bogs, Ballyphallus or whatever he calls it with the river on the first floor.*[32] Further attempts to lure John Yeats back to Ireland, were unsuccessful. He told Quinn that he couldn't possibly leave before he had completed the portrait of Quinn he had been working on for seven years. Quinn assured him that he was happy with the picture but John demurred. The old man died on 3 February 1922. Quinn sent a telegram to the Yeats sisters in Dublin:

Regret your father passed away this morning seven o'clock. He had good day yesterday, free from pain, and was cheerful. Talked last evening cheerfully. I left him sleeping at eleven o'clock last night, but felt end was near. He slept well during the remainder of night, waking at intervals. The end came in sleep without pain or struggle. After conference please cable desires about burial. If resting place to be Ireland, temporary vault can be arranged here until spring. Everything was done for his comfort and peace of mind and he had best possible medical attention.[33]

The Yeats family could not afford to have the body returned to Ireland. It rested in the Woodlawn Cemetery vault in Westchester, New York for the winter. Willie then accepted Mrs Foster's offer to have their father buried in her family plot in Chesterton Rural Cemetery, in July. Mrs Foster chose a stone made from Vermont marble, with a Celtic cross cut in the top. The inscription, written by his eldest son, read:

In remembrance of John Butler Yeats of Dublin, Ireland. Painter and Writer. Born in Ireland Mar. 16, 1839. Died in N.Y. City Feb 3, 1922.[34]

BL Reid writes that John Quinn described the surroundings to Willie thus: *When we reached the pine grove it was noon, a sunny day, with blue skies and white rolling clouds. Service was blurred by the wind in the needles and pierced with birdcalls.*[35] However, Mrs Foster writing in 1968, says that *Quinn was too ill to come.* She reported that no mourners arrived for the ceremony.[36] Mrs Foster, who was Quinn's last mistress, continued her efforts to have the body repatriated to Ireland. When Oliver Gogarty's remains were repatriated from America in 1957, she wrote a letter to the President of the Irish Senate in 1958. Her letter was passed on to An Taoiseach, whose secretary declined her request.[37]

Though Quinn had close associations with Willie over such a long period, other Irish artists had already dedicated publications to him. Douglas Hyde dedicated his *Connacht Half-Ranns* to Quinn and George Russell had done likewise with his *Imaginations and Reveries.* At Lady Gregory's prompting, Willie now followed suit with his *Trembling of the Veil*, the second volume of his *Autobiographies.* The dedication read, *To John Quinn my friend and helper and friend and helper of certain people mentioned in this book.*[38]

In 1924 Quinn auctioned his extensive library and extensive art collection, realising seventy two thousand dollars. He died on 28 July of that same year. Willie wrote to the grieving Mrs Foster: *I have known no other so full of over-flowing energy and benevolence ... I mean his benevolence expressed him as a work of art expresses the artist.*[39]

Mrs Foster was concerned about the long-term care of John Yeats' grave. She gave that responsibility to her executor, Dr. William M. Murphy. She wrote to him on 6 June 1957:

I felt that you would look after the Yeats plot and monument and that your children would carry on in the future. I wrote Mrs William Butler Yeats but as she never had very much liking for the father of her late husband, she has no interest in looking after the grave plot and monument.[40]

Late in her life, Mrs Foster had the pleasure of receiving several visits from Senator Michael Yeats, the poet's son, and members of his family.[41]

CHAPTER 4

MACHIAVELLI AT THE ABBEY

In his study of the Abbey Theatre in 1979, Hugh Hunt wrote:

Yeats has been criticised for the devious way he 'nudged out' those whose usefulness appeared to be declining or who appeared to be a threat to the authority of the Board. Such criticisms are partly true: Yeats was both devious and ruthless in his methods. Even before the departure of the Fays, Martyn, Moore and Russell found themselves out-manoeuvred into positions where they could no longer continue to serve. Nor can it be denied that both he and Lady Gregory were autocrats.[1]

In January 1897, Willie Yeats raised the idea of an Irish Celtic theatre at a meeting of the Young Ireland Society. This idea was followed up later that same year at Coole Park, when he wrote a manifesto outlining the idea of a season of plays in Dublin by Martyn, Moore and O'Grady. This theatre would be an experimental and literary theatre, unlike those found in England, where the actor was supreme. From the start, Yeats was influenced by French theatre, where the writer was paramount in a literary exercise. He was seeking £300 to begin and was already promised £150.

At a meeting of the National Literary Society in January 1899, Yeats announced the Irish Literary Theatre. The Anglo-Irish ascendancy unionists and Maud Gonne backed it. Arthur Griffith's *United Irishman* described it as an attempt to produce a really high-class Anglo-Irish drama, adding that such plays could never be popular. They were too far above the ordinary peoples' heads.[2] The project received much publicity. Yeats then set about finding professional actors for a May production of his own verse play, *The Countess Kathleen* and Edward Martyn's *The Heather Field*. Frank Hugh O'Donnell attacked Yeats' play before production as a blasphemous calumny on Irish nationalism, and Yeats himself as a meandering decadent,with a diseased mind. He said the play made the Irish nation out to be just like a sordid tribe of black devil worshippers on the Congo or the Niger.[3] The controversy upset Marytn, who was a devout Catholic. He threatened to withdraw his own play and his financial backing for the season, until assuaged by a Catholic priest. Maud Gonne, for whom the play was written with the hope that she might agree to act in it, and to whom the play was dedicated, had no sympathy for Martyn, writing to Willie on 28 March 1899:

I am sorry to hear of all the bother you are having. It is too horrid for words on Martyn's part; what a contemptible creature. You must go on with Countess Kathleen all the same. I really believe it will have much greater success alone without Martyn's very heavy & rather indigestible 'Heather Field'.

You must get a short Gaelic piece acted with it – which will answer the support of all the Gaelic people who are growing in influence & numbers daily.

The season was a success. Advanced nationalists were outraged. The drama critic of the

Frank Hugh O'Donnell

United Irishman, Frank Fay, wrote, *Mr. Yeats has proved himself to be an artist: we know him to be patriotic; nevertheless he has exhibited a startling misconception of the character of his countrymen.*

The second and last season of the Irish Literary Theatre took place late in 1900. A version of *Diarmaid & Grainne*, produced collaboratively by Yeats and George Moore, was a major flop. The Unionists were hostile to Yeats, due to his recent objection to the late Queen's Irish visit. The advanced nationalists objected to the importation of an ensemble of English actors – Ben's Company- to perform in the main play. The second play, by Douglas Hyde, *Casadh An tSúgáin,* was produced by Willie Fay, using Hyde's Gaelic League players. The ensuing row between Moore and Martyn finished the experimental theatre. Yeats realised that using imported English actors was a mistake. He also realised that plays consisting of chanted verse were not viable, and that subsidies were essential. Henceforth, a literary movement would develop into a theatrical company.

The Fay brothers amateur company, The Ormond Dramatic Company, continued producing Irish and English plays. Willie Fay acted and Frank directed. They were both experts in their fields. Discussions took place during the summer of 1901 about establishing a national theatre company. James Cousins introduced George Russell to the Fays. Russell was also friendly with Maud Gonne's Inghinidhe na hÉireann and offered his play *Deirdre* to them jointly. Frank Fay was an advanced nationalist, closely allied to Arthur Griffith and suspicious of Yeats. The latter attended rehearsals of *Deirdre*, but his proffered advice was firmly rejected by Frank Fay. Willie Fay has said *the preparations for production of an Irish play with a completely Irish cast for the first time in history were under way. The Irish National Theatre was born.*[4]

Yeats had earlier seen Fay's Amateur Company perform Alice Milligan's *Red Hugh* and, as he wrote himself, emerged from the theatre *with my head on fire.*[5] He wanted desperately to see his new unfinished play, *On Baile's Strand,* performed in a Dublin accent. Yeats and Lady Gregory realised that collaboration between themselves, the Fays and Inghinidhe na hÉireann, might be a vehicle to advance their own ambitions. They had completed the highly nationalist play *Caithlin ni hUalachain,* and felt, correctly, that it could be used to tempt Inghinidhe na hÉireann and the Fays to become associated with them.

On 6 January Maud inquired from Willie: *Have you decided anything about Kathleen yet? I think Fay will be able to manage it & I am sure it will be better than with English actors, possibly we might get miss Young to act with Fay.* Maud Gonne's own manoeuvrings, and particularly her offer to play Caithlin, sealed the deal when the matter was discussed in London on 13 January 1902. Though Willie Fay, with good reason, did not cherish the notion of producing a play with such a personage, and a friend of Yeats to boot, playing the lead. Rehearsals were very difficult, with George Moore attending and Maud arriving late. Yeats wisely remained on in London.

Yeats's play, together with Russell's *Deirdre,* was performed from 2nd to-4th April 1902 at St. Teresa' Hall, Clarendon St, under the auspices of Fay's Irish National Dramatic Society. Yeats resented Russell's play, as it became a favourite for the players. Maud Gonne had written to Willie on 6 January saying: *Russell's*

St. Teresa's Hall, Clarendon St., Dublin.

65

*Deirdre is very good. He & Miss Young acted it at Mrs Coffey's last week –
Moore was very struck with it.* Maud Gonne gave a famous performance in
Caithlin that went into Irish folklore as a piece of nationalist propaganda, as
she intoned the words, *They shall be remembered forever, They shall be alive
forever, They shall be speaking forever, The people shall hear them forever.*
Gregory and Yeats played only a peripheral part in the proceedings. She
attended one rehearsal before departing for Venice. Yeats arrived quite late
in Dublin and succeeded in drumming up publicity in the *United Irishman.*
A banner with the name of *Inghinidhe na hÉireann* was draped by the stage.

Yeats immediately spoke with the Fays about future collaboration. He
promised that he would get the plays and they should train actors. Both sides
favoured a 'method' style of acting and placed artistic independence above
pure nationalism. The Irish American patron of the arts and friend of
Yeats's, John Quinn, had offered to subsidise a first season of the new group
for £25, and £50 thereafter. Yeats became honorary President of Fay's Irish
National Dramatic Society, by default on 9 August. WG Fay wrote, *The
reception of our first venture was so cordial that we gained many new
members and we offered the presidency of the society to A.E. He said Mr.
Yeats was more suitable for the office, and Yeats accepted our invitation.*[6]
Lady Gregory, George Russell, Doughlas Hyde and Maud Gonne became
members of the board of directors. It was essentially a combination of Fays'
Ormond Dramatic Company, the Irish Literary Theatre and Inghinidhe na
hÉireann. George Moore and Edward Martyn were now outsiders. The
patronage of Cumann na nGael, an umbrella organisation of a variety of
nationalist groups, was clearly recognised by Yeats, writing in *Samhain,* as
most essential to the project. The first season was in fact organised and
financed by Cumann na nGael. Frank Fay described it as, *a Dublin political
body.*[7] Gonne and Griffith as an offshoot from the Gaelic League formed it,
because the latter was constitutionally unable to become involved in
political interests. The plays performed during that October season, were by
Yeats, Russell, James Cousins, Fred Ryan, Lady Gregory and P.T. McGinley.
Even at that early stage it was apparent to some that Yeats was in the process
of staging a coup d'etat. James Cousins, one of the founders of the group felt
that Yeats acted as if *we were contributors to him and not he to us.*[8]

Maud acted somewhat naively as she wrote to Yeats in September 1902,
alerting him to concerns that Fay had not affiliated to Cumann na nGael and
did not wish to be seen to be *too strongly political.* He had withdrawn Yeats's
play *Hour Glass* from Cumann na nGael's Samhain Festival that autumn,

wishing to keep it for the National Theatre Company's opening of its own Camden St theatre. She wrote to Willie suggesting that he make contact with Fay on the matter and offer them another of his plays instead. The Samhain Festival took place in the large Antient Rooms, while the Camden theatre was only a very small venue. She said she doubted that Fay would be so foolish as to antagonise the Cumann na nGael, adding, *Anyhow, you are President & Doughlas Hyde & myself are vice presidents of the National Theatre Company & both acting ladies are Inghinidhe so I don't think we need be too anxious on that score.* Willie soon replied, reassuring her that everything was going smoothly with the Fays.

William Bulfin wrote that Yeats' physical presence alone was overpowering. He:

Pervades the hall. He wanders about like a troubled soul. He is an original character. Everything he does seems to stir up some rancour, and he is nearly always doing things. I have done my best to find out from my conversations with him whether he unconsciously goes around driving poles into beehives or whether he does it purposively, simply for the sake of notoriety. I have not been able to convict him of doing it purposely. He wanders in the realms of the mind, just as he does in the physical world –taking little note of where his steps are leading him.[9]

Yeats was an expert in generating publicity both, in Dublin and London, for whatever his purpose. His method was to start a controversy by giving a lecture or writing a controversial article. One of the main attributes he held over those he collaborated with was his vision. He knew where he wanted to go, what he wanted to achieve. He was a long-term thinker and an excellent short-term manipulator of people and situations. Bulfin was therefore mistaken in his opinion of Yeats. Already he was plotting to deal with one of those who he felt might stand in his way.

Within weeks of the first season, Yeats had decided that James Cousins had to go, telling Frank Fay that it was better to regard Cousins as an enemy. Yeats was exercising his own petty jealousies, probably against George Russell, in this matter. Cousins had had two plays produced in their first season. He was a good friend of Russell's, and was on the artistic wing of the Company. He can be rightfully recognised as one of the founders of the new theatrical movement. Yeats' tactic was to be so severely critical of Cousins' new plays that the latter abandoned the company.

The choice of new plays was often a cause of great division with the varying elements of the Company vying for position. Maud Gonne's Inghinide na hÉireann and Cumann na nGael, were clearly interested in nationalism first, and theatre second. Yeats' supporters put artistic freedom and artistic standards first. The Fays, without thinking carefully enough about their own future, joined the Yeatsian view, and abandoned their erstwhile allies on the nationalist side. Though Padraig Colum's play *The Saxon Shilling*, was a prizewinner at a Cumann na nGael competition, and thereby backed by the nationalists, the Fays sought major revisions before they would produce it. Arthur Griffith resigned from the company in protest.

Maud attended one of the rehearsals, and in front of the company told Fay that his changes made the play absurd. Maud wrote to Willie that she might have to resign in protest over Fay's (Willie) treatment of Colum's play, as the case involved a matter of principle. In a letter, dated January 1903, she wrote:

Last night in Russell's the Fays both said it was an affair for the stage manager & I had no right to give an opinion before the Company. I said I offered no opinion on the acting which was the affair of the stage manager, but that I or anyone had the right of expressing our opinion about the merit of a published play & and as vice president I had certainly the right of expressing an opinion before the company, that the alterations made destroyed the play. Mr. Fay said it rested with no one but himself, that the rest of the Company's opinion didn't count, and finally he handed back the manuscript of the play to Colum saying it shouldn't be acted at all ... I merely said that Inginidhe na hEireann will produce it.

Willie Fay told Maud directly, that his opinion was final on the altering, cutting, & choosing of plays, despite her position in the company[10.] *The Saxon Shilling* was produced in May by Inghinidhe na hEireann, with an entirely new set of actors, to a resounding success at the Rotunda.

It was clear that some streamlining of the National Theatre Company decision-making powers, particularly the choosing of plays, was necessary. As was often the case Russell, was brought in as an honest broker. He suggested that a new forum was required to decide on new productions. In February 1903, he introduced a new constitution. The new body was to be called The Irish National Theatre Society. The aim of the new body was:

To create an Irish National Theatre, to act and produce plays in Irish or English, written by Irish writers on Irish subjects and such dramatic work

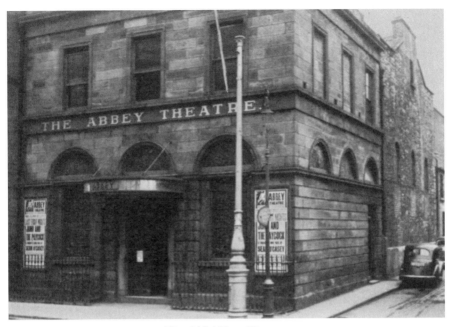

The Old Abbey Theatre.

by foreign authors as would tend to educate and interest the public of this country in the higher aspects of dramatic art.[11]

Russell was first elected as president, but refused the position. It was with great difficulty that he persuaded the company to elect Yeats instead. Maud Gonne, Russell, Douglas Hyde became Vice Presidents. Willie Fay was stage manager and Fred Ryan became secretary. A Reading Committee, which was to be of vital importance, was set up. It consisted of Yeats, Russell, Gregory, Column, Griffith, Gonne and Ryan. It generally met at Gregory's rooms in the Nassau Hotel, thus giving her an immediate advantage. The executive nominated plays and a 75% vote was required for staging.[12]

The power the Fays had in their own company was no more. They had been out-manoeuvred, and Yeats' prints were not to be seen on the evidence. He had been in London during most of the negotiating, and though he did not believe in democracy in artistic matters, he was far-sighted enough to see that the plot was moving in his direction. The Fays were not happy with this development and it served to bring them even closer to Yeats' vision. This would also make them even more beholden to him, which was a dangerous state. The power was initially with the Reading Committee. So it was that

69

Yeats' opposition to Cousins' play '*Sold*' was consolidated, and Colum's play *The Saxon Shilling*, was withdrawn. The first season of the new company choose Yeats' own *Hour Glass*, which was produced exactly as he wanted it, and Gregory's *Twenty-five*. They went on at the Molesworth Hall on 14 March.

Yeats and Gregory were, like some others, essentially interested in having their own plays produced. Other members were interested in different aspects of the theatrical enterprise.

It should be noted at this stage that Yeats was suffering the devastating indignity and embarrassment of losing Maud Gonne to Major John MacBride. He endeavoured to carry it off with his usual aplomb. Maud continued to write to him in her normal friendly terms, though she was not averse to harassing him about theatrical matters. Yeats and Gregory were now clearly centre stage in the company.

In April he spoke at the Contemporary Club, saying that a permanent hall was required. Rehearsals were being held in a room at the back of a butcher's shop on Camden St.

Yeats continued to commute between Dublin and London. In London, much to Lady Gregory's distress, another of those wealthy women anxious about his welfare, Annie Horniman, was ministering to him. She was also keen to collaborate with him on theatrical matters, if, as with Gregory, he was not yet interested in matters romantic. In May the Irish National Theatre Society (INTS), played a season in London with *Hour Glass* and *Twenty-five*. It was assisted in the exercise by the London Irish Literary Society and received good reviews. Willie Fay's production was praised and Yeats acknowledged him as *founder of the Society*. The fashionable set, however, still zoned in on Yeats and Gregory, as the main people in the company.

In Dublin Yeats was still treated with suspicion. The *United Irishman* and the *Irish Times* both attacked his sincerity and his contempt for ordinary people. The *Leader* wrote:

He is one of the most complex personalities we have. There is the touch of the real poet in him and a spice of the amateur politician ... he is as handy a man as any under the sun at successfully 'planting' his literary wares, 'no flies on him there'.

Then, not quite out of the blue, but of fundamental import, the plays of John Millington Synge began to arrive at the INTS. Yeats had earlier met Synge at the Hotel Corneille in Paris and introduced him to Maud Gonne. She sought to enlist him towards her political motives, but Synge did not like her, or her proposed methods of freeing Ireland. Yeats has suggested that it was his suggestion to Synge, that he should *"go to the Aran Islands and live there as if you were one of them"*, which led Synge to do so. WJ McCormack in his biography of Synge, *Fool of the Family*, disputes that, saying that Synge's decision had as much to do with family and personal matters. He writes, *He had returned from Paris, renewed a proposal of marriage, been rejected and two weeks later headed west*[13]. McCormack also argues that Yeats tried to present Synge as an aristocrat, which he was not, though he was from a well-off Protestant family. Synge did become a regular visitor to the Aran Islands. His first two one act plays, *In the Shadow of the Glen* and *Riders to the Sea,* convinced Yeats, and others that here was an authentic new Irish voice of genius. Yeats immediately decided to bring Synge on board his theatrical mission as a partner, and invited him to Coole. But controversy was immediate. *In the Shadow of the Glen* was read to the INTS, though not to the Reading Committee. The story line upset some. Many believed that no Irish lady ever eloped with a tramp, even if her husband, stick in hand, ordered her to get out. More rows developed as James Cousins', *Sold,* backed by Russell and Column, was reintroduced for consideration.

Yeats, backed by the Fays, threatened resignation. Cousins like Edward Martyn and others, then gave their plays to rival theatrical groups in the city. The Inghinidhe na hÉireann group within the INTS, were furious and regarded the Fays as traitors. Synge, too, came under attack.

In September, Maud, now signing herself as 'Maud Gonne MacBride' since her marriage in February, wrote to Willie saying:

I still think it best for me to cease to be the vice president of the theatre Co, I won't undertake any but National fights, & the Theatre Co. does not seem inclined for such fights. I have no wish to injure the Co. so please let me know how to gently withdraw without harming it – From all I can hear Synge's play [In the Shadow of the Glen] is horrid & I will have no responsibility for it – It was forced on the company by a trick. They were told the Reading Committee had accepted it & they had no choice in the matter & yet Russell told me as far as he knows it was never submitted to the Reading Committee. He certainly never saw it or was consulted about it.

The naming of Russell as Maud's informant would not have endeared him to Yeats. But Russell never had any difficulty in confronting his old 'friend'. Willie, who now knew that he could never 'capture' his muse, did not accept Maud's version of how the Theatre had developed. He outlined his interpretation in a letter to her. This drew a furious response from her as she rejected his revisionism of the facts. She wrote:

From your last letter to me you evidently do not understand or forget what has taken place.

Fay having succeeded in a certain measure through you & your friends (many of whom are unionists) has lost his head and thinks he can insult the National Societies who created him...*you forget the existence of the National Theatre Society was originally due to Inginidhe na hEireann & Cumann na nGael. If these societies had not taken Fay up he would still be contentedly playing vulgar English farces in the Union Jack Coffee Palace. ... He came to me & said he would rather act for Nationalists if he could get Nationalist pieces & we introduced him to Russell who gave him or rather gave us his 'Deirdre' to act. Have you forgotten how both Russell & I urged you to let us have your 'Kathleen', how you said Lady Gregory thought you should not – & how at last to make things smooth I consented to act Kathleen. It was Inghinidhe na hÉireann & Cumann na nGael who financed each of Fay's first attempts at National performances ... because we wanted a National Theatre Co. to help us combat the influence of the low English theatres & music halls.*

It is absurd to say that you did not know all this from the beginning though I believe you have forgotten it all now & have grown to think that it is you & Lady Gregory & her friends who started the National Theatre Co. Undoubtedly lately you have given it great financial help & all its London publicity ... It is somewhat hard to see an instrument we fashioned at considerable sacrifice of time & money quietly taken possession of for another purpose by people, who to say the least of it, are not militantly national. You, who are looked on as a friend, have taken the instrument we formed, from us; your conception is different from ours.

Willie had suggested the text of a letter of resignation Maud might write. But she rejected his text as possibly indicating that she was becoming less committed to the cause of Ireland. She declared that she had no intention of narrowing her activities in the future. She wrote that Ireland was in a life-and-death struggle with England. Most of the men and women engaged in that struggle have not the time or energy for purely literary and artistic movements, unless they could be made to serve directly the National cause.

Maud sent Willie a copy of a short letter of resignation addressed to George Russell, still a Vice President of the National Theatre Society. It read:

I wish to resign my position as Vice-President of the N.T. Society.

When I joined the Society I understood it was formed to carry on National & propagandist work by combating the influence of the English stage.

I find it has changed its character & ideals & while I shall always be interested and glad of its success, I can no longer take an active part in the direction & work.

When *In The Shadow of the Glen* was produced that October. Maud, with some friends, staged a dramatic walkout from the Molesworth Hall. But Yeats and the Fays ignored their protest. The costume designer for the production of *The King's Threshold* was the redoubtable Annie Horniman. She wrote gushingly to Yeats, *Do you realise that you have given me the right to call myself 'artist'. How do I thank you?* Yeats already had his answer prepared. It would be in cash, lots of it. Douglas Hyde and several of the actors left the INTS at that time. Yeats was then in the driving seat, free of any cause and with the Fays at his mercy. He was ready to take on allcomers, including the Catholic Church.

Yeats spent the next five months in the USA on a lecture tour. He told the *New York Daily Tribune* of 15 November 1903, *we have a National Theatre – of which I am the head, which is making actors, and good ones too, of young Irish working people.* The Society functioned well in his absence.

Annie Horniman was a wealthy English woman who first met Yeats at a meeting of the Order of the Golden Dawn in London in 1890. She was very interested in theatre and Willie cultivated her. She became his unpaid secretary in 1903 and offered to provide a hall for his INTS. It was clear from the beginning that her interest was in Yeats and not in any way in Ireland or Irish drama. Yeats, sent her proposal for a theatre in the Mechanics Institute on Dublin's Abbey St., to Russell, who had remained on as a Vice President throughout all the infighting. She was prepared to adapt the hall and subsidise the productions, pay the actors salaries and the cost of touring. But she wanted to be closely involved with what was to become the Abbey Theatre.

Now that Yeats had assumed control, he became more direct in his dealings with many people. He regarded himself and his peers as an elite class who should not be bothered by plebeians. He wrote to Russell, *Neither your character nor the character of any of us need defence. We should not discuss such things with any but our equals.* He was critical of actors whom he regarded as mere clerks and shop-girls. He criticised some of the leading actresses as not having sensitive enough bodies to portray high emotion. He backed up Horniman's view that seats at the Abbey should cost one shilling, though six-pence was the norm in Dublin. He insisted that the Society adopt strict rules and introduced new byelaws for the Reading Committee, against some of the Directors' opinions.

The first season in the Abbey opened on 27 December 1904 with plays by Yeats, Gregory and Synge. Gregory was ill in Coole, so Willie took all the limelight. Though the crowds later dropped off alarmingly, the opening night was packed and a triumphal occasion for Willie. Though the whole enterprise had many parts, Roy Foster has written, *as far as posterity was concerned, they were irretrievably swept aside into subordinate roles by by WBY's increasingly powerful sense of his own history.*[14]

Despite the sudden news from Paris of the ending of Maud Gonne's marriage, and her beseeching Yeats to help her, he intended to forge ahead with attempting to wrest total control of the Abbey. He wanted a professional theatre, giving the directors complete control. The actors and others would be offered contracts. Though Russell had, in sheer exasperation, finally resigned the company the previous April, Yeats turned to him to write a new constitution, changing the Society from a cooperative to a professional limited liability company. Its members would be authors and other nominees. An executive of three would have the real control. Russell favoured the notion that those who refused a salary would retain membership of the Society. Yeats turned this down flat. Russell knew exactly what has happening and was totally distraught after so many arguments, over so many things with Yeats. He told him, *Why the devil do you talk of the new rules as a compromise? What do you want? I shall have no further part in it. Who on earth is there to oppose you?* Lady Gregory was nervous about the changes, as she realised that they depended on her rival's, Annie Horniman's money. They both wanted to be Yeats' main collaborator. Synge convinced her that since they, with Yeats, would be the executives, they would retain complete control. The new Company came into being at a general meeting on 22 September. The three directors, Yeats,

Gregory and Synge, had one hundred shares each, while the actors had one share each.

Russell later wrote to Gregory bitterly, saying:

The facts are that the Society was not started by Yeats but by the actors, that I drew up the rules and that I had a considerable difficulty in inducing the members to elect him as president. These members subscribed a certain sum every week for some time towards the use of a hall ... the members opposed to Yeats were as you may remember in a majority and it was important to him to get them to resign and as I recognised his right to control the theatre which Miss Horniman gave him, I took a great deal of trouble in arguing and persuading those members opposed to Yeats to go. It is very unfortunate that Yeats should arouse such savage enmities among people who long ago had every inclination to serve him and it would do him no good to have this matter made public. He would wreck anything he is concerned with by his utter incompetence to understand the feelings or character of anybody he is dealing with. He has no talent for anything but writing and literature and literary discussions. If I were an autocrat I would give him £20,000 a year if at the end he had written two hundred lines of poetry – if he opened his mind or mouth on business or tried to run any society, I would have him locked up as dangerous to public peace.[15]

By December 1905, one of the best-known actresses in the company, Máire nic Shuibhlaigh had refused to sign a contract and demanded more money. This lead to a furious row with Willie, during which he berated her viciously. She was a close friend of the Yeats family and fled to them for protection. Willie threatened to sue her. This led to a walkout by several nationalist-minded writers and actors who later formed The Theatre of Ireland. Willie wisely facilitated the group of secessionists, and with Horniman's money bought them off with £50 each and a selection of costumes. He thus retained control of the name of the INTS and the remnant of the company. Crucially, the Fays remained with the Abbey.

Annie Horniman began to demand more of a say in all aspects of the workings of the INTS, since it was her money that was keeping it afloat. This caused difficulties all round. It was generally left to Yeats to handle her as best he could. She decided to join the company on its Scottish tour of May 1906. It was very successful but Horniman was outraged by the behaviour of some of the company. They were a group of young people away from home, out to enjoy themselves. Frank Fay was courting the actress Brigit

O'Dempsey, and Synge was in love with another young actress, Molly Allgood. Horniman wrote scathing letters to Yeats in London complaining about the vulgar behaviour of the Company. As usual, she was brandishing finance as a weapon. She renegotiated her subsidy downwards, and began to distance herself from the Abbey. Yeats had to mollify her and antagonise the Fays, resulting in Willie Fay losing his role as business manager.

Yeats was essentially a writer who wanted to see his material performed. He realised that his verse plays were not popular, and therefore had not much of a future at the Abbey. He was dissatisfied with the Abbey's production of his work, believing that an English company or at least English actors would do them much better. He believed that the Abbey was best doing 'peasant' plays, but needed to widen its production. Casting was Willie Fay's area of expertise, and he was antagonised when Yeats tried to substitute Sara Allgood in a play. Frank Fay, too, became annoyed. When Horniman offered finance for a new post of Managing Director, and the inclusion of international masterpieces in the repertoire, Yeats gleefully accepted it, criticising the theatrical limitations of both the Fays. He wanted to bring the famous actress, Miss Darragh, over from England to star in his version of *Deirdre*. Lady Gregory and Synge both knew that the Fays produced and acted their plays to an extremely high standard, and were reluctant to see them demoted to suit Yeats' own theatrical ambitions. Yet, they both succumbed to their fellow director and agreed to appoint a Managing Director, to the Fay's indignation and revulsion.

However Synge's new play, *The Playboy of the Western World*, which to Yeats' everlasting credit he recognised immediately as the work of genius it was, arrived at the Abbey. In the resulting public furore on its production in January of 1907, Yeats famously took on allcomers in defence of artistic freedom and defended Synge's play. This led some few months later to Maud Gonne attacking Willie for his role, as she defended the *peoples'* righteous anger. She wrote:

And as to you Willie, we are such friends you will not misunderstand me when I say you have done things such as calling in the police & witnessing for the Crown that give them cause to hate you & it is a healthy sign they do … You who believe in the super man why do you grow indignant with the crowd because they don't think as you do, because their virtue is not your virtue, you should not want them to think as you do. It would be a misfortune if the crowd began worrying over subtleties for it would be an end of action.

Synge himself, not being very self-assertive, was badly shaken by the resulting riots. He never indicated to Yeats or Gregory what he thought of their work. Indeed, Yeats bemoans the fact in his *Journal* that neither he or Gregory ever received a compliment nor thanks for the work they did for him.[16] Willie Fay thought Synge *the first of the Irish dramatic realists,* with *Riders to the Sea, likely to outlast any play written in Ireland since.* Fay added perceptively that *the Playboy of the Western World, written as a high comedy, ceases to exist when played as a farce.*[17]

Annie Horniman, though still tied into subsidising the Abbey, decided to transfer her energies to a new theatrical venture in Manchester. She took the new Abbey Manager, Ben Iden Payne with her. She asked Yeats for permission to perform his plays. He refused in a letter which it must have been very difficult for him to write, as it meant losing the pot of gold. The letter shows him as devoted to his country and its people He declared that he had considered her request carefully, but that he was not of an age where he could readily change his nationality. His plays would not find an immediate audience in England. His own people understood him, as he did them. He realised that the theatre might yet fail, but whatever happens:

I shall write for my own people – whether in love or hate of them matters little - probably I shall not know which it is.

Roy Foster rightly describes this letter as one of the best letters Willie ever wrote.

Payne's letter of resignation to Yeats illustrates clearly the tensions between the three Directors concerning interests in having their own plays produced to maximum effect. He wrote:

When engaged by you it was clearly stated that for obvious reasons the peasant plays should not come under my control, but that my energies were to be devoted to the verse plays and foreign masterpieces. My experience with the Company has brought me to the conclusion that their capacities are, on the whole, unsuited to your verse work ... and that it is only fair to you and your work to let you clearly understand this.

Willie Fay was again back as manager, but with his authority somewhat undermined. The appointment of Payne had demonstrated that the directors could and would move against him if necessary. The most recent summer English tour had brought great critical praise on the actors, and they were not disposed to being treated again as minions by Fay. During the following winter tour, Fay found that discipline within the company reached low ebb.

Very soon again Yeats began to resent Fay and planned to strip him of several functions, including the right to re-engage actors. Yeats wanted discipline tightened and the Company dedicated to intellectual drama, no matter how unpopular that may be. He began plotting against Fay with his fellow directors who, because he produced their plays so well, were essentially favourable to Fay. But Fay undid himself by offending both Gregory and Synge. He produced Gregory's play, *Gaol Gate,* in Galway without consulting her. She was unhappy with the timing and location. Agrarian tension was then current in Galway and she feared her play might be used as a direct incentive to violence. Fay began to harass Molly Algood, who was then Synge's fiancée, thus also annoying most of the other actors. Yeats saw his opportunity to oust Fay by allowing the enmity of the actors to take its course and bring to an end any link with the old National Dramatic Company.

Fay foolishly put forward five proposals, which could be read like an ultimatum, by the Directors. These were:

1.   That the directors put up a notice shortly that all contracts terminate on such a day. That people wishing to re-engage write to Willie Fay.

2.   That all engagements be for a season only and terminate by a fortnight's notice on either side.

3.   That where the directors require special actors for their performances I should engage them on terms to be decided between the directors and myself.

4.   That the powers of dismissing those under my own contracts shall rest with me after due consultation with the directors in case of principals.

5.   There shall be no appeal to any other authority than mine by the people engaged by me on all matters dealt with in their contracts.[18]

The directors refused to accept Fay's proposals, while agreeing that discipline must be restored. They also insisted that:

This Theatre must go on as a theatre for intellectual drama, whatever unpopularity that may involve ... if any member find himself unable to go on with us under the circumstances, we will not look upon it as unfriendly on his part if he go elsewhere, on the contrary we will help him all we can.[19]

Fay knew exactly what they were saying to him. He was out of sympathy with the literary policy of the directors. Thoroughly disillusioned, he saw his situation as having *trained several companies and arrived at the age of thirty-five and made nothing. Had he worked fourteen hours a day for over five years in America, he would have been a rich man today and not a poor fellow without a copper.*[20] Within days he wrote to Yeats:

Dear Mr. Yeats,

I regret that under present circumstances I do not see my way to continue my engagement with the National Theatre Society. I herewith give one month's notice. My engagement will terminate on Thursday 13th *February 1908.*

I am, faithfully yours

William G. Fay.

Frank Fay also resigned, though like his brother, not from the Society. Willie Fay's actress wife Brigit O'Dempsey also resigned. These departures caused a sensation in Dublin, with all insiders realising what had really happened, despite Yeats pouring praise on them in the press. Almost immediately, the Fays travelled to London to seek work, and Yeats cunningly offered them the short-term use of his Woburn apartment. Within a few months the Fays were playing in New York as, The Irish National Theatre Company. Yeats

The Abbey in 2003.

79

considered asking his friend, John Quinn, to seek an injunction against them for using that name, but decided against it. Instead on 18 March, both the Fays were suspended from the Society. Their pioneering work at the Abbey has been overshadowed and almost forgotten.

George Moore could write some years later in *Vale, The brothers Fay rose in revolt against Yeats' management, accusing him of hindering the dramatic movement by producing no plays except those written by his intimate friends ... They resigned...it was presumptuous for Willie Fay, an amusing Irish comedian and his brother to set themselves up against a poet.*[21]

Susan Mitchell, so close to all the Yeatses, and George Russell's lover, wrote of the Abbey rows in *Sinn Féin* on 8 May 1909, praising Máire nic Shiubhlaigh's performance at a Theatre of Ireland production, thus:

"She looked beautifully and spoke beautifully at the Abbey, but she has never been allowed to act there; I remember her then, no Yeats' painted angel, no statuesque instrument for reciting beautiful words, but a magic temperament for the first time struggling with the bonds of convention. Oh Yeats! Yeats! With your broken kneed heroes and bargaining heroines, even your drawing-room Deirdre, tender, appealing, complex as she was, did not save your talk of tradition, have only succeeded in producing on Kiltartan French and pigeon English, some few passably competent comic actors and actresses. I feel very sad for you and for your loss in the possibilities that your futile dictatorship flung away.

Pull yourself together, Man of Genius, save your theatre. There is yet a little time.[22]

CHAPTER 5

SECTARIAN SNOB

Willie Yeats came from Protestant stock, from which the Yeats family contributed *a line of intellectual Puritan divines*.[1] His mother's people were well-to-do merchants in Sligo, which was ominously known to its inhabitants as 'little Belfast'.[2] Neither side of the family had much time for the majority religion of Roman Catholicism. Religion meant little for Willie or his father. It was a social and cultural badge of distinction, making them superior to Catholics, whose religion they both heartily despised. Due to his father's futile attempts to become a successful artist, Willie's family were very poor Protestants. Yet, they had notions of a proud high-born ancestry, which had left the family landlord to a small estate at Thomastown in County Kilkenny. George Russell once remarked that Willie believed that he was related to the Dukes of Ormonde and should have inherited the title, if right was right.

While still a young man, Willie received some seminal advice from his mentor, John O'Leary. The latter told him that to get on in Ireland, one needed both the backing of the Catholic Church, and the Fenians. He warned Willie that the former would always be impossible for him. Yeats accepted this reality and never sought to treat with that body or allow it to inhibit him in any way. He therefore was regularly exposed to criticism as not being in touch or in sympathy with the *Catholic people*. A taint of suspicion hung over him from early in his career. He was attacked in *The Freeman's Journal* and *The Irish Times*. The advanced Catholic nationalist editors of the *Leader* and the *United Irishman,* saw Yeats' opinions as *The simple product of galloping snobbery and the original sin of Protestant descent*.[3] Roy Foster qualifies this by adding, *But snobbery is never simple being founded on an insecurity that can be psychological as much as social*. This may true 'of Yeats' social, if not his sectarian snobbery.

Yeats' difficulties with Catholic Ireland came to full public prominence with the publication of his first full-length play, The Countess Kathleen and its first production by the Irish Literary Theatre in May 1899. *The Countess Kathleen* was a verse play written for Maud Gonne. The story was set during an early famine, when a Countess sells her soul in return for food to feed her starving people. A trailer of the play was produced in Dublin in January and the plot appeared in the press. Edward Martyn had some misgivings about its theology, though a Catholic priest later assuaged these. But an erstwhile colleague of Yeats', Frank Hugh O'Donnell, now a bitter opponent, saw an opportunity to attack him in public. He did so through letters to the *Freeman' Journal*, and a publication called *Souls for Gold*, a pseudo-Celtic drama, which was widely distributed in Dublin, and through lectures.

This negative publicity led to *The Daily Nation* newspaper publishing a long and theologically-sound attack on the proposed production. It expected *those Catholics, who may form a portion of the audience, will so give expression to their disapproval as to effectively discourage any further venture of a similar kind.* It warned, the *promoters of the Irish Literary Theatre would only have themselves to blame for the consequences that will ensue if "Countess Kathleen" is presented on Monday night.* The next day's paper published a stream of letters from Catholics, supporting its stand against *anti-Irish* and *anti-Catholic monstrosities.* On the first night, Yeats hired over twenty policemen in case of trouble, which was not that unusual at the time. They, however, were not needed, as the night passed with minor barracking from the audience. Arthur Griffith, supporting Yeats in this instance, brought supporters to protect the players. Yeats, flanked by Maud Gonne and probably Lady Gregory, sat nervously. John Kelly, in *The Collected Letter of WB Yeats,* observes amusingly that, WBY *in such company had little need of the police.* Most papers gave it favourable reviews, though the *Irish Times* declared it offensive to Irish people. A letter from Royal University students appeared in the *Freeman's Journal,* saying that Yeats *represents the Irish peasants as a crooning barbarian, crazed with morbid superstition, who, having added the Catholic faith to his store of superstition, sells that faith for gold or bread.* One of the signatories was Francis Skeffington, while a first year student, James Joyce, refused to add his signature to the letter.[4]

Cardinal Logue was drawn into the controversy when contacted by the *Daily Nation* for his opinion. It published Logue's letter on 10 May. It stated;

You invite my opinion on the play of Mr. Yeats .. All I know of this play is what I could gather from the extracts, which are given in Mr. O'Donnell's pamphlet and your paper. Judging by these extracts, I have no hesitation in saying that an Irish Catholic audience, which could patiently sit out such a play, must have sadly degenerated, both in religion and patriotism.

Yeats often pointed to this controversial episode as creating his reputation as anti-Catholic. John Kelly argues rather that it crystallised doubts that had long been growing and developing. He no longer got the benefit of any doubt and his audience became less tolerant of his inherent and wilful anti-Catholicism. As late as 1923, as he delivered his Nobel Lecture in Stockholm, Yeats told the Royal Academy of Sweden that; *My 'Countess Kathleen' was denounced by Cardinal Logue as a heretical play.*

In his *Autobiographies,* Willie said he had observed that Irish Catholics lacked the good taste, domestic manners, civility and decency of the Protestant Irish. He equated peasantry with Catholicism, even in the persons of his erstwhile close collaborators, the cousins, George Moore and Edward Martyn. He dubbed them peasant sinner and peasant saint.[5] He wrote of Martyn's awkward body as looking like that of a Parish Priest, betraying the origin of his *mother's peasant blood.*[6] He was not fond of the Catholic mother, blaming her for keeping her stock down in the mire. He said that these women refused to marry Protestants, thus stultifying their offspring's possibility of becoming acquainted with refinement and sensibility. He was of the opinion that not a single Catholic family developed, nor could have developed, a tradition of culture like that at Coole Park since the middle Ages.[7]

Yeats was particularly critical of Catholic schools, saying that they had no feeling for style or for life, rather were they only interested in facts and figures. He saw them as destroyers, like their church.[8] The most common anti-Catholic theme in his writings is reserved for *the priests*, whom he blames for creating a *terror of culture.*[9]

Protestant Ascendancy was very much on the decline during Yeats' lifetime, as the overwhelming Catholic population sought to claim its democratic rights to land and positions of power and influence in their own country. The challenge for much of the Protestant class, facing a marginalisation, was to leave, or seek a future for themselves in their own country. For the poorer Protestants, the latter was their only option. Many of the better-off, also remained, though staying aloof in their castles or houses. The Yeats family did not even own a house.

When Willie became an almost semi-permanent occupant of Coole Park, he had found what he thought his rightful inheritance ought to have been. It became a safe haven from those ruffian Irish Catholics that he and Lady Gregory looked down on. This haven at Coole also offered him the opportunity and capacity to reclaim an Irish identity for himself, his family and all Protestants, who wished to belong. Gregory, too, had little sympathy with Catholicism. She had attended the Pope's mass in Rome during the time of her affair with Wilfred Scawen Blunt. She wrote of the mass afterwards as:

A mummery as usual, the rites looked altogether pagan, and His Holiness drinking all the wine that had been consecrated had a ludicrous look. Attending another mass she wrote, *feel more indignantly Protestant than ever.*

Yeats had, earlier in his career, been close to George Moore and they had collaborated on several theatrical endeavours. Yeats had put Moore's name forward for membership of the Irish Literary Society in London, only to have it rebuffed by the formidable Chairman, Barry O'Brien. Yeats tendered his own resignation in solidarity with his friend and would later have his revenge on O'Brien. Moore was a very difficult person, a Catholic aristocrat and landowner, which Willie thought to be a contradiction in terms. When Moore sinned against Yeats, his Catholicism, which meant little to him, was an obvious a target of attack. Moore eventually put himself outside the pale for Yeats and Gregory, when he published his famous memoirs, *Hail and Farewell*. The three volumes cover 1901-1911, which Moore spent living in Dublin. In the last volume, he proceeded to offend Lady Gregory by alluding to her family's earlier endeavours as proselytisers, and in his reference to her as *an ardent soul-gatherer* in county Galway. But after paying due homage to Yeats' role in Irish artistic life ,and stating mistakenly that the latter had all his great work behind him, he proceeded to deliciously ridicule the vain, glorious, lout.

At a meeting in Dublin to whip up support for Hugh Lane's proposed art gallery, which was attended by his artistic and social peers, Willie, took to the podium in fighting form. Moore wrote of Willie's performance:

We have sacrificed our lives for Art, but you, what have you done? What sacrifices have you made he asked, and everybody began to search his memory for the sacrifices that Yeats had made, asking himself in what prison Yeats had languished, what rags he had worn, what broken victuals he had eaten. As far as anybody could remember, he had always lived very comfortably, sitting down to regular meals and the old green cloak that was in keeping with his profession of romantic poet he had exchanged for the magnificent fur coat which distracted our attention from what he was saying, so opulently did it cover the back of the chair out of which he had risen. But quite forgetful of the coat behind him, he continued to denounce the middle classes, throwing his arms into the air, shouting at us.[10]

Yeats answered Moore in his poem *Closing Rhymes,* by comparing his own work to *a post, passing dogs defile.* He also described Martyn as a man carved out of a turnip.[11]

Ironically, Patrick Kavanagh believed that the best portrait written of Yeats was by Moore in *Hail and Farewell.* Kavanagh wrote, *Yeats disliked it at the time, yet it is very affectionate, and even at that time when Yeats was under forty, with his best work yet to come, Moore recognised his genius.*[12]

Edward Martyn had first brought Yeats from Tulira Castle to meet Lady Gregory at nearby Coole Park. He also collaborated on and funded their Irish Literary Theatre. Martyn was a very conservative Catholic, who could only support *The Countess Kathleen* after being counselled by several priests. It was first produced together with Martyn's own play, *Heather Field.* Despite his continuing desire to see his plays produced, Martyn's religious scruples, together with his withdrawal of sponsorship, saw the early demise of The Irish Literary Theatre. Nevertheless a friendship between Yeats and Martyn continued, especially as Martyn converted from Unionism to nationalism, becoming in fact a one-time President of Sinn Féin and the founder of Dublin's Feis Ceoil and the Palestrina Choir. When Yeats set out to buy his tower in county Galway in 1916, Martyn, whose neighbour he then became, assisted him and offered him free temporary accommodation. Despite all this, Oliver Gogarty, a mutual friend, felt able to write:

Yeats hated Edward Martyn because he was a Roman Catholic. There was in Yeats, derived doubtless from his parson grandfather, a bigotry that could not have been discovered in the grandparent, but which brooded in Yeats. This, and of course the jealousy of the "household of continuance".[13]

Yeats' *Oxford Book of Modern Verse* in 1935, proved a very controversial choice for a variety of reasons. One critic wrote, *the selection from the poets is capricious to the point of eccentricity. I cannot feel that either the introduction or the selection was the result of Mr. Yeats' best powers.*[14] WH Auden wrote, *I challenge anyone in this court to deny that it is the most deplorable volume ever issued.*[15] He surprised many by including no less than seventeen of Gogarty's poems.

A letter to *The Irish Times* on 6 December 2001 possibly throws some light on this. It read:

My father, Myles Dillon, knew Gogarty very well and he also knew Yeats. He used to always remark, when this subject arose, that of course one had to remember that Gogarty had helped out Yeats on a couple of occasions when he was strapped for cash. More importantly, he had just given Yeats a motor-car.

It was widely believed at the time that the gift of the motor-car greatly increased Mr. Yeats' appreciation of Mr. Gogarty's poetic skills.

Andrew Dillon, whose father Myles Dillon, an internationally renowned Celtic scholar, died in 1972, penned the letter. Andrew Dillon assures me that he has no reason to doubt the authenticity of the story.

It was in Yeats' most difficult personal crisis that his genuinely-held anti-Catholicism surfaced most clearly. Willie had met Maud Gonne in January 1889 and, as he said himself, his troubles began. He pursued her privately and publicly, though she told him she was unattainable. He did not see through the deceit of her Parisian life, and foolishly fed in to her need to believe in reincarnation after the tragic death of her baby boy, Georges. Even after she bore another child to her lover, Willie remained an innocent, a believer in the fairies. When that affair ended, and she confessed all to Willie, he still loved her, still wanted and needed her. She convinced him that he should settle for a 'spiritual marriage' with her.

Maud often told him he was getting something out of their strange relationship, as she was. She had become his muse and he had composed some of his most beautiful verse about her. He had given her immortality, and she was well aware and grateful for that. She regularly reminded him that he was essentially a poet, and a muse was necessary to him. Their appearances together in Dublin became important events, socially and culturally, especially as their advanced political views appeared to be so close. It was one of these causes that eventually led to the greatest calamity of Yeats' life.

A man named John MacBride had co-founded an Irish Brigade to fight alongside the Boers in their war against England in 1899. The cause of the Boers and of the Irish Brigade were taken up in Ireland by Maud Gonne, Yeats, Arthur Griffith, John O'Leary; Michael Davitt and a host of leading parliamentarians also subscribed. After one year the Brigade was stood down. MacBride, by then a national hero, was unable to return to Ireland. He went to live in Paris and was met by Maud Gonne. The woman of action soon fell for the man of action, then a commissioned 'Major' from the Boer

86

army. They toured America together collecting funds for the Boer and Irish causes. When Willie heard the news of their imminent marriage in 1903, he was devastated, traumatised and humiliated. But worse, much worse, his muse, his queen, was to convert to Catholicism. He had to act.

In four letters, only one of which survives, in draft form, he poured out his vitriol against the Catholic church, and what it would do to his icon and her standing among the Irish people. Blinded by his own hatred, he did not realise that Maud herself was in fact very familiar and at ease with Catholicism. She would soon tell him that she found, *the Ritual of the Catholic Church beautiful and inspiring.*[16] *It has greater and far more tradition that the English church and as the head of one's church I prefer the Pope to Edward VII.* Terence Brown writes of Willie's *letter: is a painful document indeed. Yeats' caste snobbery, never very far from the surface in his personality, boils up as a noxious anti-Catholic elitism, as if the nightmare of Gonne's apostasy had released bile he did not customarily allow to influence his feelings. He does not appear wholly in control of himself in this bitter, admonitory letter.*[17]

Willie felt that because of their spiritual marriage, he had a right and a duty to save Maud from demeaning herself and destroying her influence as a leader. He begged her to heed him in her moment of great peril and not fall into a lower order, giving the priests power over her. She belonged to a superior class, above the people, and was going to marry one of the people. This would thrust her down socially and rob the very same people of her leadership. It would be a great betrayal, a denial of God. Willie associated himself with the upper-class leadership position to inspire others and uplift the nation. Her conversion would betray the truth and abandon her role as one of the Gods. He asked her would the 'priest' lead the people in their hour of need. 'No, no' he assured her, the priest will betray the people again, as he did in 1800, when the Irish Parliament was amalgamated with Westminster, and later by condemning the Fenians. He told Maud, who advocated the use of physical force, that the priest will always caution against violence and emasculate the pride of the young men of Ireland. He will say *be quiet, be good Christians, do not shed blood.* Then he told her that she had articulated these truths and she was now about to betray them and herself.[18]

W.B. Yeats famous speech on divorce in the Senate in 1925 has been described by Terence Brown as aggressively sectarian, causing great offence in the chamber and in the country. This is dealt in greater detail in Chapter 10.

As late as 1927 Maud told Willie that:

You hate the Catholic Church with the hate of the Daemon condemned by the old monk of the Mariotic Sea & when you take your stand on certain papal Encyclicals you always remind me of Satan rebuking Sin ... For your poetry you will be forgiven, but sin no more.[19]

CHAPTER 6

JOHN O'LEARY'S GRAVE

In his book, Yeats and Artistic Power, *Phillip Marcus writes,* O'Leary died on March 16, 1907, and in 'Poetry and Tradition', finished in August of the same year, Yeats treated his death as the watershed between the era of the leaders and the era of the clubs. *In this essay, which might be considered a scenario for 'September 1913', O'Leary served as the epitome of the 'old romantic conception of Irish Nationality' – on which Yeats noted, his own art had been founded.*[1]

Few people played such a pivotal role in the life of the developing young writer WB Yeats, as did John O'Leary. O'Leary provided him with inspiration as well as much basic practical assistance. Indeed Terence Brown in his life of WBYeats says *O'Leary began to occupy the role of substitute father for the poet.*[1a] O'Leary was thirty-five years older than Yeats. He was an intellectual who had become involved in Fenianism as a young man. He had served a long jail sentence and then been exiled to Paris. He returned to live in Dublin in 1885 and met the twenty- year old Willie that same year. He was an impressive looking man, with *a noble head* and a long beard. For Willie to meet such a man of action was thrilling.

John Yeats, seeking to give his son some experience in public speaking and to broaden his horizons, had brought him along to the Contemporary Club, in a first floor room at the corner of College Green and Grafton St. It was an open forum where male unionists and nationalists discussed contemporary issues, in an informal 'club' setting. O'Leary was one of the most famous members and a friend of John Yeats. Among the regular members were Douglas Hyde, George Russell, John F. Taylor, Stephen Gwynn and George Sigerson. Another member, TW Rolleston, had launched a new literary magazine, the *Dublin University Review* which published Willie's earliest poems during 1885. The poet first recited them at the *Contemporary Club,* where the members would criticise and take a vote on their merits.[2]

Willie was pleased to discover that O'Leary lived a short distance from their own home. One evening he called unannounced to O'Leary's at 10 Ashfield Terrace in Terenure. John was out, but his sister Ellen, who was playing cards with some females, insisted that Willie join them at the card table. She was a poet herself and was very interested in the young man. This visit led to him being invited to attend the O'Leary's 'At Home' literary evenings, where he met Katherine Tynan. She and her father also held similar literary evenings on Sundays at their home in Clondalkin. Willie became a guest there also.

John O'Leary
as a prisoner
in Mountjoy.

At a very early stage in their relationship O'Leary recognised the potential of Yeats to become a great poet. He consciously set about 'capturing him for Ireland'. At that time Willie was quite ignorant about any Irish cultural heritage. O'Leary began to lend him books from his extensive personal library. It was from these books that Willie first became acquainted with Irish legends and fairy lore. People like Douglas Hyde, Standish O'Grady and Sir Samuel Ferguson, were then making them available in English translation. In his autobiographies Willie acknowledges this fact, adding that it was from those Irish books, the debates at the Contemporary Club and conversations with O'Leary, that all the work he tried to accomplish flowed.[3]

A description of O'Leary, Yeats and Maud Gonne at this time reads:

A tall lanky boy with deep-set dark eyes behind glasses, over which a lock of dark hair was constantly falling, to be pushed back impatiently by long sensitive fingers, often stained with paint – dressed in shabby clothes that none noticed (except himself, as he confessed long after) – a tall girl with masses of gold-brown hair and a beauty which made her Paris clothes equally unnoticeable, sat figuratively and sometimes literally, at the feet of a thin elderly man, with eagle eyes, whose unbroken will had turned the outrage of long convict imprisonment into immense dignity. He never spoke of that imprisonment … John O'Leary, the master, and his two favourite disciples, William Butler Yeats and Maud Gonne.

O'Leary was the symbol of the Fenian faith; he was not a revolutionary leader. Theoretically he would have freed Ireland by the sword – and he objected to dynamite! Because of his nobleness, he had many disciples, but these two, I think ranked highest in his affection, and on them he set his high hopes. In his little room in Temple Street they sat surrounded by books, books on shelves and books on piles on chairs and on the floor; and Willie Yeats said there must be more books, - new books for a new generation. The master told him to leave the Art School and write them.[4]

Though O'Leary was a nationalist, he was also a moralist, an idealist and a man of integrity. He believed that nationalism and literature were necessary to each other. A political revolution would not succeed without being backed by a cultural revival, believing that a literary revival was necessary for the achievement of nationhood. He had no doubt that the Irish nation was a separate cultural entity and set his life on achieving a political separation. His disciple, Willie Yeats, would gradually hold similar ideas and base much of his life's work on achieving such an outcome. Irish literature should be Irish in content, using the fund of lore available. The Irish language was not an absolutely essential part to this.[5]

Yeats quoted O'Leary as saying "there are things that a man must not do even to save a nation".[6] As Conor Cruise O'Brien has written, "Yeats now became what he was to remain all his life, a nationalist of the school of John O'Leary.[7] That school was a moderate one, which did not get you hanged or jailed, and that suited Willie's innate prudence and pride.[8]

In later years, when O'Leary was dead, Willie surmised as to why O'Leary had paid so much attention to him, why he had helped him so much. He thought that maybe, like himself, O'Leary had such high standards that he would eschew mediocre literature, even if it supported Irish nationalism.[9] Not all the members of the Contemporary Club were as well disposed to Willie as O'Leary. Stephen Gwynn wrote, "*Every one of us was convinced that Yeats was going to be a better poet than we had yet seen in Ireland and the significant fact is that this was not out of personal liking.*[10] Katherine Tynan also wrote of how exasperating Willie could be on his visits to her farmhouse home in Clondalkin, as even at an early age he expected to be the centre of attention.

Willie finished his first major work, *The Wanderings of Oisin,* in late 1888. He had a publisher in mind, but before he could approach him, Willie needed to be able to guarantee the sale of a minimum number of copies. Canvassing people to take 'subscriptions' was the way to achieve this. His father tried to assist him but was unsuccessful.[11] It was then that O'Leary stepped in and eventually succeeded in reaching the necessary quota, enabling Willie to approach the publisher Kegan Paul with his manuscript. Much to his disgust, Kegan Paul demanded a higher quota. O'Leary obtained further subscriptions and the book was eventually published in January 1889. It received good reviews, particularly in England, where a great poetic future was forecast. Oscar Wilde wrote;

Books of poetry by young writers are usually promissory notes that are never met. Now and then, however, one comes across a volume that is so far above the average that one can hardly resist the fascinating temptation of recklessly prophesying a fine future for its author. Such a volume Mr. Yeats' ' Wanderings of Oisin' certainly is. Here we find nobility of treatment and nobility of subject matter, delicacy of poetic instinct, and richness of imaginative resource. Unequal and uneven much of the work must be admitted to be. Mr. Yeats does not try to 'out-baby' Wordsworth, we are glad to say, but he occasionally succeeds on 'out-glittering' Keats, and here and there in his book we come across strange crudities and irritating conceits[12].

By June, the book had only sold twenty-eight copies on the open market and Kegan Paul was threatening to sue Willie. With O'Leary's assistance, he paid £2.3s.10d to the publisher as a settlement. O'Leary also negotiated that the publisher T Fisher Unwin would take the remaining books and republish them in May 1892.

In January 1889, the Yeats household in London, through the O'Leary connection, received a visit from Miss Maud Gonne. Ellen O'Leary had met Maud in Dublin, en route back to her Paris home after defying landlords in county Donegal. Ellen told Maud about the brilliant young poet she knew and whom Maud should meet. Ellen wrote to Willie saying that she had given "a *new lady friend of ours, and a new convert to Ireland*" a letter of introduction to his father.[13] Ellen was sure that Maud, "*so charming, fine and handsome*" would not fail to be admired by the Yeats' family, as she already was by the O'Learys. The only member of the Yeats' family smitten by their visitor was Willie. He soon told the O'Learys that if Maud Gonne founded a Flat Earth Society he would happily join. The turmoil of his life had begun.

Later that same year came the shocking news of the sudden death of Ellen O'Leary, aged fifty-seven. Her brother wrote to Willie, 'a *horrible calamity has come and the light of my life has gone out*'.[14]

Willie was always short of money and, like many another Irish writer, depended on family, friends and acquaintances, for funds. During his long courtship of Maud Gonne, he was lucky, for, as he assured O'Leary, the lady usually insisted on paying her own way. On a visit to Howth, however, when she was in a state of turmoil, she forgot about paying and Willie, to his horror, found himself spending ten shillings! This, he later assured O'Leary, as he tried to borrow from him to make up the shortfall, was a very great sum of money indeed.

O'Leary helped Willie get work that would pay. He introduced Willie to

John Boyle O'Reilly of the *Boston Pilot*, and the *Providence Sunday Journal*, which both accepted his material. O'Leary himself was the Literary Editor of the GAA's, *The Gael*, and it too paid Willie for contributions. O'Leary and Katherine Tynan were regular visitors to the Yeats household in London. O'Leary usually stayed with his friend, Dr. Mark Ryan, a Fenian leader who lived at 15A Gower St. He looked up old friends, especially Richard Barry O'Brien, a main stay of Irish nationalists in London. O'Leary himself, though owning property in Tipperary, was not well off, particularly when tenants refused to pay rents during the Plan of Campaign. He survived mainly on a substantial loan from Dr. Mark Ryan, and on an insurance policy inherited from his father. On one occasion O'Leary discovered Willie had been in Dublin and had not called to him. O'Leary let Willie know of his annoyance at this. Willie wrote assuring him that it was entirely due to a misunderstanding and a lack of time on his part.

O'Leary was held in such high esteem that he almost automatically became the figurehead of a variety of organisations. He became a Patron of the GAA and of the Young Ireland Society. He was a co-founder and first President of the National Literary society in 1892. He was President of the Centenary Committee to celebrate the 1798 Rising. He was closely involved with Willie in this enterprise, in a variety of rows and intrigues. As the foundation stone of a monument to commemorate Wolfe Tone was laid at the Grafton Street entrance to St. Stephen's Green before tens of thousands of people, the speakers included Willie and John O'Leary. When Willie launched his Library of Ireland project, clashing with Charles Gavan Duffy, O'Leary had advised against it. Eventually Willie had to abandon his plans, and felt let down by Maud Gonne herself in the matter.

O'Leary was always rather cautious about Maud, being aware of the allegations that she might have been an English spy. He knew how Willie was so smitten with her and told him that essentially Maud was a beautiful woman, seeking excitement.[14a] Willie often sought O'Leary's assistance on Maud Gonne's behalf, particularly when Irish nationalist enemies in France were assailing her. O'Leary strongly advised Willie against spending so much of his time on matters of the occult. Rather, he wanted the poet to concentrate more on his poetry. O'Leary tried to influence Willie in moderating his own stance on nationalism, away from Maud's extremism. Indeed, on a famous occasion, Maud criticised O'Leary and Michael Davitt to Willie, for not joining her and her militant confederates in a public protest at the visit of the Colonial Secretary, Joseph Chamberlain, to Dublin in 1899.

In a letter to Willie, she refers to O'Leary and the parliamentarians holding a meeting in the safety of the rooms of the Celtic Literary Society. On Maud's arrival, Davitt explained that he and O'Leary considered it foolish and senseless going to Beresford Place in such a fashion as to draw the police batons on them. The protest was in connection with the Boer War. Maud and O'Leary and Griffith had played a leading role in the *Irish Transvaal Society,* with Willie assisting on occasion.[15] A variety of organisations came together to form an umbrella organisation called, Cumann na nGael, with O'Leary as President, a post he held until his death.

In early 1900,opposing a visit by Queen Victoria to Ireland, Willie courageously, wrote a letters to the papers. He told the *Freeman's Journal;*

"I propose that a great meeting be summoned in the Rotunda on that date, to protest against the Union and to disassociate Ireland from any welcome that the unionists or the time-servers may offer to the official head of that Empire in whose name liberty is being suppressed in South Africa, as it was suppressed in Ireland a hundred years ago. I propose that Mr. John O'Leary be the Chairman, and that all Irish members be upon that platform.[16]

It was out of this agitation concerning the Boer War that Maud Gonne came to know Major John MacBride when he came to live in Paris after his service in South Africa. Willie was already slightly acquainted with him, while O'Leary knew and liked him. Gonne, MacBride and Yeats could be described in their own individual ways as disciples of O'Leary. Maud told O'Leary that by marrying the national hero, MacBride in 1903, she felt that was marrying Ireland.[17] When their baby, Sean MacBride, was baptised in Dublin in April 1904, O'Leary was their choice as godfather, though his public agnosticism did cause complications at the christening ceremony.[18] Two months later Maud travelled to London for the annual Wolfe Tone celebrations. She was supposed to share a platform with Willie and O'Leary, but Willie cancelled at a late stage. He was nervous of meeting Maud, as he had recently been presented to Queen Alexandra.

Even at that early stage, the Gonne-MacBride marriage was in a terminal state. Unable to travel to Ireland or England, MacBride went on an extended stay to America, only returning at his wife's entreaties.[19] Within a few months of his return, matters between them deteriorated, as the lady informed him of some details of her past life. MacBride abandoned Paris and returned to Ireland, risking arrest there. He preferred to take this chance, rather than continue in the marriage. Maud then decided to end the marriage, and made third party accusations against her husband, to her family solicitor in London. From late December 1904 to January 1905, intensive negotiations took place in London between their respective advisors. The main sticking point between them was the custody of their baby. John MacBride's main advisor was Richard Barry O'Brien, who had earlier forced Willie's resignation from the Irish Literary Society, over its refusal to allow George Moore become a member, on his proposal.

Maud knew that MacBride would garner much support from Irish nationalists. Realising O'Leary's stature there, she wrote directly to him on 9 January, appealing to him that unless MacBride accepted her terms for a separation a scandal was inevitable. She told him that it was her intention to return to live permanently in Dublin. She ended her letter by writing, *Your Godson is beginning to walk.* O'Leary was perturbed by the situation. He replied immediately:

17 Temple St.
Dublin.
13/1/05

My Dear Mrs Gonne MacBride,

Knowing your husband as I do, I cannot believe that he has done anything that would make it impossible for you to live together, but whatever he has done, or whatever you think he has done, is a matter, which as far as I can at all see, need not enter the question of separation at all.

Since both of them wanted to separate, O'Leary thought that should be straightforward, save for, *the terms of the boy's custody ... as to going into law, it would be a great scandal to all your friends ... such a course would be simply disastrous to yourself and no doubt extremely painful to your husband.*[20]

Willie contacted Barry O'Brien directly in London to ascertain whether MacBride would accept Maud's terms. He was informed in the negative. Willie was critical of what he termed O'Brien's tendency to favour MacBride. O'Brien insisted that he was acting as an honest broker, to seek to avoid a catastrophe for Irish nationalism should two of its icons divorce in a public court.

In June as the divorce case proceeded, a group of advanced Irish nationalists visited Fontenoy, the scene of the famous charge by the Irish Brigade which had brought French victory in the War of the Austrian Succession in 1745.

John O'Leary and John MacBride at Fontenoy, 1905.

Though aged seventy-five, John O'Leary made the trip. He was famously photographed, seated in a railway carriage alongside Major John MacBride. This picture appeared in the Irish Independent, indicating clearly where O'Leary's sympathies lay.[21] Maud wrote to Willie that same month:

The trial ... will drag on till the Autumn but I should think that after the first trial John MacBride's power for harm will be considerably diminished & he will not be able to get people to be photographed with him [as] he did at Fontenoy. I was really sorry to see poor Mr. O'Leary's photo with MacBride just now in the papers.

Judgement was delivered in the divorce case in August of 1906, with a legal separation the outcome, and with MacBride having liberal access to his son. As she had promised, Maud made an early visit to Dublin to appear alongside Willie in the Abbey Theatre for the opening night of Lady Gregory's *Gaol Gate*.

O'Leary died the following March. His passing was widely reported in Ireland, England and America. The *Daily Telegraph*, regarded as a Tory organ wrote of him as:

An ardent and incurable revolutionary – gentle but persistent in his fanatical gospel, rigid, consistent, incorruptible, as modest in desire as in means.

John Devoy in the *Gaelic American* wrote:

No man of his generation and no man in the last one hundred years has left a brighter example of steadfast adherence to principle and purity of life. Alice Milligan wrote in the American *Donhioe's Magazine; He stood for principle against compromise, and denounced the methods of continental anarchy in a few instances introduced into the Irish struggle. He was not very sanguine of immediate success, had seen enough of failure to daunt the bravest heart; but he taught us that in spite of failure we should not surrender.*

His funeral was organised by the '98 Centenary Committee, on which Willie had been so prominent. Among the organisations represented were the IRB, Cumann na nGael, the GAA, the Parnell Commemorative Association, Irish Parliamentary Party.

As major funerals went in Dublin, it was not a great one. It took place on a public holiday Monday, and the rain beat down incessantly. James O'Connor MP, PT Daly, John O'Hanlon and Major John MacBride carried the coffin. All his erstwhile colleagues and admirers were present, save for Willie Yeats. The latter was available and could have attended the funeral of a man, to whom he owed so very much, but he chose not to do so. Roy Foster has correctly described Yeats' absence as *in Irish society, a notable and deliberate gesture*[22] on his part. It was left to John Yeats, a life long friend, to redeem the family honour. He wrote a short letter to the *Freeman's Journal,* saying, *to tell the unwelcome truth to one's own countrymen and one's own friends … John O'Leary possessed this courage. But for him and his like the nation would have perished.*[23]

Yeats explained his absence later. He admitted that he shuddered to see about the grave those who aspired to a form of nationalism neither he nor O'Leary could share. In an article entitled, *Poetry and Tradition*, he associated those who would attend the funeral, with those who would have participated in the recent attack on Synge's *Playboy.* He likened O'Leary to a man whose personality, aristocracy and artistry made him a natural born leader, *like himself.* In O'Leary's passing he saw a watershed between the era of traditional leaders and those of the clubs then proliferating in Ireland. He

97

saw natural elite leadership being overtaken by a new class of shopkeepers, clerks and school-masters, whose poverty, ignorance and Catholicism, made them a poor substitute[24].

Willie joined Lady Gregory and Robert Gregory on a visit to Italy shortly after O'Leary's death. There, particularly in the walled town of Urbino, he recalled Castiglione's *The Courtier*, and longed for a return to artistic order and labour. Romantic Ireland was dead and gone.

John O'Leary

CHAPTER 7

AN OLD BELLOWS, FULL OF ANGRY WIND?

Maude Gonne was the person with whom Willie Yeats had the longest and most intense personal relationship. He entertained hopes of marrying her for nearly thirty years. Despite some very serious differences their friendship endured.

Willie, at twenty-three years old, was one year older than Maude Gonne, when they met for the first time in January 1889, at the Yeats family home on Blenheim Road, London. He was a naïve young poet, encountering an experienced woman of the world. Maude was a recent convert to Irish nationalism and determined to make her mark in that milieu. Ellen and John O'Leary had told her that the poet was destined to play a major cultural role for Ireland. He was poor and dependent. She was rich and independent. Her fashionable clothes, and the fact that she left the hansom cab in which she arrived, waiting outside the house for her return journey, did not endear her to the females of the house. Willie's father, John Yeats, was somewhat taken aback, that on her first visit to the Yeats family home, she should express such firm views on Irish nationalism. Her report of the work she was doing in Donegal on behalf of the peasant tenants against rack-renting landlords was met with silent embarrassment. John Yeats was himself a landlord of a small farm at Thomastown in county Kilkenny.

The tall beautiful lady, incongruously wearing slippers beneath her Parisian gown, quickly smote Willie. She was quite used to overwhelming men by her beauty and found such reactions rather tedious. She was interested in the poet for his potential. She accepted his invitation to meet him for dinner on the following evening. They met on successive evenings for a week, and talked about their ideas and vision for the future of Ireland. She told him that she was an actress whose only family member, a sister Kathleen, lived in London. He offered to write a play for her and would soon begin work on *The Countess Kathleen*. As suddenly as Maude came into Willie's life, she departed it.

She lived in Paris and, without any warning, announced that she was returning there. As he saw her off at the boat train, he wanted to lay hands on her and kiss her lips, but he dared not.[1] To commemorate their meeting he wrote a poem called, *The Arrow,* in which she is the arrow smiting his very marrow. He did not hide the fact, with family or friends, that he was in love with a goddess, but he surmised how could a poor student hope to marry such an enchanted being.

Maude was then the mistress of a French politician, a dedicated follower of the radical General Georges Boulanger, named Lucien Millevoye. They had met at the spa town of Royat in the Auvergne district some years earlier, and they soon became lovers. Their relationship was secret, as he could not afford any public scandal. Maude had her own apartment in Paris and Millevoye lived with wife and his family.

Maude saw Willie as a young upcoming poet who could be useful to he, in her career in Ireland. She would cultivate him on that basis and become his muse, thus becoming part of Irish cultural life. She would use him to further her various endeavours, knowing how he was so smitten by her physical beauty, and his aspiration of capturing her hand in marriage. She was the prince, the person of action; he was the princess, the thinker, the writer, and the poet who would immortalise her.

Maude was in love with Millevoye and became pregnant by him shortly after her return to Paris. Some months later, she made an unannounced visit to her ill sister in London. On hearing of her presence there, Willie turned up on the doorstep, to the consternation of all within. There was no option but to admit him and risk him recognising Maude's state. The innocent poet however did not notice anything inappropriate and was soon sent on his way, quite happily. Maude delivered a baby boy, Georges, in Paris. That event was kept very private in Paris, London and Dublin, apart from close family members.

To the consternation of Millevoye, Maude soon resumed her life of travelling to Ireland to help the downtrodden tenants in Donegal. He made a brief, though abortive journey to Donegal, entreating Maude to return to their baby son in Paris. She also continued to meet Willie in Dublin and London. He proposed to her in Dublin, in the summer of 1891, to which she responded by saying that she would never marry. She would not elaborate on her reasons. He commemorated this time by writing of a trip they made to Howth in the poem, *The White Birds*. As on their first meeting, Maude suddenly announced, without any explanation, that she had to return to Paris urgently. She had received a message from Millevoye saying that baby Georges was ill with meningitis. The baby died and Maude was demented thereafter.

Willie persisted in writing to Maude, and after a few months she travelled to

Dublin to meet him, being a passenger on the same boat that carried the body of Parnell home for burial. She told Willie in fine detail of the death of the baby in Paris, though she did not identify herself as the mother. She explored Willie's occult beliefs, hoping there was a possibility that she would one day meet Georges again. Willie introduced her to his good friend, George Russell. Russell told Maude about reincarnation, assuring her that Georges would live again. Willie and Maude later travelled together to London to begin her induction into the Golden Dawn spiritualist movement of Madame Blatavasky. He hoped that Maude's interest in the occult would bring them closer.

In 1893 Willie tried to start a Library of Ireland project, which floundered amid great rivalry with Sir George Gavan Duffy, J.F. Taylor and George Sigerson. Though Maude had given him a lot of help in the work, he felt that she let him down when matters got difficult, and she returned home to Paris. As would happen so often throughout their relationship, their rows were usually short-lived, with each quite ready to acknowledge the other's differing views and move on. Though sorely wounded by the library episode, Willie soon travelled to Paris to review a play, *Axel,* by Villiers. Maud attended the play with him, and Millevoye. Willie, in his innocence, and ignorance, was disappointed to find that his usual intimacy with Maude did not occur.

Maude's second baby with Millevoye, Iseult, was born in August 1894. This time Maude remained at home in Paris to look after her infant. It was not until more than two years later that, on a visit to Paris, Willie found that his old relationship with Maude was rekindling. As Iseult grew older, her mother gradually resumed her visits to Ireland, getting involved in political events again, usually in the company of Willie. They became heavily involved in the preparations for the centenary celebration of the Rising of 1798, and the opposition to Queen Victoria's Jubilee Day celebrations in Dublin. The latter brought them both into contact with the socialist James Connolly.

Maude and Willie stayed in different hotels in Dublin, to avoid malicious gossip.

On an occasion in 1898 they each had separate but simultaneous dreams of each other in which they were married. When Willie called to Maude's hotel the next morning, they exchanged details of their dreams, and as he later wrote in his *Memoirs*, for the very first time, she kissed him *with the bodily*

Maud Gonne

mouth. The next morning she was quite upset and confessed all to Willie about her secret life with Millevoye, which she said was all but ended. Willie thought that she would surely agree to marry him, but she replied that she would never marry, adding that she had a hatred of physical sex. She prevailed on him to enter into a form of spiritual marriage with her, in which their souls would unite.

The relationship continued on that basis as they pursued common activities, related to the Boer War and the eventual production, with Maude in the leading role, of *Caithlin ni hUalachain* in 1902. Out of the Boer War came John MacBride, and the fulfilment of Henry Nevinson's prediction, that the first man of resolute action whom she meets, will have her at his mercy.[2]

As usual, Willie made some beautiful poetry out of the devastating pain, caused by his muse. He wrote, *Never Give All The Heart* and *O Do Not Love Too Long.* His public humiliation and personal misery were not to last too long, as Maud soon re-established contact and confessed that she had made a horrendous mistake by marrying. As a divorce case ensued, Willie became her mainstay and support against her husband, insisting that she hold fast for the divorce and rid herself of MacBride forever. Within a few years he published his poem, *Reconciliation.* Though some people may have blamed her for what she did to him, he would not, writing:

Some may have blamed you that you took away the verses ... He hoped that he could still capture her.

The intensity of their love comes through in many of her letters to him, and it truly must have been, for him, beyond any understanding or even acceptance, as to why she would not marry him. On 26 July 1908 she wrote:

It is not in a week but in a day I am writing to you. I had such a wonderful experience last night that I must know at once if it affected you & how?

Last night I thought I would go to you astrally ... at a quarter to eleven last night I put on this body & thought strongly of you & desired to go to you. We went somewhere in space I don't know where ... I only saw your face distinctly & as I looked into your eyes & your lips touched mine. We melted into one another till we formed only one being, a being greater than ourselves who felt all & knew all with double intensity ...

Six months later Maud wrote, in terms which must have been excruciating for the love-lorn recipient:

Dearest,

It was hard leaving you yesterday, but I knew it would be just as hard today if I had waited. Life is so good when we are together & we are together so little!

You asked me yesterday if I am not a little sad that things are as they are between us – I am sorry & I am glad. It is hard being away from each other so much there are moments when I am dreadfully lonely & long to be with you – one of these moments is on me now – but beloved I am glad & proud beyond measure of your love, & that it is strong enough & high enough to accept the spiritual love & union I offer –

I have prayed so hard to have all earthly desires taken from my love for you & dearest, loving you as I do, I have prayed & I am praying still that the bodily desire for me may be taken from you too. I know how hard & rare a thing it is for a man to hold spiritual love when the bodily desire is gone & I have not made these prayers without a terrible struggle that shook my life though I do not speak much of it & generally manage to laugh.

That struggle is over & I have found peace. I think today I could let you marry another without losing it – for I know the spiritual union between us will outlive this life, even if we never see each other in this world again.

Among their later letters, however, it appears that there was at least one instance of physical love between them, during the summer of 1909. It was not a happy encounter for Maude, as she quickly reverted to her stated horror of physical lovemaking. Willie was forced once again to be satisfied with another episode of their spiritual marriage. This theory is based on a letter written in May 1909 as Maude travelled by boat to Ireland. Her emotional letter speaks of their love, yet she admits to have spoken unjustly to him *yesterday evening* and proffers an apology:

I forgot that those who would distribute life or death must be purer than the angels & that I was full of human passion & weakness. On me alone the blame lies for the forgetfulness of that spiritual marriage long ago! She again renounces carnal love writing, *My loved one I belong to you more in this renunciation than if I came to you in sin. Did you not say yourself that our love must be holy?*

Maude's home remained in Paris; as she felt it might be unsafe to travel to

Ireland with her young son, Seaghan, lest her husband reclaim custody. The presence of her daughter, Iseult Millevoye, would also demand some explanation in Dublin. Willie began to spend long summers staying with Maude at her summer-house in Normandy. He became very fond of young Seaghan, but especially so of Maude's beautiful daughter, Iseult. Maude herself still travelled to Dublin and remained involved with her own women's organisation, Inghinidhe na hÉireann. One project she invested much time and effort in was to seek to extend school meals to children in Dublin. Among the subscribers to her fund was Willie. When the Dublin Workers' Strike of 1913 occurred, Maude began fundraising for the strikers and their families. She wrote to him in the Autumn of 1913 saying:

Money is needed for starving children. It is horrible to think of the misery & hunger in Dublin. Iseult & I are going over to do what little we can to help the people.

She wrote again on 29 November:

My Dear Willie, Thank you so much for your generous subscription to the children's dinners. It is very kind of you. I hope this will be the last this year I shall have to beg for this object.

One recurring theme in Maude's letters to Willie was her lament that he was spending so much time on matters other than composing poetry.

When the *English Review* came out in January of 1914, it contained extracts from George Moore's forthcoming third volume of *Hail and Farewell*, titled, *Vale*. It provoked a crisis for several people, including Willie and Maude. It contained damaging information about many public figures in Dublin whom Moore had known and worked with. *Vale* would 'out' Edward Martyn as a homosexual. It indicated Hugh Lane to be homosexual and a transvestite. It exposed George Russell's affair with Susan Mitchell. Much of the information, and especially that concerning Willie and Maude, had been given to Moore in the greatest of confidence, in private conversation. Some years earlier, Moore, and Willie had been on a train journey together from the Broadstone Station in Dublin to Westport.

Moore took the opportunity to question Willie about his relationship with his muse. What he really wanted to know, he asked Willie, was how far did he get with the lady? Did he actually bed her? Willie was foolish enough to indicate to Moore that because of his youth and inexperience, he did not, having had to be content with a platonic affair. Moore commented in his text,

So why jeer at Yeats for his humanity, when it is so common for men to behold divinity in the women they love, and as in the case of Yeats, believe that the stars *could tell us everything.* Moore added, *Yes, I understand, the common mistake of a boy; and I was sorry for Yeats and for his inspiration, which did not seem to have survived his youth, because it had arisen out of an ungratified desire.*[3]

Moore was of the opinion that Willie, whom he so admired as an artist, had completed his best literary work. When Willie read the offending article in London, he was duly horrified that his indiscretion in discussing his intimate affair with Maude was laid open. That he himself had done so to a man like Moore added to his sense of betrayal. After a period of panic, he thought it politic to write to Maude and warn her. His letter to her does not appear to be extant, but her reply to him is. In this letter, it is clear that all he informed her of was that she had suffered a personal insult, supposedly in words ascribed to himself by Moore. It appears that in his letter, Willie did not necessarily deny uttering those words. For Maude, in her reply, says that if he had made a denial, it complicated matters for her. She was somewhat put out that he had not sent her a copy of the offending article, which she set about acquiring immediately. She warned him to keep her letter to him a secret, until she could read the article carefully and consider her position. Her initial reaction was that if she were so badly insulted, she would horsewhip Moore. Willie also mentioned to her that, by way of reply to Moore, he had written a poem. She was glad to hear of that, though she surmised, the article must have therefore appeared some considerable time previously. She asked him to send her Moore's address. The poem referred to was *Closing Rhymes*, in which Willie refers to himself and his treasures as a *post passing dogs defile.*

Maude succeeded in getting a copy of the article on the same day she had replied to Willie. Having read it carefully and considered her position, she wrote another letter to him. She made it clear that she understood fully, how and why he was so worried and upset by the piece. She was glad that he had been able to write a good poem in reply. Maude realised well, how indiscreet Willie had been in discussing their relationship with Moore. Having decided that she could live with the piece, she made no objection, nor did she utter the mildest chastisement to Willie. Rather did she comment supportively to him, saying that the best things in life often come out of adversity.

The outbreak of World War One changed life on the Continent totally. At its outbreak, Maude and her family were marooned at Argeles in the Pyrenees.

She wrote Willie that the war was race suicide and inconceivable madness. She and Iseult began to nurse the wounded soldiers during the early months of the war. In 1915 she reported to Willie that her nephew had been killed. She later noted the death of Hugh Lane on the *Lusitania*. Back in Paris, she tried to get Willie to visit, saying that she, Kathleen, and their cousin May, were working in a military hospital. Lucien Millevoye's son was killed in action. Iseult was then working in her father's aviation factory.

Maud kept closely abreast of political happenings in Ireland, north and south, but like most people was *overwhelmed by the tragedy and the greatness of the sacrifice our countrymen and women have made,* in the Easter Rising of 1916.[4] Willie wrote almost daily, sending newspapers to Maud. As executions commenced of men she had known so well, she commented on her husband's execution, *he has died for Ireland ... by his death he has left a name for Seaghan to be proud of. Those who die for Ireland are sacred.*[5] She expressed the wish to Willie that she could travel to Dublin immediately to nurse the wounded, but knew that she would not get a passport from the English authorities.

During the summer of 1917, Willie spent much time in Normandy with Maude and her family. He thought after the execution of John MacBride, Maude might reconsider his proposal of marriage. He was disappointed but then secured her permission to propose to Iseult. The latter prevaricated but also refused him. Maude decided to travel with the family and Willie, as far as London. On arrival at Southampton, as she had suspected, she was forbidden to travel on to Ireland, under the Defence of the Realm Act. She stayed in London and enrolled in an art college in Chelsea. Iseult got a job and Ezra Pound became Seaghan's tutor.

Within a couple of weeks, Willie married Georgie Hyde-Lees, with Ezra Pound as his 'best man'. Willie's own family were unable to attend due to the short notice they received. The couple had met several years earlier through their common interest in the occult. Georgie was very keen on Willie. He was fifty-two years old and she twenty-four. Her mother realised that Willie was marrying her as a second or third best choice. She tried to abort the marriage, but was dissuaded from doing so through Lady Gregory's intervention.

Willie wrote to his father shortly before the wedding to inform him of the event. He wrote that it was only decided *a few days ago.* He describes Miss Hyde Lees as, *comely and aged twenty- four.* He told his father that she had enough money to keep the two of them, with the prospect of more. He said that mutual friends had long wished for the marriage. He felt that because the girl's mother wanted the marriage, *I might marry so young a girl and yet not do her wrong*[5a].

While on honeymoon, Willie wrote to Iseult saying how unhappy he was. Iseult replied immediately, consoling him. In an act of almost total incomprehension, he showed that letter to his wife. For Georgie, that was a moment of near panic. Her mother was proved right. Willie had married her on the re-bound.

It was only ten days after their wedding day. Georgie was faced with the most crucial decision of her life. She was married to a man who clearly did not love her. She considered leaving and returning home, but she wanted the marriage and was prepared to fight and work for it. She decided that she would have to win her husband on her own merits. That same afternoon, she began the 'rouse' of free association in automatic writing, which intrigued and enthralled Willie. It became a complete therapy for him, as he saw Georgie as a medium that delivered a *foundation for his system of philosophy and a well of symbols for his poetry*[6]. This ongoing interplay between them would later become the volume, *A Vision*. Of more immediate import, Willie was soon to tell Georgie that his aches, depression and weariness had vanished, along with his impotence. Georgie had a large sexual appetite and was able to arouse her husband in tandem and saved her marriage. She looked after the great man well, in a myriad of roles over the next twenty years, often putting up with his preference for other women.

Willie wrote of his love for Iseult in the poem, *Owen Ahearne and his Dancer*. He wrote of her:

How could she mate with fifty years that was so wildly bred?

He wrote of Georgie:

I did not find in any cage the woman at my side,

O but her heart would break to learn my thoughts are far away.

The wedding had taken place so suddenly that both family and friends were intrigued to know more of the lady. John Quinn felt that, *It all seems very sudden and suggests she is furniture for the castle*[7]. Ezra Pound, who soon to begin an affair with Iseult, thought that Willie might have done a great deal worse. He wrote that *she seems attractive and sensible: at least she would not be a flaming nuisance.*

Maud had written from her flat on the Kings Road in Chelsea to congratulate the groom:

I think your betrothed charming & I am sure that we will be great friends. I am so glad of this, it would have been dreadful if you had chosen someone who would have broken our friendship. I feel Georgie will not, I think she will enter it & add to it. I find her graceful & beautiful, & in her bright picturesque dresses, she will give life & added beauty to the grey walls of Ballylee ...

Iseult likes her very much, & Iseult does not take to many people..

The Yeats sisters reported that Maude Gonne and Lady Gregory were both pleased, adding that they both had had their own 'whack' of Willie. When Willie decided to take his bride to Ireland to visit his tower and meet the family, there was great interest in the visit. In the meantime Maude moved into Willie's, Woburn Buildings' rooms for the duration of his stay in Ireland.

In February of 1918, Maude decided to ignore the order against her travelling to Ireland and, heavily disguised, travelled there with her fourteen-year old son. A friend, Helena Maloney, met her. As with her husband before her, she hoped that when her presence became public, the police would not trouble her. She bought a house at 73 St. Stephen's Green and called herself Madame Gonne MacBride. She joined the 1916 Widows' Association.

The mood in Ireland then was for total independence under Sinn Fein. As the government actively contemplated introducing conscription, it decided in May to make a pre-emptive strike against Sinn Féin, arresting seventy three prominent Sinn Feiners. Two days later Maude was arrested and taken to Holloway Jail in London, where she was to spend nearly six months. As usual when trouble struck, she turned to Willie for help. She wrote to him on 14 June:

I live, eat & sleep in a cell 7 feet by 13, a small window so high one can't see out, only about ? foot air opening ... we are allowed to write & receive 3 letters a week, but I have received no answers to those I have sent. Each letter must not exceed 20 lines & reply 30 lines. I am wild with anxiety about Seaghan, this day week I hunger strike unless I am allowed to see him. If I die, my death will give America & the world a striking example of English justice ... Send me a small translation of the Summa of St. Thomas Aquinas

*for one needs sound doctrine to prevent imagination going wild in
meditation. Do what you can for Seaghan & Iseult.*

Goodbye love to George & yourself
Your old friend
Maud Gonne

Maude found the prison regime intolerable, and was unable to adjust to the
regime of being locked up for twelve hours every night, and receiving only
one hour's exercise daily. Kathleen Clarke, the widow of Tom Clarke (at
whose wedding John MacBride had been best man), described her thus, *She
was like a caged animal herself, like a tigress, prowling endlessly up and
down.*[8] The only concession made to Maude was to allow her to have her pet
canary in her cell with her, which she spent most of her time talking to.
Willie was distraught, fearing that she might go mad. Maude received the
news of the death of Lucien Millevoye in the office of the prison governor
in Holloway. Willie tried to use his establishment contacts to have her
released, all to no avail.

He and Georgie went to London and moved Iseult into Woburn Buildings.
He told Maude that she could have it rent-free for one year. Willie returned
to Galway, where he was supervising the renovation of his tower. Seaghan
lived there with him until Willie decided on a suitable boarding school for
the boy. Later in the year, Willie moved to Dublin, renting Maude's house on
St. Stephen's Green. His wife was pregnant and he wanted the baby to be
born in Ireland, and within easy distance of the maternity hospitals.

Willie redoubled his efforts to have Maude released as the autumn arrived.
He approached the Chief Secretary, Edward Short, hoping to have her
released without parole. It was against the rules of Sinn Féin prisoners to
accept release on parole. Short advised him to take this up with the Home
Office. He was advised that the best chance of release would be on medical
grounds. It was felt that an assessment by a Home Office doctor would not
be helpful. A battle to get agreement on an independent medical examination
commenced, with George Bernard Shaw's help enlisted. Willie, in
exasperation, asked Short whether the Government wanted to make a martyr
of *her* too. Eventually, Short agreed to recommend such an independent
examination. The independent medical examination stated that she had
tuberculosis and needed a warm climate.

One night late in October, as Maude was going to bed, the Governor
appeared at her cell, saying that she was to be moved immediately to a

nursing home for one week. Seaghan and Iseult met her there. When Maude discovered that her release might be temporary, and that she would have to pay the cost of staying in the nursing home herself, she decided, in contravention of her release conditions, to travel to Woburn Buildings. She wrote immediately to Willie thanking him for all he had done for her and her children. Her health was very fragile, she told him. Kathleen wanted her to live with her in Switzerland. Maude was adamant that, whatever she did, her family had to stay together. She was certain that Dublin was the best place for them to live. Kathleen Clarke's reaction to Maude's release was, *All through her imprisonment she was kind, gentle and very courteous; she had very charming manners. I missed her, but was glad she was out of it.*[9]

In November 1918, at the end of the war, Maude discovered that passport requirements for travel to Ireland were lifted. Though she was still forbidden to travel under the Defence of the Realm Act, she decided to go to Dublin. She dressed in the uniform of a Red Cross nurse accompanying Iseult and Seaghan. She had told nobody of her plan and arrived off the boat train at Kingstown early in mid-November. At that time Georgie Yeats was seven months pregnant and in poor health. Taking a cab, Maud arrived outside number 73 St. Stephen's Green. Leaving her two children in the cab, she knocked on the front door of the house. After some minutes, Willie opened the door in his night attire. He was aghast to see Maude there. After a moment's thought, he became furious that, after all he had done to have her released, she was putting herself, her children, his pregnant wife and himself in jeopardy. Though realising that it was her house, he feared that if he allowed her stay, as she demanded, he ran the risk of having the police raid the house, with possibly terrible consequence for his unborn child. He told her that she could not stay, that he would seek alternate accommodation that same day, and undertook to hand the house back to her. The house was big enough for them all, Maude retorted, but Willie was adamant. He could not take any risk. Maude turned on her heels and rejoined her waiting children. She told the cab driver to trot on around the Green, while she thought of where else she might go. She decided to again go to her good friend Helena Maloney.

Iseult, who had become a close friend of Georgie's, later reported the incident to Ezra Pound, saying that both were *equally to blame and in need of keepers.*[10] Knowledge of what had happened became public in Dublin. The militant Cumann na mBan, charged Willie with conspiring with the Chief Secretary, Mr. Short, to have Maude rearrested and deported. This most serious and potentially deadly charge, in the circumstances then prevailing in Dublin, was luckily later withdrawn. But the episode was most embarrassing to the two protagonists.

Lily Yeats, no friend of Maude Gonne's, wrote of this episode to Mrs Jeanne Robert Foster on 20 November. She said that Maude wished to go to bed in the house and make her arrest more dramatic - *dragged from her dying bed I suppose* - Willy described the whole thing as *absurd*. When a doctor arrived and said such a proceeding could endanger Georgie's life, Lily wrote: *Still the lunatic refused to go - Willy had a scene with her and turned her out - the new Irish patriot is a pest.* Not content with disparaging Maude, Lily describes Iseult [whom she names as 'Isolde'] as *a pretty number, something of a ..... boy in petticoats* and Shawn as *a ... spoilt child, scruffy and untruthful.*[10a]

After the birth of the baby, Willie wrote the poem, *A Prayer For My Daughter.* Writing in his tower home, with Baby Anne fast asleep amid an Atlantic storm, he prayed that the child would be beautiful, though not like some beauty he had known, without wisdom and marrying foolishly. He hoped that she would not know intellectual hatred, for he had seen *the loveliest woman born* degenerate into *an old bellows full of angry wind.*

Despite the contretemps on the doorsteps of No. 73 St. Stephen's Green, Maude and Willie soon returned, in their own inimitable fashion, to intimate ways. In early 1920 Iseult married the very young Francis Stuart in difficult circumstances. Maude wrote to Willie that *the marriage is a tragedy.* She then reprimanded him, in her own well-mannered way by adding *She certainly took your advice of taking no notice of what I might think or advise.*[11] As Stuart was an ardent admirer of Yeats, Maude sought to have him influence her son-in-law, who was according to Maude, beating Iseult.[12]

Willie intervened and visited Iseult in Wicklow. She had by then separated from Stuart, and discussions took place about an end to the marriage, when Iseult discovered herself pregnant. Maude was distraught when Iseult later decided to return to live with Stuart. Meantime Sean MacBride had been arrested and was in Mountjoy Jail. Maude naturally looked to Willie for moral support. Her house had been raided by the military. She expressed relief that Willie was coming to Dublin, albeit for an operation to have his tonsils removed by his friend Oliver Gogarty. Her letters kept Willie up-to-date on the horrors of the War of Independence and the activities of the Black and Tans. On 24 August 1921, she offered congratulations to Willie

A Bronze head of Maud Gonne by L. Campbell from the Hugh Lane Municipal Gallery, Dublin.

and George on the arrival of their son, Michael. Iseult's baby had not lived.

At first Maude supported the Anglo-Irish Treaty and assisted the new Government, though her son opposed it. When the new government began to take harsh measures to secure the country, and imprison and execute prisoners, Maude turned against it. Because Willie supported the Free State and became a senator, their long-term friendship ended and regular contact ceased for several years. In 1926, when Sean was arrested on suspicion of being involved in the assassination of the government strongman, and friend of Yeats's, Kevin O'Higgins, Maude again wrote to Willie looking for help. That gave Willie the opportunity to reiterate that, *your husband was never one of my heroes - his brave death did not abolish his treatment of you - but he is a hero to these men.*[13] Yeats assured her that the Cosgrave government would never execute the son of John MacBride. In reply Maude excoriates him for supporting Government measures responsible for vicious treatment of prisoners. They exchanged sometimes recriminatory to letters during 1927-8, with Willie writing *we will never change each other's politics. They are too rooted in our characters.*[14]

He wrote of her in *Quarrel in Old* Age, commenting that:

> *I had forgiven enough*
> *That had forgiven old age*

The last letter Maude wrote to Willie was in June 1928, and concerned their attitudes to impending old age, while again identifying their respective personal unchanging characteristics:

Oh how you hate old age - well so do I, I see no redeeming features in it, but I, who am more a rebel against man than you, rebel less against nature, & accept the inevitable & go with it gently into the unknown – only against the sordidness & cruelty of small ambitions I fight until the long rest comes – out of that rest I believe the Great Mother will refashion great beauty & life

again. While we sleep she will work in the stupendous energy of Creation –
but till sleep comes our souls & bodies fight – in weariness, which is old age
– at the awakening it will be with the glory & joy of youth again.

Maude and Willie last met in late 1938 when they had tea together at his home, Riversdale, in Rathfarnham. It was not a happy conclusion to a lifetime of intimacy. Maude wrote, *as we said goodbye, he, sitting in his armchair from which he could rise only with great effort...the whirlpool of life had sent the current of our activities wide apart.*[15]

When Willie died in the south of France in January 1939, Maude like many others was most anxious that he be buried in Ireland. This was not to occur for several years. In early February a Memorial Service was held in St. Patrick's Cathedral in Dublin. The President and Taoiseach were both represented. In the congregation were all the Yeats family, including Jack and his wife. Among the many messages of sympathy received, were those from Madame Gonne MacBride and Mr. and Mrs Francis Stuart.

After the war preparations were made to repatriate Willie's remains for burial in Sligo. It transpired that his grave at Roquebrune had been interfered with and his remains removed to another quarter of the cemetery. This happened despite George having bought a ten-year plot in 1939. Attempts were made locally in Roquebrune to dissuade the family from exhuming the remains, due to the uncertainty of the precise location to which they had been transferred during the war. External pressures on the family, and their own desire to have the remains re-interred at Sligo, necessitated that a somewhat uncertain exhumation went ahead.[16] The remains had to wait for a further five months before arrangements were made for their transfer by Irish naval corvette to the port of Galway, as the port of Sligo was unable to afford the *Macha* a safe berthing. At Galway a problem occurred at the quayside, when it was discovered that the coffin would not fit into the body of the hearse. The naval ratings solved the difficulty by removing hinges from the hearse. The cortege than travelled through the counties of Galway and Mayo. As it passed, people harvesting in the fields stopped to bless themselves. At Sligo the James Connolly Pipe Band flanked the cortege with draped drums. At the request of the family there was no State ceremony except for a Military Guard of Honour. From Sligo it travelled to Drumcliff. As it did so, a veil of mist hung over the bare head of Ben Bulben and soft grey rain swept in from the sea to the tiny churchyard.

The chief Government representative with the cortege, and the person responsible for the whole operation, was the Minister for External Affairs, Sean MacBride. He was also there in a personal capacity, representing his mother, Maude Gonne, who was unable to travel from Dublin. Two other Government Ministers attended, James Everret and Joseph Blowick, as did the Leader of the opposition Eamon deValera. At the graveside the Mayor of Sligo said, *today we have fulfilled the expressed desire of WB Yeats that he might rest in the shelter of Ben Bulben.*[17]

A family prays at the grave in Drumcliffe.

CHAPTER 8

GLORIOUS WILLIE YEATS

WB Yeats merits the adjective, *glorious,* for his sublime yet accessible poetry, and for his life long devotion to the Irish nation.

Patrick Kavanagh, writing in 1962, argues that WB Yeats had a desperate desire to be thought of as Irish. He says that:

Yeats took up Ireland and made it his myth and theme. And you can see him today standing in the centre of that myth, uneasy that he doesn't fully belong. Now we can see that he does fully belong to the exciting affair with the Nation, and with Pearse and Connolly, and the others. But the fact remains that he never was at ease.[1]

While there may be some truth in the latter point, it may have more to do with his genius than with his nationality. Willie, like each member of his family, knew that he was Irish. If there ever was any doubt on that point, the family's bitter experiences of living in London, reinforced their certainty of being Irish. A part of Willie's greatness, developed from those early days when he identified his life's work, and continued to see it through, in good times, and in more difficult times. He understood and accepted the sectarian challenge John O'Leary conveyed to him at an early stage, that to get on in Ireland, one needed the backing of the Fenians and of the Catholic Church. The latter proved impossible. As Kavanagh so rightly said, he was and is an integral part of the Nation, *with the others.*

Leon Kellner was an Austrian writer, specialising in English literature. He had often noticed Willie in the British Museum, though not realising who he was. Ernest and Grace Rhys, mutual friends, invited Kellner to meet the leader of the Celtic Movement in 1899. To Kellner's surprise, he recognised the *dark-eyed ascetic of the British Museum, the very slight sleek-haired young man with the large deep-set eyes.* Kellner and Willie took tea at the Rhys' home and a very civilised English conversation ensued, which deeply disappointed Kellner. As Kellner was preparing to leave, Willie asked him what direction he was going in. Kellner replied, *towards the Park,* and Willie said, *I will go with you.* Kellner was taken aback at the directness, writing that this was *the only out of the way, un-English remark, made by Yeats during the whole afternoon.* The two men spent the entire evening together.

Some four years later Kellner wrote about the experience, painting a not uncritical picture of a wonderful young man. He wrote:

As soon as he warmed up and began to speak of Ireland, it was no longer possible for me to get a word in edgeways and I think he did not care to know if I was listening. Never before have I listened to such a wonderful, enchanting, repellent, contradictory flow of language. He spoke of Ireland's glorious past and still more glorious future, of the mission of the Irish people in history, of the curse and blessing of the present foreign yoke, of the ancient kith of the Irish peasants which is also his own, of the spirits of the water and of the air, which he [Yeats] hears and feels when he is in his Irish home, and with whom in moments of inspiration he feels himself one, as with all Creation: he names names out of Ireland's past, with the deepest reverence, as a believer utters the name of God. Angus, Aedh, Deirdre and Grania, Fergus and Oisin – these and other names fell from his lips and I felt that as he pronounced them, that he was speaking of then as a good child speaks of his parents and brothers and sisters. He spoke of his dream-world as if in a dream and it was indeed strange, almost uncanny in the midst of the noise of the West End of London, in the every day prosaic surroundings of shops and omnibuses, in the midst of ugliness and vice, to listen to old Irish legends and Utopian enthusiasm for the future

Though Kellner was so impressed with Yeats' performance, he was aware of the apparent absence of social conscience for the appalling conditions of so many Irish people then alive in Ireland. This would be one of the judgements made later against the poet by WH Auden. Kellner continued:

Yeats is not of this world. His inner life is entirely filled by the thoughts of Ireland's past and Ireland's future. The poverty of the Irish today, the terrible decrease in the population: over forty thousand people emigrate from Ireland every year, to settle in America and the Colonies – the all powerful influence of the Roman priesthood, that impoverishment of the soil, and whatever evils are under which the Celtic element in Ireland is suffering. – All that is to Yeats of secondary importance, a fleeting space of time in Ireland's history. That must all pass over, such is his conviction, and if only Celtic spirit can be kept alive he is not afraid for Ireland's future. The star of godless, materialistic brutal England is on the wane – the Sun of pious spiritually minded Ireland is rising.

This is to the Poet Yeats an article of faith. Like his Spirit-world and his Catholicism, and one must bear this in mind in order to understand his

117

writings. Yeats is, as William Archer says, not the Incarnation of Irish Celticism, but the quintessence of the old Celtic spirit. It is as if the poet Oisin, the favourite hero of the poet has been reincarnated in him- so far are his feelings and thoughts removed from our time.

I did not always find him intelligible … his poems address themselves exclusively to the tenderest, most delicate side of the human soul.

Yeats is a kindred spirit of William Blake – that is true not only with regard to what is mystic in their natures but also in regard to the naïve childish and elementary strain in their writings. Blake's, "Tiger Tiger", is to be found in all the English National Schools reading books and has almost become a 'Volkslied'; and Yeats has written some nursery songs which are unique in literature, e.g. 'A Cradle Song'.[1a]

Though Yeats was destined by fate to spend up to half of his life in England, he was at pains to avoid writing about his urban existence there, save for *The Lake Isle of Innisfree*. Though he came to detest that poem later, for understandable reasons, it was an Irish poem, distancing him from London and aspiring towards a rural existence. The absence of English place names in his work, can be seen as the greatest indication of that significance. Though he lived there for so long, he moved about sparingly. Even the London Oxford nexus remained a foreign land for him, noticed by a foreign eye, picking out the strange and not as in one's own country the familiar things, for interest. The effort to remain true to cultural, political and artistic independence must have been difficult. He lived in England because he needed its tradition of publishing houses and writing to make a living.

Kavanagh later asserted that Yeats did not belong to Sligo, but possibly more to London. This is not so. Despite his unhappy relationship with his mother, Sligo was family. Given his peripatetic life style, Sligo could even be described as home for early periods of his life. He later he discovered a mother substitute and collaborator, and he transferred his allegiance south to county Galway.

In 1885 WB Yeats met the paroled John O'Leary and his mission in life gradually unfolded. He adopted the moderate politics of O'Leary. He strayed into a more extreme form of nationalism for a period in the company of Maud Gonne and other advanced nationalists. After the trauma of her marriage and divorce case, he reverted to his moderation and cultural work. The shock and excitement of the Easter Rising aroused his nationalism. After his marriage, he wanted to live safely and rear his family in Ireland.

118

He devoted much of his energy to the new Irish Free State, becoming a Senator in the Oireachtas.

Maud Gonne often chided Willie for spending too much time involved in peripheral activities, which took him away from his primary work as a poet. She knew how long and laborious his composition was, writing to him on 12 November 1909:

What makes the extraordinary charm of your poetry is the terrible though unseen effort of its creation. This somehow makes the atmosphere of a precious jewel about it. Like a gem it is the outcome of a terrible & hidden effort.

At an earlier meeting between her sister Kathleen, Maud and Willie in London, the two sisters had presented a contrasting picture to him. Maud looked tired and rather dishevelled, unlike her well- groomed sister. They spoke of poetry. Willie said that a good poem must appear and read as if the words flowed readily. Yet the reality could be that one line might take several hours to complete. People of the world, teachers, priests, and financiers, often regard poets as idlers, though their work may be as difficult as those engaged in stone-breaking. Willie's message led to Kathleen comparing the poet's lot to that of women who have to constantly appear at their best. This episode is captured in the poem *Adam's Curse*.

In July 1911, when Maud heard that Willie was going to America to promote an Abbey tour, she was angry, writing:

Really Willie you have no right to waste your time like that. There are a hundred of theatre managers & the coarser & rougher they are the better they succeed, but there are one or two poets at most in the world capable of producing literature that will live as a crown to their nation & you are one of these & it makes me quite wild to think you are going to America simply as advance agent to the Abbey Theatre Company. Don't think I under rate the value of your theatre but it is NOTHING in comparison with your poems...

Like most poets, Willie sometimes wrote spontaneous verse, making little if any subsequent alterations. His main method of composition was so very different though. He often wrote prose drafts of a subject fit for a poem. Later, in Louis MacNeice's phrase, he *made himself a poet and as poet, he was essentially a maker.*[2] His verse went through many versions as he chanted it aloud, searching for the right word to give meaning, but also to fit into the metre and rhyme he sought. This may be in part why WH Auden criticised his poetry as being too technical. The result is surely what matters. The poems are best understood and enjoyed when read aloud. Yeats himself intended his poems to be read aloud, to be performed.

Of course, his practice of composing often caused great distress to those who were within earshot of his continuous chanting. His sister Lollie was put under great strain in their house in Harold's Cross by his interminable chant. While staying in Maud Gonne's house in Normandy one summer, James Cousins was left alone in the house with Willie. Cousins knew that Willie intended to work, so he remained very quiet. He wrote that he began to hear *a queer monotonous murmur* permeating the house and continue for the next three hours. Cousins decided to investigate and observed Yeats *sitting on a chair in the corner of the kitchen with his head bent low into the corner*.[3]

Sir Ian Hamilton, a cousin of Lady Gregory's, wrote, with little sympathy, of observing the ambience that the lady provided for her guest at Coole.

Yeats and I were the only two guests in the big house. Yeats, unfortunately for my enjoyment, was in the throes of composition and was being thoroughly spoiled. No one can have ever heard anyone grumble so much about the pangs and pain of producing a line of poetry and no one ever heard anyone play up to him like Lady Gregory. Thick rugs were laid to prevent the slightest sound.[4]

The first version of Willie's verse was often of a personal nature, which in the next version became more generalised. In seeking to establish his original mood and thought, the prose drafts and the earlier versions are fruitful to study. Because his poetic gifts far outweighed his intellectual strength, he often lost intellectual control of his subject to the power of his symbolic imaginings.

It is almost universally accepted that WB Yeats was a great poet, and possibly the greatest poet writing in English of the twentieth century. One who debated this was the poet WH Auden, who proposed arguments for and against Willie in 1939. Auden admitted that Yeats had talent but denied that he was a great poet. He did not see the gift for a very high order of memorable language, and posed the question as to the number of Yeatsian poems people could recall. Auden also expected to see a keen understanding of the times Yeats lived in, as well as empathy for progressive attitudes. He held that Yeats failed miserably on both these counts, having a *feudal mind*. He allows him some minor credit for assisting Irish nationalism. He chides him for wallowing in irrational superstition, as opposed to accepting scientific methodology. Auden said Yeats believed in fairies and rejected social justice, reason,and hoped for war in the end.

For the defence, Auden, while accepting that Yeats was a conceited snob, a physical coward, and unscientific, also accepted that he was still a great poet. Willie reacted to his world in ways that produced good poems throughout his entire life. Auden believed that poetry and other art forms, effect little change for people. Poetry involves language and it is there that Yeats is great. Auden also alludes to the remarkable fact that Willie wrote some of his best poetry later in life, after freeing himself from the Gonne muse. In his elegy, *In Memory of WB Yeats,* Auden wrote:

> *You were silly like us;*
>
> *But your gift survived it all:*
>
> *For poetry makes nothing happen...*
>
> *Let the Irish vessel lie*
>
> *Emptied of its poetry*[5]

On Auden's own memorial stone at Westminster Abbey, are carved two lines from that elegy on Yeats:

> *In the prison of his days*
>
> *Teach the free man to praise.*

One example of Willie's actions in standing up publicly for his country, while in his 'advanced nationalist' state, occurred early in 1900. The Boer War had begun the previous year and two Irish Brigades had been formed in South Africa to fight alongside the Boers. In Ireland the Irish Transvaal Committee, headed by Maud Gonne and Arthur Griffith, used the unpopularity of the war to whip up anti-English sentiment around the country. Queen Victoria was due to make a visit to Ireland, ostensibly to celebrate her golden jubilee, but in reality to effect support for enlistment into the English army. Advanced nationalists were utterly opposed to the visit. WB Yeats became embroiled in public controversy on the matter after writing a series of letters to the press. This exposed him to vitriol from some of the English papers.[6]

He wrote to the *Freeman's Journal* on 20 March 1900:

Dear Sir,

> *Let any Irishman who believes the Queen's visit to Ireland to be non-political buy the current number of Punch. He will find there a cartoon*

representing the Irish members gazing, in various attitudes of terror, at a proclamation announcing this visit, while a picture of President Kruger, who is made to look as much like a chimpanzee as possible, lies at their feet, having fallen from the shaking hands of one of them. The Irish members are made as hideous as President Kruger is made, and the whole is inspired by national hatred. The advisers of the queen have not sent into Ireland this woman of eighty-one, to whom all labours must be wearisome, without good reason, and the reason is national hatred; hatred of our individual national life; and as Mr. Moore has pointed out, the necessities of Empire. She comes, as Mr. Moore has said, to do the work her recruiting sergeants have failed to do, "with a shilling between her finger and thumb and a bag of shillings at her girdle", and it is the duty of those who believe that Ireland has an individual National life to protest with so much courtesy as is compatible with vigour…

On 3 April he wrote from London to the *Freeman's Journal* in even more strident tone. Of the Queen he said, *She is the official head and symbol of an Empire that is robbing the South African Republics of their liberty, as it has robbed Ireland of hers. Whoever stands by that roadway cheering for Queen Victoria cheers for that Empire, dishonours Ireland and condones a crime*

Annie Horniman, among many others, is often poorly served in Ireland, when juxtaposed with WB Yeats, as founder of the Abbey Theatre. She came from a middle-class English family which was interested in art and the theatre, having become wealthy from Horniman' Tea. Her father had a private museum in London. She was very much an individualist, cycling alone across the Alps on a man's bicycle. Opinionated and outspoken, she was completely out of sympathy with Irish nationalism. A feminist, she was interested in astrology, but most of all loved the theatre. She was a shrewd businesswoman, interested in becoming an *artist*. She met WB Yeats at the Order of the Golden Dawn in 1890 and became infatuated with him. She financed the production of his first play, *The Land of Heart's Desire,* in London in 1894. Willie persuaded her to subsidise his theatrical ambitions in Dublin. She became an integral figure in the development of the Abbey Theatre, though at all times her own motivation was to further Willie's ambitions. Without her money the Abbey may not have happened. Lady Gregory saw her as a rival for Willie's attention and treated her in an inimical fashion. Willie had a difficult task in handling Horniman, as she insisted in playing a hands-on role at the theatre. One continuing row she had there was over the cost of the cheapest seats. She refused to allow the traditional sale of sixpenny seats. All treated her as an intruder. But Willie, who needed her money, played up to her, as the promise of ever-growing largesse was dangled before him. He even got the Directors to agree with her demand to appoint an English managing director, Ben Payne.

In 1907, after WB Yeats had refused to attend the funeral of John O'Leary, he joined Lady Gregory on a trip to Italy to restore his mangled mind. The Abbey Company meantime was on an English tour, managed by Annie Horniman. By this time she was feeling very disgruntled at her treatment at the Abbey and determined to end her relationship there. She had written to JM Synge after the *Playboy* riots and Yeats' magnificent defence of the play, saying, *I feel myself a worm not to have come over, but the Directors took no notice of my offers to come and join the fray.*[7] She had had enough of Ireland, and planned to begin a theatre in Manchester and take Ben Payne with her. Willie, not unnaturally, was very upset at this prospect. He sought to persuade her to stay with his theatre by offering to open a second company in Dublin which would stage the kind of international plays both she and he wished to see performed. She refused his offer, though she agreed to continue her commitment to the Abbey, but only on a short-term basis. Willie realised that this was very important, as it meant that he still would have time to influence her long-term role in funding. She then repeated a request that he would give his plays to her new theatre in Manchester. Willie knew how much that would mean to Horniman, and that without this 'reparation' on his part the chance of extra money from her was remote. As usual, he took Gregory's advice on this important matter. In a letter, which shows Willie in a truly glorious light, he answered his patron, telling her that her proposal was impossible. Like all writers, he wished to reach an international stage, nevertheless, giving up his plays to an English audience would amount to his giving up his nationality. His immediate audience, in everything he wrote, was his own race. He would not change that, even though it could be a love or hate relationship. While the Irish theatre still needed him, and he might yet need his corpus of plays to attract donors, he could not let them go. For the few remaining years of her subsidy, Miss Horniman became more and more critical of Abbey personnel, and eventually her sale of the Abbey lease to the National Theatre Society had to be arbitrated on by CP Scott of the *Manchester Guardian*. In his letter to her, Willie had shown his true colours! As Roy Foster writes, *it is, in its way, one of the best letters he ever wrote.*[8]

When news of the Easter Rising broke, Willie was staying with his artistic friend, Sir William Rothenstein, in Gloucestershire. The latter recalled that his guest fretted at the news, saying that he had not been consulted about it. He was very moved, describing it as a poets' revolution, all about innocent theorists sacrificing themselves, and without doubt paying the penalty. Maud Gonne wrote to Yeats from France, desperately seeking accurate information. They both agreed that the postponing of Home Rule at the start of the war had led to the Rising.

As the executions begun in May, Gonne quoted the lines from *Caithlin ni hUalachain* about the executed; *the people shall hear them forever,* and in her own words wrote, *the deaths of those leaders are full of beauty and romance.* She told Willie that a tragic dignity had been restored to Ireland by those sacrificed. In a letter to Lady Gregory on 11 May 1916, Willie confessed that he had no idea that any public event could move him so deeply. He said that he was trying to write a poem about the executed, using the phrase that *terrible beauty has been born again.* He was very despondent about the future. At the same time he had indicated to Rothenstein that he could not unequivocally support the Rising. He spent July and August in France with Maud Gonne and her family. Since she was now a widow, after the execution of her husband, Willie felt free to propose to her again. In late August, Lady Gregory wrote to Willie, expressing her puzzlement by his apparent indifference to Ireland, telling him that:

I believe there is a great deal you can do, all is unrest and discontent— there must be some spiritual building possible—You have a big name among the young men.[9]

During September Willie read a draft of *Easter 1916* to Gonne on the beach in Normandy. In November he sent her a copy of the poem. She disliked it, deeming it unworthy of its subject, feeling it did not do justice to men of genius like Pearse, MacDonagh and Connolly. Ironically she told him that:

It is not a great whole, a living thing which our race would treasure and repeat, such as a poet like you might have given to your nation and which would have avenged our national failures by its spiritual beauty.[10]

Though I will deal with it later, it is worthy to note here that the reference to her husband in the poem, may not have commended it to her. Neither may the repeated phrase, *a terrible beauty,* with its almost internal contradiction, have pleased Maud. The phrase can be read as referring to Maud herself, as well as to ordinary men being cast as heroes. As Terence Brown has noted, though Gonne is not mentioned directly, she is *a presiding spirit* in the poem.[11] Elizabeth Cullingford identifies the character of Countess Markiewicz in the second stanza as really that of Maud Gonne, who might have been among the leaders and those executed, had she remained active in Dublin. The poet feared that her fanatic heart would lose its femininity and *trouble the living stream,* as a new stone, or *a terrible beauty.*[12]

Some commentators have accused Yeats of "getting in on the act" with *Easter 1916,* inferring gender politics at work again, with Willie playing the role of 'Princess' or 'mother' to Maud's 'Prince'.[13] Terry Eagleton adds, in acclaiming the poem,

He puts on the mask of tragic chorus, and out of the slow impersonal contemplation of a particular event in which idealism, folly, heroism and destructiveness were intermixed, fashions an image which stands for all such events in human history.

WH Auden described it as a masterpiece, but in the context of, t*o succeed at such a time in writing a poem, which could offend neither the Irish Republicans nor the British army, was indeed a masterly achievement.*[14] Declan Kiberd sees the poem as *an imperialist's elegy for a headstrong but contaminated foe. In it, the Irishman is still a child … The rebel's play was staged to gather an Irish audience and challenge an English one.*[15] Kiberd adds that the theatricality of the Rising appealed to Yeats. He felt that he had to be part of it. He realised that though he had helped to wind the clock he had not been present to hear it strike. But he could endorse it only with severe qualification. In the end, he did fulfil his bardic duty and name the dead heroes. But the important word for Yeats is *terrible.*

As Yeats tried to explain to his upper-class English hosts why Irish people might have felt it necessary to rise out against England, suspicions were aroused that he might be pro-German. Terence Brown writes that *there was even talk that his Civil List Pension might be withdrawn.*[16] This would assuredly serve to make him very cautious in his public life. In May he wrote to Maud about the danger of the times, adding that Dublin would not be a safe place for anybody who wishes to speak his mind. In England, people were occasionally arrested for speaking against recruitment in some hotel bar. He suggested to Maud that in Ireland everybody in the hotel would be arrested.[17] When he was pressurised to write a poem about the Great War, he resisted, saying that *I think it better in times like this, we poets keep our mouths shut.*

Willie was perspicacious enough to realise that publication of such a poem as *Easter 1916* could be a politically-fraught exercise. On 28 March 1917, he had twenty-five copies printed for close friends. It was not published publicly in Ireland until St. Patrick's Day 1919, and in England only in October 1920, in the *New Statesman*. Lady Gregory had worried that its earlier publication might have hurt their theatrical endeavours. Yeats has been much criticised for his timidity in publication. Conor Cruise O'Brien saw it as an example of his cunning. O'Brien wrote;

Yeats could be fearless on issues where artistic integrity was involved … But on national politics, even where he felt passionately, he usually acted prudently; and even at this point, although he acted with unusual boldness, he did not allow himself to be carried away.[18]

Terence Brown termed O'Brien's portrait of Yeats as *a man who combined passion and a strategic self-serving political cunning through most of his life* as *'iconoclastic'*. Brown also found that O'Brien's assessment of Yeats's stance in the autumn of 1920 and the winter of 1921 'lacks generosity'.[19]

The poet had good personal and political reasons to consider. He had committed himself to living at least part-time in Ireland, as far back as March 1917 when he purchased Thoor Ballylee, moving in there in September 1918. He, of course, also continued to live in Oxford. Maud Gonne's harsh reaction to *Easter 1916* had to be considered, particularly as he began to woo her daughter, Iscult, after Maud's usual refusal of marriage. He also had the ear of the English Establishment and hoped to do good there. In December 1916 he and Gregory had dined with the Prime Minister Asquith and discussed the Lane picture problem. In October 1918 he lobbied Lord Haldane against the imposition of conscription to Ireland.

Willie and Georgie had spent the first half of 1920 in the USA. In August she suffered a miscarriage, and he had had his tonsils removed by Oliver Gogarty. Lady Gregory kept him informed about the dastardly actions of the British forces in the country. So, during the War of Independence, in October 1920, a very dangerous time in Ireland, he released *Easter 1916* to the *New Statesman* for publication. He thus demonstrated where his allegiance lay, as the English were making it abundantly clear, that they would not *keep faith*. The next month he allowed publication of his three Easter Rising poems in *The Dial* in America.

During Easter 1916 and afterwards, Willie had been to some extent equivocal about the Rising; subsequent events, however, made it clear to him that the tragic sacrifice of the *terrible beauty* had been necessary after all. The argument that they should have waited until the end of the war and German defeat was futile in the circumstances of the *Sixteen Dead Men*. They had joined the Pantheon of earlier patriots and the course to be trod was clear: the time for give-and-take was past. In the third of his 1916 trilogy, Yeats is even more forthright. After a dialogue between Patrick Pearse and James Connolly, he concludes that the blood sacrifice is necessary for the *Rose Tree*.

> *There's nothing but our own red blood*
> *Can make a right Rose Tree*

As the Anglo-Irish War got more brutal during the winter of 1920-21, many of Maud Gonne's letters to Willie, who was then living in Oxford, were about the atrocities committed by the British. She mentioned several cases where she was convinced that torture had taken place after court-martial and before execution. These included the university student Kevin Barry, who was hanged in Mountjoy Jail. She wondered to Willie whether it would be possible to get some prominent person to write to *The Times* in protest.

Maud herself was too heavily involved at various levels. The Red Cross in Geneva and the British Red Cross refused material assistance to those affected by the war. The American Red Cross sent £5 million aid. Dublin's Lord Mayor invited Maud to sit on an executive committee to distribute this aid, under the auspices of a non-political White Cross. She helped with school meals in Dublin and Donegal, as well as with assistance for people with disabilities. She was actively involved in trying to get sentences of death commuted and the lot of prisoners eased. The Sinn Féin Government had a publicity department, headed by Desmond Fitzgerald, to which Maud lent support. When Fitzgerald was arrested in 1921, his wife was refused permission to visit him. Maud enlisted Willie's help and visits became possible. She passed on Fitzgerald's admiration for Willie's poetry to him.[20] She told him of Iseult's suggestion that the Abbey should revive Fitzgerald's play, *The Saint*, adding that she believed that Lady Gregory approved of the idea. Fitzgerald was a London-born poet who had fought in 1916 and was to play an important role in the emerging State, as well as fathering the future Taoiseach, Garret Fitzgerald. As Fitzgerald and Arthur Griffith were interned in Gloucester Gaol, a regular topic of conversation between them was the poetry of WB Yeats. Griffith began to speak of the forthcoming important date of 13th June, which the internees would have to celebrate. Much to Griffith's amusement, Fitzgerald did not recognise the date as Yeats' birthday. Griffith succeeded in getting the prison governor to recognise the day as an important one for the prisoners. It was marked by a special dinner with entertainment, including the recital of the great man's poetry.[21].

Willie realised only too well that Maud Gonne expected him to take some public stand about the situation in Ireland and specifically about the activities of the notorious *Black and Tan Auxiliaries*. An opportunity and a challenge arose on Willie's own doorstep, when in February 1921 the Oxford Union, decided to debate the motion;

This House would welcome complete self-government in Ireland and condemns reprisals.

Willie received an invitation to speak for the motion. John Stewart Collis proposed it. He subsequently wrote of Willie's speech, in terms that assures one that he learned well all those years previously at the Contemporary Club. Collis wrote:

He stepped forward with some passionate exclamation of denial concerning something that had been said. Then with extraordinary vehemence he arraigned the English — (unclear word in manuscript) and scattered the speaker who had just resumed his seat. Gathering impetus from his increasing rage he left the Treasury Box and strode up and down the aisle between the Ayes and the Noes, waving his arms and shaking his fists at the audience, pouring out a sustained flow of eloquence. At first the house was changed into a theatrical audience but as the speech progressed, became more and more beaten and subdued until finally everyone was convinced that England was a brutal monster and Ireland a betrayed angel. Yeats eventually sat down amidst unexampled enthusiasm; the fourth speaker was completely dished and the motion approved by an overwhelming majority, 219 to 129. Yeats had the powerful lower lip, which reveals the born orator and the born pugilist – a certain pugnacity, a certain disdain being necessary to the great orator.[22]

Willie's speech received much publicity and the next letter from Maud reflected this, as she congratulated him;

I was so glad to see your speech at the Oxford Union & the big majority for Ireland obtained in the debates – It must be uphill work in England, but all the same it is telling and the forces against us are falling apart in their desire to shirk odium & responsibility & shift the blame on one another.[23]

128

That same month saw the publication by Cuala Press in Dublin of the three Easter Rising poems.

Henry Moore sculpture, St. Stephen's Green.
Erected in 1967 by admirers of W.B. Yeats.

CHAPTER 9

ASSASSINATING JOHN MACBRIDE

In WB Yeats' poem, *Beautiful Lofty Things,* from *Last Poems,* he writes of the important people in his life, John O'Leary, his own father, Standish O'Grady, Augusta Gregory, Maud Gonne, and concludes with the line,

All the Olympians; a thing never known again

Patrick Kavanagh, writing in 1962, poses a rhetorical question. He asks, *But was it not he who made them Olympians?* Kavanagh refers to Yeats as *the god, the authority; the Mother Mind to whom all things could be referred. Any person possessing this myth-making quality can transform a commonplace society into an Olympian one.*[1] Kavanagh's assertion has stood the test of time as the power and influence of Yeats' poetry grows ever stronger. The Yeatsian world-wide industry has seen to that. This chapter is concerned with one, whom the poet sought to and succeeded in traducing down the years, one excluded from participating as an olympian. Yeats' acolytes, with a very few honourable exceptions, have clung, limpet-like, to those offending lines from *Easter 1916,* as merited, ignoring the historical record, and the unyielding hatred which inspired their creation.

This other man I had dreamed
A drunken, vainglorious lout,
He had done most bitter wrong
To some who are near my heart …

Yeats rarely names the targets he sets out to mock and destroy. Yet throughout his writings lie 'direct' and 'indirect' vitriolic allusions to John MacBride and his marriage to Maud Gonne. He told John Quinn on 14 January 1904 that Maud Gonne's marriage to John MacBride was the single worst event of his life.[2] In a later poem about Iseult Millevoye, *To A Young Girl,* he wrote that *her mother had broken his heart.* His earliest poetic response to the marriage, and his own loss, came in the 1904 collection, *In The Seven Woods,* which contained two poems describing the pain of his loss and his advice to lovers, *O Do Not Love Too Long* and *Never Give All The Heart.*

His attitude to the successful suitor came in early and unpublished lines:

My dear is angry that of late
I cry all base blood down,
As though she had not taught me hate
By kisses to a clown …

John MacBride

John MacBride was three years younger than Yeats and two younger than Gonne. His father had been a ship's captain from Glenshesk in Antrim, who had settled in Westport County Mayo, married a local girl and set up *a* merchant business on the Quays. John, the youngest of five boys, was educated locally by the Christian Brothers and at St. Malachy's College in Belfast. His brother Anthony and he were contemporaries at St. Malachy's of Eoin Macneil.[3] Anthony studied medicine and practised in London with Dr. Mark Ryan. The latter was a native of Galway and a leader of the Irish Republican Brotherhood. He initiated Maud Gonne and possibly WB Yeats, into that secret society. Anthony MacBride initiated John into the IRB. Both doctors were activists in London's Irish nationalist and literary organisations. As such, they were contemporaries and colleagues of WB Yeats. John MacBride worked at a wholesale chemist in Dublin. One description of him at that time comes from Arthur Lynch, later to command the second Irish Brigade to see action in the Boer War. Lynch wrote:

At a noted London hotel, a small committee of Irishmen had met to consider the question of a propagandist paper. Amongst those was John MacBride then a chemist's assistant in Dublin, an active and determined young man, of ruddy countenance and with reddish hair, with something of eagerness and determination and unflinching courage in his expression. We had separated and had drifted apart and though there was no falling out between us, he became unfriendly.[4]

One of the very active nationalist societies flourishing in Dublin in the 1880's was the Young Ireland Society, which met weekly and was attended by all the leading literary and nationalist figures of the day. It was probably at this society that MacBride first met WB Yeats. The minute book of the society lists the presence of both at meetings during 1885.[5] It was at a meeting of the Leinster Literary Society, later to be called, the Celtic Literary Society, that MacBride first met the serious and shy Arthur Griffith and his friend Willie Rooney. Maud Gonne participated in their activities, though Rooney had the embarrassing task of informing her that women could not actually become members.

John MacBride's main political work was within the IRB, which was constantly scheming and planning for a distant revolution. He was a keen admirer of Parnell, and was one of two thousand Gaelic Athletic Association members, who, ignoring the condemnation of the Catholic Church, escorted Parnell's remains to Glasnevin Cemetery. Yeats had refused to accompany Gonne to the funeral, though he had met her off the boat, which carried the dead hero's body back to Ireland. The IRB was constantly riven by splits and conspiracies. One breakaway group was the Irish National Alliance. MacBride and Yeats became members. MacBride attended an INA convention in Chicago in 1895 as a Dublin delegate. A Police file on him that same year, described him as a *Clerk in Hugh Moore & Co., aged about thirty, 5 ft.' 6." In height, of medium build, reddish hair, grey eyes, fair eyebrows, reddish moustache, said to be active in Secret Societies and one of the intimates of Fred J. Allan.*[6] Allan was head of the Supreme Council of the IRB and remained a life long ally of MacBride. MacBride visited America again in 1896 as a delegate at an IRB convention.

Later that same year, MacBride travelled to South Africa. Maud Gonne was subsequently informed that this 'excursion' may have been inspired by the IRB as a way of sorting out difficulties at home. Arthur Griffith soon joined him.[7] The centenary of the Rising of 1798 became a major international occasion for Irish nationalists, with centenary committees formed world-wide. Willie Yeats was heavily involved in the London and Dublin organisations. In Johannesburg John MacBride was the main organiser and sent one delegate to the central celebration in Dublin. At a parade in Johannesburg on 15 August 1898, he proposed the toast to *The Memory of the Dead.*[8]

It was at a meeting of this, still-functioning, '98 Centenary Committee chaired by MacBride, on 3 September 1899, that the decision was taken to hold a public meeting to put the idea of the foundation of an Irish Brigade to fight alongside the Boers should war break out with Britain. Other national groups made similar plans.[9] MacBride wrote of that meeting;

I issued a manifesto to my fellow countrymen to form a Brigade to assist the Boers … a vast meeting was held in Johannesburg and Irish from Praetoria came. I, as permanent president of the organising committee was moved to the chair. The scene was full of enthusiasm. I was immediately offered the position of commander, but the high honour I had to decline on account of my lack of military training and experience. Mr. Gillingham said he knew of a Mr. Blake in Pretoria, a lieutenant from the USA. I interviewed him and took him to the next meeting and proposed him as Commander.[10]

Blake was injured at an early stage of the war, and MacBride became commander for most of the hostilities. The formation of the Brigade and its campaign alongside the Boer army received much publicity in Ireland, where Arthur Griffith was then editing the *United Irishman*. Griffith and

The officer corps of the Irish Brigade. MacBride is on the right of back.

Maud Gonne, assisted by Yeats and other advanced nationalists, used the Brigade as a tool to promote a renewed spirit of nationalism. The Boer War engendered much anti-English sentiment throughout the country, despite the fact that a high proportion of the British army in South Africa, were native Irish. As early as 30 September 1899, Yeats was writing to Lady Gregory, apologising for having to delay visiting her, as he had to wait on in Dublin, lest Gonne needed him to speak at a meeting about the Transvaal situation. Gonne and Griffith were among those who had set up the Irish Transvaal Committee in Dublin on 10 October. Its aims were to collect funds for the war effort and send an Irish flag out to MacBride. In preparation for another public meeting, which would be banned and broken up by the police, Yeats assured Gonne that he was with her and hoped for a Boer victory, adding: *I am not English, and owe England no loyalty.*[11] Yeats continued to support the Irish Transvaal Committee in public, much to the annoyance of some British newspapers. One Frank Hugh O'Donnell intercepted funds collected by Gonne from the Transvaal's representative in Belgium, for his own purposes. Yeats and Gonne had to discourage one faction of the IRB from executing O'Donnell.[12]

The Irish Brigade participated in the war for a full year, fighting very effectively alongside the Boer Army. MacBride's leadership of the Brigade and his bravery in the heat of several battles, made him a national hero in Ireland. Ballads were written about him, sporting teams adopted his name. One example was: *'John MacBride's Brigade'.*

The second verse reads:

Three thousand Transvaal Irishmen, with spirits brave and free,
They struck the Saxon foemen down at Glencoe and Dundee.
From Ladysmith to Spion Kop their flag victorious waved,
And well they wreaked revenge on those who Erin's Isle enslaved.
With guns and bayonets in their hands, their Irish flag on high,
As down they swept on England's ranks out rang their battle cry-
Revenge! Remember '98, and how our fathers died.
We'll pay the English back to day, cried fearless John MacBride.[13]

Another Mayo born man, Michael Davitt, resigned his seat in the House of Commons, in a protest against the war. The bye-election in South Mayo was set for February 1900. Advanced nationalists decided to run MacBride as a candidate, knowing that if he won he would be automatically disqualified. They expected that the recently reunited Irish Parliamentary Party would acquiesce in 'loaning' them the seat until the forthcoming General Election, due in September. Unfortunately, after the bitterness of the Parnell Split and its aftermath, the Parliamentary Party, despite its admiration for MacBride and the Irish Brigade, did not give MacBride's candidature a free run in South Mayo. This was a missed opportunity for Irish parliamentarians to conciliate a new generation of separatists and forestall the growth of Sinn Féin.[14] The advanced nationalists were furious and bitter as MacBride was heavily defeated. He himself read the news in a local Transvaal paper, *The Standard and Diggers News*, where it was headlined, *Ungrateful Mayo.* MacBride himself said his defeat was *proclaimed in every British camp with joy.*[15]

The set back for the advanced nationalists did not stop Willie Yeats from proposing, almost immediately, that a sitting M.P. in Dublin should resign his seat and allow MacBride a free run in the ensuing bye-election. Tim Harrington had been an M.P. for Dublin since 1885.Harrington was a long time nationalist who had been imprisoned twice. He had been Parnell's barrister in the Commission on Parnellism and Crime. Willie mentioned his proposal to Gonne in a letter. She replied:

The Harrington MacBride idea is excellent. Harrington will be a fool not to accept for his popularity is at very low ebb in Dublin just now.

If elected, MacBride would be disqualified and the seat could be returned to Harrington in the forthcoming general election.[16] Nothing came of this suggestion.

Though 1900 was a very busy year for Gonne, she sought to keep in close touch with Willie. In July she chided that she had not heard from him for a long while. In September, she told him she would be in Dublin soon and wanted him to meet her there for a week, to do some work in the occult and Celtic mysticism.

The British had difficulty defeating the Boers and poured a vast army into the country. It developed into a form of guerrilla war. The Irish Brigade was not suited to this development and was stood down. MacBride received two testimonials from the Boer authorities, one from State secretary Reitz and one from Commandt-General Louis Botha. The former read:

In the name of the Government of the South African Republics, I hereby express my hearty thanks to Major MacBride and the Irish Brigade for the valuable service rendered to our country during the war.[17]

The South African authorities paid for the safe passage of the Brigadiers to neutral countries as they could be charged with treason if they returned to Ireland or Britain. MacBride decided to travel to Paris. He was met there by a delegation, including his mother and brothers, Mark Ryan, Arthur Griffith, Stephen McKenna, John O'Leary, and Maud Gonne. Maud described him as:

A wiry, soldierly-looking man, with red hair and skin burnt-red by the South African sun.[18]

Maud recalled MacBride and Griffith talking, as she sat *in an armchair smoking cigarettes and listening.* She was thrilled to hear of Irishmen actually fighting England. The capture of English officers in particular delighted her. She felt that, *that little band of Irishmen in the Brigade had done more for Ireland's honour than all those at home.*[19]

Griffith and Gonne advised MacBride he should do a lecture tour of the USA, dealing with his experiences of the war and collect funds for Griffith's *United Irishman.* Maud and MacBride composed a set of speeches. MacBride sailed for New York with a letter of recommendation to John Devoy from John O'Leary. The New York Irish acclaimed MacBride as an Irish hero. Though staying at the Vanderbilt hotel and being feted everywhere, he soon tired of it all. He wrote to Gonne, saying that he wanted her to deliver on her promise, that she might join him later if necessary. He told her that otherwise he would not continue with the tour. She had terminated her long time relationship with the French politician, Lucien

Millevoye, some months earlier and decided to join MacBride.

In early February 1901, Willie Yeats received what should have been a disconcerting letter from Maud. She told him that she was leaving for America to join MacBride for a two-month lecture tour. The poet had spent some twelve years, at that stage, devising ways of capturing his muse in marriage. She sought to soften the news by adding that, she *hated going away so far from all my friends.*[20] Eight weeks later she wrote from Michigan:

Oh the weariness of an American tour! The constant being on show! The receptions, meetings, banquets etc - no you don't know the weariness of it all & to have to go through all this for money. I who despise money but have realised that money is necessary to carry on the work in Ireland. MacBride is going around with me, & is very good & saves me all the worry & fatigue he can, he is becoming quite a fine speaker.

She added that they were extending their tour until they had reached their financial target. She asked him to write to her at the 5th Avenue Hotel in New York City.[21] MacBride wrote to his mother about his companion; *Miss Gonne astonishes me the way in which she can stand the knocking about. For a woman it is wonderful.*[22]

Maud Gonne wrote later that John proposed marriage to her in America, but she put him off by saying that she wouldn't marry while there was a war on, adding that there was always an Irish war in progress. Donal P McCracken writes that *She later claimed that it was on this coast-to-coast tour that John proposed to her. If this was so, MacBride was no doubt flattered and dragooned into it.*[23]

The premature death of Willie Rooney in Dublin had a shattering effect on Griffith. He wrote several letters to Gonne, beseeching her to return to Dublin. She decided to leave the lecture tour and let MacBride continue on to the West Coast himself. She returned first to London and then to her home in Paris. It was around this period that Willie met Maud at her sister's house in London, when she looked so tired compared to Kathleen. He wrote the poem, *Adam's Curse,* comparing the work of the poet to that of a woman presenting herself at her best:

We sat together at one summer's end,

John MacBride completed the tour and returned to New York where he spent some time. Maud received a letter from him saying that he was returning to

Paris, and he asked her to meet him there. She knew that he could have made a good living in New York if he had remained there. In Paris she found him quite despondent that the state of Ireland was so passive after the excitement of the war. He told her that he hoped to earn a living in Paris, while waiting for the *chance of a fight.*[24]

In March of 1902 Maud was due to take the stage in Dublin for Willie's *Caithleen ni hUalachain*. It was to be the high point of their mutual collaboration in the cultural and nationalist field. Many difficulties occurred in the rehearsals. Maud insisted that Willie come to Dublin and attend some of them. Despite the fact that he had his own firm directorial views, Maud played the role her own way, acting herself as many thought. Willie was thrilled by her acting, writing to Lady Gregory that she played magnificently and with weird power.

The *United Irishman* was again experiencing dire financial circumstances and in danger of closing down. Willie decided to write a letter of congratulations and support for the paper to Maud. This would then be published in America and hopefully draw funds from there. Maud asked him to address the letter to Griffith but to send it to her. She told him that *Major MacBride will forward it, it is better not for my name to appear in the matter.*[25] Maud knew how highly John was held in America, especially by John Devoy and Clan na Gael. The tactic worked, as within a few months MacBride received 2,540 Francs from Devoy for the *United Irishman*. He acknowledged receipt from Devoy, adding, *I will send it on to the Editor immediately and forward a receipt when it arrives.*[26]

Maud herself had a very high opinion of John, as an astute and careful man who could be trusted, unlike some other young Irishmen in Paris, who were morbidly sensitive about their lack of money. She used often entertain him in her fashionable apartment on Avenue d'Eylau. John himself, who had a tiny attic flat in Rue de Lussac, near the Pantheon and Irish College, always took Maud to a café when she travelled to his quarter. She began to suggest to him that they could have tea in his room rather than always going to a café. She recorded, with some amusement, his shock at her proposal, until she assured him that such an attitude was a narrow English one. She found his room neat but sparse. He became an expert at tea making as they talked of about all kinds of plans to fight the English and expel them from Ireland. They both agreed that physical force, preferably on English soil, would remove the English. At times Maud was suspicious that John was not telling her of his entire involvement with and knowledge of activities against the English.[27]

138

It remains unclear at what point it dawned on Willie that he had a rival in his long-time quest for the hand of his muse and spiritual spouse. It is hard to believe that he could be so obtuse as to the inherent dangers in the ongoing interaction of Maud and John in Paris. Yet it appears that he did not realise what was happening. Henry Nevinson, a journalist and admirer of Maud, had predicted some years earlier that, *the first man of resolute action whom she meets will have her at his mercy.*[28]

In July of 1902 Maud told Willie that she was staying at the convent in Laval with Iseult, reminding him that Iseult was baptised a Catholic. She then admitted that she herself had considered becoming a Catholic, but had decided against it, lest it meant *limitations of thought.*[29] It was not too long later that he heard that Maud had changed her mind and decided to become a Catholic. His reaction to this came in the form of a dream, which he confided to St. John Irvine. Yeats saw Maud entering a room full of beautiful people. She walked around the room, looking at these beautiful people, who all smiled and smiled but said nothing. And suddenly in his dream, Willie realised that they were all dead … He woke up and said to himself that, *she has joined the Catholic Church.*

In truth, when Maud wrote the above to Yeats, she had already decided to marry John MacBride and become a Catholic. The previous month she had written to her sister Kathleen, and explained her reasons. She confessed that her life had been hard but she preferred to be envied than pitied, so she kept her secret thoughts to herself.

Now I see the chance, without injuring my work, of having a little happiness and peace in my personal life, and I am taking it. We are made that way, that we need companionship and with Iseult growing up, I cannot get this companionship outside marriage. Marriage I always consider abominable but for the sake of Iseult, I make that sacrifice to convention. Now my dearest, MacBride and I are interested in the same work and the Irish movement is a people's movement.[30]

Kathleen begged Maud not to marry the penniless soldier, but rather to marry Yeats, who could give her a most agreeable life on a high social and cultural level. Maud replied reassuring her that marriage to MacBride was the best thing for her. She was not interested in social life, which she considered:

Dull and unprofitable and a waste of time. My mind is quite made up. As for

Willie Yeats, I love him dearly as a friend, but I could not for one moment imagine marrying him. I love John MacBride. MacBride is a man I know very well. I have seen a great deal of him for the last two years and I know he is thoroughly sincere and honest and I can trust him entirely and I think I will always be happy ... I shall be just as independent and live my life as I always have and go on with my work in the same way ... Darling marriage won't change me now one bit.[31]

Maud knew of the devastation which her conversion and marriage would cause to Willie. He had pursued her publicly for so many years and made her his muse, and it was assumed she could never marry another. He wrote in his Journal that everyone that came near her *made me jealous.*[32] In August Maud visited John's mother in Westport. She told Willie of the pleasing time she had with Joseph MacBride, John's brother, fishing for eel at night on Clew Bay She wrote, *It was the loveliest night I have ever seen. Joseph MacBride is very nice. He lives in a charming cottage on the edge of the bay where we all took tea yesterday.*[33]

This letter sent out a clear sign of how much she was at one with the MacBride family, and therefore with John, marooned in Paris. She was inviting Willie, her close friend, to become friendly with the MacBrides. He must have read the signs. In December Maud praised an article of Willie's in the *Fortnightly Review,* saying that she would return it in a day or so, as *MacBride has it.* She spent most of January in Dublin deeply involved in theatrical matters. From there she wrote Willie a long letter on the battles then ensuing between the Fay brothers and the advanced nationalist societies. It appears that on her way back to Paris, she saw Willie in London and confirmed her intentions. Very soon he wrote a series of tormented letters begging her not to convert and marry MacBride. In one draft letter, tentatively dated January 1903, in the *Gonne Yeats Letters,* he told her that he had pondered carefully whether he should write at all, but decided because they had meant so much to each other, he had a right and a duty to speak the truth. He recalled their experiences together. He told her that she was unique, symbolic, above the people, above the priests who had betrayed the people. He begged her to remain aristocratic, to remain true, not to marry one of the people, not to thrust her soul down to a lower order. He urged her to become again as one of the gods and not to betray the truth, her friends and her own soul. He wrote in the name of their fourteen years friendship, and thought he might never write again.

Maud replied sadly, as she believed their friendship need not be diminished after her marriage. She felt she was being called by destiny. She had no aristocratic ambitions. She belonged to the people; she was the voice of the people, which as a Catholic, would only help her. She felt that she would remain in Laval with Iseult, for a time. She ended her letter:

Friend of mine au revoir, I shall go over to Ireland in a couple of months, if you care to see me I shall be so glad & you will find I think that I am just the same woman you have always known, marriage won't change me I think at all. I intend to keep my own name & to go on with all my work the same as ever.

Write to me sometimes for I want your news & I want to keep your friendship always.[34]

Roy Skene wrote that *when Yeats received word of Maud Gonne's marriage to MacBride in February 1903, he abandoned plans for the Irish Mystical Order.* Skene quotes Norman A. Jeffares *once she was married there was nothing to look forward to, even with diminished hope. The puzzle to him had been that, when they went to see the LIA Fail, Maud had appeared to understand his plans, especially for the Castle of Heroes, to be built of Irish Stone ... It seemed impossible to him that she should not marry him, knowing his love and his plans for Ireland. Her marriage carried conviction that all hope of achieving the loveliness of his dream was gone.*[35]

Elizabeth Cullingford wrote that *Red Hanrahan, first published ten months after Maud Gonne's marriage, is a thinly disguised account of Yeats's failure to win her for himself. She is compared to Venus, and thus identified with carnal rather than spiritual love.*[36]

It was not only Yeats and Kathleen Gonne who objected to the marriage. Arthur Griffith, a close friend to both parties for many years, begged them not to do it. John's own family advised him that there was too much difference between them for a successful marriage. MacBride's mother and brother Joseph wrote from Westport. Most importantly of all, Maud's seven and a half year old daughter, Iseult, objected, telling her mother that she *hated* MacBride. Iseult made an enormous scene at the convent in Laval when Maud informed her. Maud tried to console her by promising that, when she returned from her honeymoon, she would have a big party for Iseult at the convent. As Maud wrote, Iseult would not be reassured, as *she had only cried the louder and clung to me, and Sister Catherine had had to drag her away.*[37] This traumatic experience was to linger with the little girl, and she remained hostile to, and fearful of, her stepfather for the rest of her life.

141

Indeed Iseult and her husband, Francis Stuart, both retained a life-long hatred of John MacBride. In a Yeats Symposium in 1989, Stuart referred to Yeats' line, *'a girl who knew Dante once, and lived to bear children to a dunce'*, as a reference to Maud Gonne and her late husband.[38]

Maud had a dream in which her beloved father, Tommy, spoke to her saying that she must not marry. She told John of the dream. He then produced his mother's letter, advising that the marriage was not sensible. Mrs MacBride praised Maud as a brave and beautiful woman, but warned that she would not make John happy. He also showed her Joseph's letter. He said that Maud was older than John, so used to being independent and wealthy, while his brother had nothing. Joseph said a man should only marry a woman that he could keep. The couple then reread Griffith's letter, where he begged them, for their own sakes and, very perceptively, for Ireland's sake, not to marry. Griffith described John as *full of convention,* while Maud was the opposite.

They both sat silently for a time contemplating, until Maud broke the silence remarking that those whom the gods love die young-a short life and a merry one would be their motto if need be.[39]

Within a few days of their return from their honeymoon, John wrote that Maud *went to Laval to ask the Chanoine Dysalt to induce me to receive Millevoye at our house. I refused. All this lack of delicacy naturally led to friction.*[40] Iseult naturally wished to be with her own father and saw MacBride's arrival as stymieing that possibility. Maud wanted to please Iseult by inviting her father to the house. It was natural that MacBride would see things differently. Maud did keep in touch however with Millevoye for Iseult's sake.

When Yeats was dealing with the resulting trauma, he was, as so often, taken in hand by Lady Gregory at Coole Park. There he began to work on a book of poems to be published that summer. In that book, he wrote *I made some of these poems walking about among the Seven Woods, before the big wind of 1903.*

Maud wrote to Willie three days after her marriage. She told him that he was quite right to have written so frankly to her. She assured him that he would find little change in her. She spoke about theatrical matters and asked him to thank Lady Gregory for her *kind & thoughtful letter.* She told him to write to her and ended her letter with, *Always dear Willie, Your friend, Maud Gonne MacBride.*

Maud, baby Seaghan, John MacBride.

Maud, Iseult, Seaghan.

Two months later Maud replied to a letter from Willie, telling him how happy she was to hear from him. She wrote arranging to take tea with him in London. She spent two hours at his Woburn Buildings apartment. She explained to him why she had married. She said that Millevoye had made her position impossible, consorting with actresses, making her look ridiculous. He had also visited Iseult while she was away and this annoyed her too. In a fit of anger against Millevoye, and in an effort to keep him out, she decided to marry. Willie reported the story in detail to Lady Gregory, saying, *poor Maud Gonne was here yesterday for two hours. I am afraid she has been more foolish than any of us imagined.*

Willie treated this reunion as a lifeline for himself and proclaimed it so in his frenzied poem, *Reconciliation,* with the last two lines particularly, terminating the equivalent of a primeval scream.

> *But, dear, cling close to me; since you were gone,*
> *My barren thoughts have chilled me to the bone …*

In, *No Second Troy,* it is obvious that the poet attaches no blame to his erstwhile muse, for whatever she had done; the blame must lie with *ignorant men.*

The London soiree with Yeats became a source of great annoyance to Maud's husband. She had pretended to him that the meeting took place at the Grosvenor Hotel. When he discovered that this was untrue, he was very upset. He wrote of this later saying:

On her first journey to Ireland after her marriage she wrote to WB Yeats, London, asking him to send her a wire to the Grosvenor hotel asking him if she could go and have tea with him in his rooms. At the same time she was telling me she was writing to the gentleman in question asking him to come and dine with her at her hotel. She lied so often that I found it impossible to believe a single word out of her mouth unless I knew absolutely she was telling the truth.[41]

This event did not endear Yeats to MacBride, but served to make the latter bitter, suspicious and insecure about his marriage. During this London trip, Maud also told her sister Kathleen that her marriage was a mistake. Maud and Willie continued with their usual variety of collaborations, until Maud delivered a baby boy, the future Sean MacBride, winner of Nobel and Lenin Peace Prizes, in January 1904.

Yeats began writing his *Deirdre* on 12 June 1904. *Deirdre,* the Irish Helen was reminiscent of Maud Gonne. Women most deserving of praise choose powerful men, because the secret of mastery must involve what is antithetical in such a woman's nature. Although we are so delicately made, Deirdre declares, there is something brutal in us, and we are won over by those who can shed blood. Harold Bloom says that Yeats is certainly thinking of MacBride's victory over him. Bloom adds that even much later in Phase 16 of *A Vision*, Maud Gonne was presumably one of the *some beautiful women*. Bloom writes: *Here too are beautiful women, whose bodies have taken upon themselves the image of the True Mask ... They walk like queens and seem to carry upon their backs a quiver of arrows, but they are gentle only to those whom they have chosen or subdued, or to the dogs that follow at their heels. Boundless in generosity, and in illusion, they will give themselves to a beggar because he resembles a religious picture.* Bloom adds that out of phase they are Venus and choose Vulcan as Maud Gonne choose MacBride.[42]

Of the rewrite by Yeats' of *On Baile's Strand*, Richard Ellman says that it centres

The play's entire thematic structure squarely on the conflict between values of Cuchulainn and the values of Conchubar. This conflict owes much of its vividness to the soul-searching Yeats underwent after finding he had lost Maud Gonne to John MacBride ... Yeats blamed his own timid, critical intellect for restraining his impetuous nature so that when he should have embraced he feared and qualified and idealized. He had lost the capacity for acting on instinct which men like MacBride, lacking the critical mind, possessed. Maud Gonne's marriage was therefore an indictment: instead of condemning her, he condemned himself: took all the blame out of reason'.[43]
Maud was enthralled with her new baby, seeing him as the reincarnation of her dead baby, Georges. The marriage was proving an unmitigated disaster. John MacBride could not risk going to Ireland without the danger of being arrested and tried for treason. Instead he went to America on another lecture tour. After about five months there he returned to Paris, *in deference to the pleadings of my wife*. Matters did not improve between them and by late October, MacBride had decided to leave the marriage and take his chances in Ireland. He left a letter for Maud, who was then travelling back to Paris from Ireland, while he journeyed in the opposite direction. He reckoned that the police in Ireland would not expect him to make such a move at a time like that. He reached the family home at Westport in safety.

John's letter annoyed Maud greatly. They exchanged several letters, before they agreed to a family meeting in Dublin on 18 December. Maud travelled as far as London with the baby. There she consulted her family solicitor with a view to separating from MacBride and gaining sole custody of their baby. She then met Dr. Anthony MacBride, making an allegation that her husband had indecently assaulted her daughter Iseult. This was the only matter Maud raised at the time, but as time progressed, her charges became incremental. She informed Anthony that a legal document for John's signature was being drawn up. If John signed it, admitting the assault, giving her full custody of the baby, and agreed to emigrate permanently to America, no charges would be brought. Failure to sign would be followed by court action for criminal assault. John travelled to London immediately, outraged at his wife's allegation. Negotiations commenced between the parties with Barry O'Brien, a former colleague and one time adversary of Willie Yeats' in the Irish Literary Society, advising MacBride. These negotiations lasted several weeks and, much to the horror of Irish nationalists around the world, foundered, mainly on the custody of the baby. Maud left London early in 1905, threatening to sue for divorce in Paris. At that stage, Maud did not mention anything about the involvement of Eileen Wilson, her half sister who was then married to a brother of her husband's, in the case pending.

At that very time WB Yeats had just completed the triumphant opening of the Abbey Theatre in Dublin. Maud had no hesitation in informing him of her situation and calling in his support at this time of crisis. Her letters to him were full of bitter allegations against her husband as she wrote:

Of a hero, I had made, nothing remains and the disillusion has been cruel … I am fighting a man without honour or scruples … the evidence against MacBride is overwhelmingly terrible and complete … the case will rest on the evidence of others, not on mine … the charge of adultery with E., I would gladly withdraw though I have complete proof.[44]

This was music to Willie's ears as the possibility of recapturing his muse arose. He was totally open to believe everything Maud wrote about her husband. He encouraged her to have nothing more to do with any settlement which did not drive MacBride totally out of her life forever in a full divorce. He knew that his name could arise in a divorce case, but was prepared to accept that. Efforts continued to avoid going to court, with George Russell, John O'Leary and Ella Young, seeking to mediate.

To Maud's credit, despite the vituperative letters she wrote to Yeats, she made it clear to him that, despite everything, MacBride remained true in his fidelity to the National cause.[45]

Willie wanted to travel to Paris to be near Maud. She cautioned against it, saying that MacBride was insinuating that every male friend of hers was a lover. She told Yeats that MacBride threatened to kill him. Willie's uncharacteristic reaction to this, in a report to Lady Gregory, was to make a joke of it, describing it as the only cheerful news he had had in several days. He declared that it added to the zest of life. Maud promised Willie that when her ordeal was over, she would meet him in Dublin. Willie sought legal advice from Lady Gregory. He sent Annie Horniman to Westport to find negative information on the MacBride family; he assisted Maud in getting John Quinn to seek derogatory affidavits from MacBride's extended visits in America.

The letters, which passed between Yeats and Gonne, are contained in the excellent publication, *The Gonne – Yeats Letters,* edited by Anna MacBride White and A Norman Jeffares. The joint editors say, *As such situations usually are, it was a nasty bitter game, but on the whole Maud Gonne's letters give a reasonable account, allowing for a certain obvious one-sidedness, and so the story unfolds in her own words to Yeats*[46]. She made her written petition to the Court in Paris on 3 February 1905. The whole sorry saga of legal proceedings lasted until August 1906, when a verdict was delivered.

Despite Maud's certainty that she had a watertight case against her husband, this was not the reality. She reported to Willie on 8 August:

Here is the verdict as far as I can remember it, not as yet having received the written copy. MacBride has succeeded in proving Irish nationality & domicile so that only separation & not divorce can be granted.

The Court now suits MacBride in his petition of separation against me -

The Court thinks the charges of immorality are insufficiently proved, but that the charges of drunkenness are manifestly proved … the Court grants Mrs MacBride judicial separation in her favour & gives her the right of guardianship of the child. It allows the father the right of visiting the child at his wife's house every Monday, & when the child shall be over 6 years old allows the father to have him one month in the year.

I am very disappointed & I shall probably appeal this verdict & change my lawyer for Cruppi neglected my affairs shockingly.[47]

The verdict meant that Maud had to continue living in Paris, for MacBride would be able to lay claim to the custody of his son in another jurisdiction.

MacBride was found innocent of the immorality charges brought against him in Court. William Murphy in *Family Secrets* writes of Maud, *She had earlier borne Lucien Millevoye's illegitimate child, Iseult, of whom the court had no official cognisance.*[48] Maud had not included any charges relating to Iseult to the court, and when challenged, refused to allow her give evidence. If declared guilty of such a charge, MacBride faced twenty years in jail. Yet it was his counsel who insisted in having this latter allegation brought out into the open in court. MacBride was insistent that he clear his name.

The charge of MacBride's adultery with *'E'*, as Maud wrote to Willie, concerned Eileen Wilson. Eileen travelled from Westport to Paris for the trial and denied the allegation. The court accepted this.

It is worth noting that Elizabeth Cullingford appears to be one of the very few academics or biographers writing in the 'Yeats/Gonne/MacBride Triangle' field, who has not prejudged and condemned John MacBride. She has inserted qualifications, which at a minimum illustrate, that unlike so many others, she is not prejudiced but open to any attempt to establish the facts. She is astute enough to write in *Gender and History in Yeats's Love Poetry* concerning Maud Gonne, of: *the battered and betrayed wife of the drunken and possibly adulterous John MacBride.*[49] Likewise she writes of Maud, in the abortive pre-divorce case negotiations in London, *in private she used his alleged indecent assault upon the ten-year old Iseult as a bargaining weapon.*[50].

These attentions to detail are examples of academic excellence, which I had firmly expected to find in Roy Foster's authorised biography of WB Yeats, *The Apprentice Mage.* In an otherwise magisterial treatment, however, I was sorely disappointed in Foster's volume, in this particular area. Foster wrote of Yeats, *He had long been hearing rumours about the marriage – some true (MacBride's drunkenness), some not (their baby Sean's epilepsy). But the truth was spectacularly shocking. On 9 January having had an interview with May Bertie-Clay, WBY wrote to Gregory. He was still reeling at the catalogue of MacBride's crimes: violence, sexual abuse, threats to children.*[51] Thus is MacBride condemned by the use of the words *truth* and *crimes.* There is no reference to the fact that none of those charges were upheld in the subsequent court case. There is no reference in Foster's text to any defence by MacBride. Foster includes a footnote reference about the court case. It concerns Maud's view of the *Evening Mail* and the *Independent's* reporting of the case. He also refers to a manuscript in the National Library of Ireland. (MSNLI 29,818) where he states, *MacBride's version is preserved in a testimonial he wrote for Fred Allan*. Foster says that MacBride stressed his wife's *impure life,* her *indelicacy,* and her *trying to force her ex-lovers on me.* Foster also includes the fact that MacBride had a major grievance concerning his wife's immediate contact with Yeats immediately after their honeymoon.[52] For *The Yeats Gonne MacBride Triangle,* I read the many voluminous and detailed manuscripts in the National Library of Ireland, containing John MacBride's papers. I have put the detail of the triangular affair into the public domain, including Maud's actual court charges and MacBride's rebuttal. One of the very surprising documents there is an affidavit from one of Maud's closest allies, Jenny Wyse Power, in support of John MacBride. Since *The Apprentice* Mage was published, several biographers, academics and journalists, continue to use Foster's book as authoritative on MacBride, and the assassination persists.

Dr. Conor Cruise O'Brien, together with Cullingford, are the only academic writers, I feel, who have been meticulous in their references to John MacBride. While recognising that Yeats's hatred of MacBride made him the *basest of the base*, Dr. O'Brien is careful to qualify it by adding, *from Yeats's point of view*.[53] A recently published novel of the relationship between Willie and Maud by Barry Shorthall, has also been very fair to the person of John MacBride.[54]

The Parisian Court declared John MacBride to be a fit father to his son. He admitted to being drunk on two occasions, but declared that, given the type of marriage he found himself in, it was a great wonder that his wife did not turn him into a drunkard. MacBride lost his counter-suit against Maud for defamation and had to pay costs. He won a libel suit against the Irish Independent in connection with their reporting of the divorce case. He was awarded one-pound damages.

Maud was later to tell Willie that her dreams had told her that MacBride had to leave her life and would inevitably do so. In retrospect she believed that if she had not pursued John as she had, their parting would have inevitably happened. She mused that she may have acted prematurely.[55]

Maud had promised Willie that as soon as the case was over she would travel to Dublin to see him. On 20 October 1906, Lady Gregory's *Gaol Gate* opened in the Abbey. Mary Colum was in the audience. She recorded the scene:

Ten, fifteen minutes passed and the curtain did not go up. Somebody or something was being waited for. At last we saw Yeats enter hastily … accompanied by a tall woman dressed in black, one of the tallest women I have ever seen. Instantly a small group in the pit began to hiss loudly and to shout 'up MacBride' … the woman stood and faced her hissers, her whole figure showing a lively emotion … Yeats standing beside her, looked bewildered as the hissing went on: his face was set in lines of gloom, but she was smiling and unperturbed. Soon a counter hissing set up, the first hissers being drowned out by another group and then I realised who she was … She was a legend to us young persons in our teens … Her height would have drawn attention anywhere, but it was her beauty that produced the most startling effect. It was startling in its greatness, its dignity, and its strangeness. Supreme beauty is so rare that its first effect is a kind of shock.[56]

Maud appealed the verdict in 1908. She was again refused a divorce, though MacBride's access to his son was reduced. John MacBride had remained in Ireland since 1905, and was never to see his son again. Maud feared that she would have to remain domiciled in France, to retain custody of Sean.

Maud and Willie resumed their peripatetic relationship and probably had at least one full sexual experience together. It was a Pyrrhic victory for the man, as it only served to highlight Maud's horror of sexual intercourse. He had to almost immediately agree to resume their 'spiritual marriage', as she wrote:

I forgot that those who would distribute life or death must be purer than the angels and that I was full of human passion and weakness …[57]

John MacBride was a leading figure in the ongoing nationalist cause, and a colleague to most of its leading figures. Willie Yeats, too, knew many of the same people, particularly its writers and poets. Both were, ironically, taken by surprise by the actual Rising at Easter 1916. The leading conspirator, Sean MacDiarmada, had sent a letter of warning to MacBride on the morning of the Rising, but it was not delivered. MacBride however, happened on the military preparations in the city.

Thomas MacDonagh, whose poetry Yeats had praised, prevailed upon MacBride to join his Jacob's Factory garrison as second in command, when he met him strolling at St. Stephen's Green. During the week the Rising lasted, MacBride again showed an extraordinary degree of courage, as witnessed by members of the garrison. Just before the surrender, he had an opportunity to escape and return home to Clara Allan, the woman he loved. He spurned the offer, in the knowledge that he faced almost certain execution. He told a group of Volunteers who were about to take their opportunity to escape;

Liberty is a priceless thing and anyone of you that sees a chance, take it. I'd do so myself, but my liberty days are over. Good luck boys. Many of you may live to fight some other day. Take my advice, never allow yourselves to be cooped up inside the walls of a building again.[58]

Máire nic Shuibhlaigh, Yeats' old Abbey adversary, was among a group of *Cumann na mBan* volunteers in Jacob's Factory. In her 1955 book, The *Splendid Years,* she recalled MacBride, writing that he, *fulfilled all expectations as a soldier of courage and resource, a gentleman, quiet, witty, always unruffled. Without exception, the Volunteers in the building admired and respected him.* When she informed MacBride that the women did not want to leave the garrison, he replied, *it would be better for you to go.* As Máire lived near Clara Allan in Glasthule, he asked her to take a special message to Clara. *Tell them too, that we had a good week of it, he added.*

After the execution of Maud's husband, Willie again entertained hopes of marrying his widow. When this hope was denied, he brought Georgie Hyde Lees into the picture and married her.

I have discussed the poetic standing of *Easter 1916* in a previous chapter. Some have claimed that Yeats had done MacBride a favour by including him in the pantheon of the leaders. It is true, as Terry Eagleton has written, that:

It is, Yeats himself who is heroising the dead republican leaders, gathering them into the artifice of eternity … It's up to him, in short, who gets in on the act; 'Yet I number him in the song' he announces with lofty condescension of his old rival John MacBride, with the unmistakeable implication that he'd thought a bit about keeping him out.[59]

Nevertheless, the negative aspects of MacBride's character, unfairly attributed to him by Yeats, are what have reverberated down the years and Yeats well knew this. He had been writing with an eye to the future for many years.

There exists the possibility that unlike Yeats, Maud Gonne's attitude to her husband had 'softened' considerably. It may be for this reason she was equivocal about his treatment in the poem. While she might be appreciative that he was among the named leaders, with MacDonagh, Pearse and Connolly, she could not have been pleased at the long passage, linking herself to Yeats, and condemning John MacBride in perpetuo: lines that I have argued elsewhere *which she may have known were undeserved and lines that were untrue.* A thaw of sorts had occurred during the year of 1910, when Maud sought to intercede personally to help her husband get a post with Dublin Corporation.[60] Though he was angry and repudiated any offer of assistance, Maud did holiday, *en famille,* in her husband's county of Mayo, during the month of August of that same year. As Margaret Ward writes;

For some reason she didn't fear MacBride attempting to kidnap her son … Maud was fond of her mother-in-law, the rift was with her husband, not the rest of the family, and perhaps for Sean's sake she wanted contact with the family to be maintained. John MacBride did not appear on the scene on this occasion.[61]

Elizabeth Coxhead in her study, *Daughters of Erin,* says, *the bad feeling blew over eventually.*[62] Maud's attitude to her executed husband went full circle, as is clear in the letters she wrote to Yeats after the Easter Rising. These sentiments could not have been welcomed by Willie, particularly, the remarkable passage:

As for my husband he has entered Eternity by the great door of sacrifice, which Christ opened & has therefore atoned for all, so that in praying for him I can also ask for his prayers & 'A terrible beauty is born'.[63]

Maud had earlier informed Yeats that she had already occasion to defend MacBride's good name by writing to the French press, countering attacks on him by the *Daily Mail.*[64] One factor that ensured that Maud had to be exceedingly careful in any defence of MacBride was that she had depended on the words of third parties in her earlier charges against him. Chief among those was the petulant Iseult Millevoye, whom Maud dared not cross.

Some years later, in *A Prayer for my Daughter,* written to commemorate his daughter Anne, Yeats returned with some harshness to the person of John MacBride. The poem's dominant figure is the unnamed Maud Gonne under the guise of Helen of Troy. In stanza four, he seeks to belittle and denigrate her husband, writing of him:

Helen being chosen found life flat and dull
And later had much trouble from a fool ...

The poem is only peripherally concerned with the future; its real focus is on the poet's past. Gradually, without accusing her directly, he exorcises the spirit of Maud Gonne.[65]

As late as 1927 Yeats was writing to Maud Gonne saying:

Your husband was never one of my heroes – his brave death did not abolish his treatment of you – but he is a hero to these men. Cosgrave was in the next cell to him in 1916 & was to have been the next executed.[66]

What could Maud say to such hatred, as she sought Senator Yeats' help, in having her son, Sean, released from prison, lest he be executed on suspicion of being involved in the assassination of Yeats' good friend, Kevin O'Higgins?

Maud wrote her memoirs, published in 1938. Despite the story ending just prior to her marriage, the treatment of John MacBride there is gentle and even wistful. It is quite unlike that painted by her for Yeats, by him in literature, and by the biographers of Gonne and Yeats, in history.

CHAPTER 10

NATION BUILDER

WB Yeats kept his options open in the poem *Easter 1916*. His attitude to the event and the participants was clouded by his words that England might have *kept faith*, and the tragic exercise may not have been necessary. If England had kept faith and Home Rule came to pass and was accepted, he could still be on the winning side. The victory of Sinn Féin in the 1918 General Election and the obliteration of the old Irish Parliamentary Party, demonstrated that a revolution had occurred. With his poetic trilogy, which included *Sixteen Dead Men* and *The Rose Tree,* Willie knew he was on the winning side, and he had the poems to prove it.

Georgie Yeats wished to live permanently in Ireland, more so than her husband did. She knew that it was the right place for him to be. In theory he did wish to live there in his tower, but his innate caution made him hesitate. In April 1921 he was working in England on the poem about the vicious War of Independence, which would eventually be called *Nineteen Hundred and Nineteen,* when dragon-ridden days and drunken soldiery rode upon sleep. The Truce between Sinn Féin and the British army occurred in July and hope emerged that a permanent cessation would emerge. Michael Yeats was born in August. As negotiations in London dragged on, Willie expected a treaty to emerge which would be accepted by a majority of the people in the twenty-six counties, for the other six had already been severed from the rest of the country. He doubted whether the 'extreme party' would accept such a verdict. The Anglo-Irish Treaty was signed in December and voted through by the narrow margin of 64 votes to 57 in the Dail in January 1922. The defeated "extreme party", led by Eamon deValera, refused to accept the vote and withdrew their allegiance. Arthur Griffith was elected President of Sinn Féin with Michael Collins becoming Chairman of the Provisional Government.

That same month an Irish Race Convention was held in Paris, with the Duke of Tetuan from Madrid, a descendant of the O'Donnell of Donegal in the chair. Its aim was to celebrate Irish artistic endeavour and discuss Irish independence. The divisions evident in the Dail transferred to Paris, with two opposing delegations attending. Griffith appointed Maud Gonne to the official side. Willie also attended and spoke on *'The Abbey Theatre, Synge and the poets of 1916'.* It was already clear that the Provisional Government

Yeats' house on Merrion Square.

valued him highly. His brother Jack B Yeats also attended, though he was firmly on the opposite delegation, being a Republican and a supporter of DeValera. Attempts to establish a permanent secretariat in Paris, foundered on the lines of the Dail division, and the new Government refused funding.

Willie remained full of confusion. He told his friend H. Das M.D., of Oxford, that *the political exigencies of his country necessitated his immediate return to Ireland to serve her.*[1] While the family decision on moving to Ireland had been made, he still surmised about going far away from England and Ireland, where his children could grow up in safety. Japan was one place he considered. His feelings and anxieties were being mirrored within the British Government, as we shall see below. The executive of the family, Georgie, travelled alone to Dublin in February, and using her own money, bought an elegant house in Merrion Square. Willie was thrilled and very proud of her initiative. The Yeats, at last, would be making a triumphal return to their own city!

At that same time, word came from America in a telegram from John Quinn that John B Yeats had died in New York. His two daughters, who had not seen their father for thirteen years, were very sad that he had died far away, alone, and in a cheap boarding house. An American lady named Jeanne Robert Foster, who had befriended him, was with him very close to the end. She and Quinn organised the funeral service. A white marble monument was erected reading, *In memory of John B. Yeats of Dublin, Ireland. Painter and Writer.* As late as 1958, Mrs Foster sought to have his remains repatriated to Ireland.[2] Willie, who had bore some of the financial cost of keeping his father, told his sister Lily, that it was for the best that their father had been

155

The author on the bridge at Ballylee.

spared a long illness. He was very sorry that his father would not see and live in his eldest son's fine house and be proud of his family. Willie and his family left England for Ballylee in March.

The political and military situations in the country remained volatile with the Irregulars refusing to recognise the Provisional Government or its National Army. It had been Winston Churchill's task to sell the Treaty to a hostile House of Commons. He had told the Prince of Wales; *The Irish event seems to turn well. Arthur Griffith and Michael Collins are men of their word ... I am full of hope and confidence about Ireland. I believe we are going to reap a rich reward all over the world and at home.*[3] The British were very nervous during the spring least de Valera and the republicans attempt a coup d'etat. Winston Churchill wrote to Michael Collins on 12 April:

The Cabinet instructed me to send you a formal communication expressing their growing anxiety at the spread of disorder in the twenty-six counties. Instead of this, however, I write to you as man to man. Many residents are

writing to this country tales of intimidation, disorder, theft and pillage …
Surely the moment will come when you can broadly and boldly appeal, not
to any clique, sect or faction, but to the Irish nation as a whole. They surely
have a right to expect you to lead them out of the dark places, and the
opportunity is one (the loss of which) history will never forgive…every day
that the uncertainty continues must be attended by the progressive
impoverishment of Ireland. Nobody can invest or make plans for production,
while the threat of civil war, or of a Republic followed by a state of war with
the British Empire, hangs over the country. I trust the end of May, or at the
very latest, the first week in June, will see the issue submitted to the Irish
people …[4]

In April the Irregulars occupied the Four Courts complex in Dublin city, thus
declaring openly their intention to thwart the authority of the Provisional
Government, as the British began to leave. Michael Collins was very
reluctant to move militarily against erstwhile colleagues in the War of
Independence. His hand was forced by the belligerence of the opposing
forces and an ultimatum from the British to take control of the Four Courts.
Collins borrowed field guns from Churchill and pounded the barricaded
complex, reducing it to ruins. This acted as a catalyst and exposed the de
facto civil war, which had been simmering around the country. Galway city
and the area surrounding Yeats' Tower and Lady Gregory's Coole Park
remained in the hands of Government forces throughout. During night-
times, bands of rebels roamed the countryside, threatening people and
property and stock. Willie wrote several letters to friends in England
describing the situation, as houses were searched for weapons and
sometimes burned to the ground. He feared for his own family and his tower,
and not without good reason. The Irregulars blew up the bridge beside his
tower, though he was given time to take his family to the comparative safety
of a protected upstairs room in the tower. He tried not to become embittered
by those terrible experiences. In his great poem, *Meditations In Time of Civil
War*, the fifth section, *The Road at my Door*, he wrote:

> *An affable Irregular, A heavily built Falstaffian man,*
> *Comes cracking jokes of civil war*

He placed much faith in nature and he soon began to *smell honey in places
where honey could not be*. The bees *began to build in the empty house of the
state*. When he got back to Dublin in September, he had little patience with
people who wanted to know 'the exact facts of the situation'.

The Irregulars were gradually pushed southwards into Munster, as civil war inflicted shocking treatment on combatants who had so recently fought together against the British. The Provisional Government won a resounding victory in a General Election. The new Dáil met on 9 September. Its new leader, WT Cosgrave, said that all arms must be surrendered. He said the Treaty would be honoured, and the new Constitution would be ready for British parliamentary ratification before 6 December, on which date, under the Treaty, the authority of the Provisional Government ceased. Ratification would mean the legal establishment of the Irish Free State.

The two foremost leaders of the Government, Griffith and Collins, were dead. The Government had had to exist under armed guard, bunker-like, at Government Buildings, unable to go home for fear of assassination. On 12 August, Arthur Griffith died at St. Vincent's Hospital, where he had been admitted under an assumed name. He had died from long years of exhaustion. Ten days later, Irregulars shot Michael Collins dead in an ambush in his native county of Cork. The new Government, literally under siege in Dublin, introduced new laws with summary execution for those caught carrying arms. They felt that the rule of democracy or anarchy would prevail. Executions and reprisals proliferated. William T. Cosgrave and Kevin O'Higgins became the two 'strongmen' of the Government. All of this chaos did not enable Willie to feel great confidence in the family decision to live in Dublin.

From an early stage, Willie was publicly honoured in Ireland. In July of 1922, Queens University of Belfast gave him an honorary degree. Far more important, on a personal basis, was a further honorary degree, from Trinity College in Dublin. This had been the *alma mater* of several members of the Yeats family, including his father. As a teenager, Willie feared that he would not be capable of matriculating and so did not apply for entry. He might also have become a professor there. Trinity College was an integral part of Anglo-Ireland.

The new Constitution, which came into effect on 6 December, laid down that Parliament would be bi-cameral. There would be an elected Dáil and a nominated Seanad constituting the Oireachtas. The President of the Executive Council, WT Cosgrave intended to use the Senate as a vehicle for illustrating that Anglo-Irish people were to be accepted as full citizens of the new State. It contained sixty members. Cosgrave nominated thirty new Senators from the Anglo-Irish community, as it might not be adequately represented in the Dail. Among the senators were names that resonated with

158

privilege and power within the old order, like Baron Glenaavy, Dowager Countess Desart, the Marquis of Headfort, the Earls of Kerry and Wicklow.

The new Senator William Butler Yeats was appointed as qualified to speak on education, literature and the arts in general. He was pleasantly surprised to discover that there was a generous stipend attached to the office. John Quinn expressed himself as very pleased with the news, but was extremely annoyed that Douglas Hyde was not so honoured also.

Willie lived in what he described as the Berkeley Square of Dublin, at the centre of political and cultural life. The Senate, National Gallery of Art, National Library and the Museum, the Arts Club, were all within walking distance. He had to have an armed guard on his house, as the situation was fraught with danger for public figures associated with the Government. Civil War still ensued. During January of 1923, thirty-four Irregular prisoners were executed, causing reprisals against the houses of Senators. Willie wrote to his friend Robert Bridges that two bullets were lodged in the frame of one of his windows. He described the state of the country as the sheep trying to control the goats, the latter being naturally the more enterprising race. His friend and colleague, Oliver Gogarty was kidnapped, but luckily escaped and avoided execution. Several Senators had their houses burned. Some writers believe that during this month of January, Willie again had serious misgivings and reconsidered staying in Ireland.[5] This would not have been so surprising, but his wife would not countenance such an invidious retreat by her illustrious husband.

While Senator Yeats was becoming a respected conservative member of the Free State apparatus, Maul Gonne was again going in the opposite direction. She had initially supported the Treaty, but as her young son, Sean MacBride became involved with the Irregulars and was imprisoned, she changed her views. She had a fundamental row with her old friend and colleague, Arthur Griffith, over the policy of the Provisional Government. Her long-term support of the plight of prisoners reasserted itself and she became a most bitter opponent of the new Government. She became the focus for agitation and public protest, defying police attempts to silence her weekly protests in Dublin's O'Connell St. Her hatred of the new Government knew no bounds, as Willie accepted nomination as a senator. Early in 1923 she wrote to him, warning that unless he denounced the new Government, their relationship was terminated forever.[6] She berated him for accepting the legitimacy of a State *which voted Flogging Acts against young republican soldiers still seeking to free Ireland from the contamination of the British Empire.*[7]

The Government banned Maud Gonne's Women's Political Defence League and arrested her. Willie was in the process of writing to Olivia Shakeaspeare when he heard the news. He told Olivia that he could not write any further, as he had to contact Iseult and offer to help. As it happened Maud was released the next day, but not before she gained first-hand experience of prison conditions, which she highlighted in her ongoing campaign against the Government. There were about twelve thousand prisoners in total, including about four hundred women. Hunger strikes were resorted to, increasing tension countrywide. In April Maud was again arrested. She immediately joined those women on hunger strike. Her imprisonment brought great pressure on the Government, including a personal appeal by Senator Yeats to Cosgrave. He told the latter that Maud was fifty-seven years old, and would not be able to stand the strain of a hunger strike like a younger woman. Cosgrave told him that women should stay out of politics and help mind the sick. He believed that it was not possible to *consider these women as ordinary females*. Finally, after twenty days Maud was released and taken home by stretcher. Later, Iseult was arrested and again Willie worked frantically for her release. The Government released all the hunger strikers as a gesture of good intention, but warned that in future those prisoners resorting to hunger strikes would be let die. The Government won a General election in August. Many prisoners were still in jail. Hunger strikes were again resorted to. After the death of two, the rest ceased their action. Among those detained in jail was Sean MacBride.

One of Senator Yeats' finest moments came on 14 March 1923, when he spoke in a very measured way in the Senate on the *Griffith Settlement Bill*. This was a modest provision which the Government introduced to assist the widow and children of Arthur Griffith. Griffith had opposed Yeats in his *United Irishman* on cultural nationalism over many years. Eight Senators, the Minister for Finance and the Cathaoirleach of the Senate contributed. Each acknowledged the stature and commitment of their deceased President. Senator Yeats who had known him longest and best, said:

I was on many points deeply opposed to Mr. Arthur Griffith during his lifetime on matters connected with the Arts, but time has justified him on the great issue that most concerns us all. He was a man with the most enduring courage and the most steadfast will. I have good reason for knowing how enduring his courage was. I first met him a great many years ago, when he and his friend Rooney were editing a little paper which they set up with their own hand as well as writing it. They also paid for the weekly expenditure on

that paper. I know how hard a struggle it was for him to edit and print that paper, and I remember in those days, on hearing how hard that struggle was, I offered to get some of his articles placed in, I think, " The Speaker", which was an English Liberal paper. I remember his reply, that he had taken a vow to himself never to write for any paper outside Ireland. That was for him a vow of poverty, and he kept it. For many years, at least two or three years, before the end, it must have seemed to him that he was carrying on an almost hopeless struggle, and when the final crisis came he showed himself a man of particular value to this country. If it were only in this, that when the final test came he gave his faith, not to an abstract theory, but to a conception of this historical nation — and we are all theory mad. On that point he kept himself thoroughly sane, and we owe, therefore, to his memory great honour, — honour that will always be paid by this country.[8]

Arthur Griffith's grave, Glasnevin, Dublin.

An unspoken name must have been foremost in Willie's mind, as he described the struggle to keep *the little paper* alive. That was the name of Maud Gonne, who greatly assisted the cause financially, and whom Yeats must have known was loved and desired also by Griffith. Hers was a name that could not be mentioned. When he had refused her request to intervene on behalf of an imprisoned militant republican female, he received threats. He reported to Lady Gregory that he *will have no more political conversations with her.*[9]

Towards the end of that year came the news that Willie was to be awarded the Nobel Prize for Literature. He famously asked his informant, Bertie Smylie, editor of *The Irish Times*, " how much is it worth?" The £7,500 prize, his Senate salary and Civil Pension, together with his literary earnings, all set him up as quite a wealthy man. The Nobel Prize consolidated his reputation internationally. When giving his Nobel Lecture in Stockholm, he declared the honour to be for his theatrical endeavours. This was not so as the citation read, *for his always inspired poetry, which in a highly artistic form gives expression to the spirit of a whole nation.* His own interpretation suited his long-term aim, to highlight the Abbey Theatre, and to entice the Government to fund it, as a national institution. He began his lecture saying:

Bust of W.B. Yeats.

I have chosen as my theme the Dramatic Movement because when I remember the great honour that you have conferred upon me, I cannot forget many known and unknown persons. Perhaps the English committee would never have sent you my name if I had written no plays, no dramatic criticism, if my lyric poetry had not a quality of speech practised upon the stage, perhaps even if it were not in some degree the symbol of a movement. I wish to tell the Royal Academy of Sweden of the labours, triumphs and troubles of my fellow workers.

Throughout the rest of his speech, which according to the website of the Nobel Foundation, he *maintained was written down from memory,* Yeats mentioned some of those workers, Hyde, Lady Gregory, Edward Martyn, Miss Algood, Miss Maire O'Neill, and John Synge. In his acceptance speech, he also mentioned his collaborators, saying:

Thirty years ago a number of Irish writers met together in societies and began a remorseless criticism of the literature of their country. I owe much to those men, still more to those who joined the movement a few years later and when I return to Ireland these men and women, now growing old like myself, will see in this great honour a fulfilment of that dream. I, in my heart, know how little I might have deserved it, if they had never existed.

Yeats met success in securing a secure financial status for the Abbey, when during the 1925-6 season the Government began to subsidise the Abbey. Willie had to accept a Government nominee on the Board, as the subsidy became an annual grant. He was quite content to see it become a State Theatre, as an incident in 1930s demonstrated. Soon after he had been conversing with Peadar O'Donnell, the revolutionary and writer, a fellow director of the Abbey informed him that posters had appeared in the city advertising a meeting in the *Abbey* for the following Sunday night, to be hosted by *Saor Eire*. Yeats deigned to be incredulous and gave instructions that such a meeting could not be allowed to occur. He said: *We are a State Theatre and we cannot admit a meeting that wishes to destroy the State. The thing is clearly impossible. No political demonstrations at all are allowed.*[10]

At home, as a Nobel laureate, Willie became the focus of great public attention. Ministers dined at his home. He paid particular attention to Kevin O'Higgins, the strongman of the Government. The Tailteann Games, an ancient sporting festival from Ireland's Celtic past, was revived. A Literary Festival included presentations by Yeats, GK Chesterton, Oliver Gogarty and Stephen McKenna.

The Senate usually sat in the afternoons. This gave Willie the opportunity to continue his practice of writing in the mornings. He told an admirer:

Of course I work. My poetry costs me endless labour. I begin every day at eleven and work steadily until lunch at one thirty ... I sit down to it like the galley slave to his oars ... My pace is now seven or eight lines a day. Writing poisoned my youth. I could have been happier if I had stopped writing.[11]

Willie took his membership of the Senate very seriously. He was an assiduous speaker in all sorts of debates. When a committee to consider a permanent location for Parliament was being discussed, he was against a move to the Royal Hospital in Kilmainham, even on a temporary basis. His concerns were for its *very great architectural importance,* and whether *the permanent value of the building will be in any way affected,* by designs for changes. He also said, *People coming from the country, we feel, will want to find themselves nearer the Parliament than they would be, if you put it out in that remote suburb.*

The allowance for members of thirty pounds monthly was regarded as a contribution towards their expenses. Senator E. MacLysaght noted that, *It is earned even by Senators who live in Dublin and have not to come up from the country,* as he introduced an amendment, *That no member of the Senate shall receive this allowance in respect of any month, which he has not attended at least half of the meetings of the Senate held during that period.* Senator Yeats objected to this measure, saying, *it does rouse in one a strong distaste. I think it should only be proposed if there has been gross abuse. I think there has been no gross abuse. (6/6/1923).*

During a debate on a scheme for the editing, indexing, and publishing of manuscripts in the Irish language, then lying in the Royal Irish Academy, Trinity College and elsewhere, Senator Yeats spoke of his own life's work. He said the advances in idealism had been dissipated by the civil war. In proposing an amendment to the Bill, he said:

I find it strange that I, who am a non-Gaelic scholar, should be left to bring this proposal before the Seanad. I may say, to give a little weight to my words, that the greater portion of my own writings have been founded upon the old literature of Ireland. I have had to read it in translations, but it has been the chief illumination all my life. The movement I am connected with, the whole poetic movement of modern Ireland, has drawn a great portion of its inspiration from the old Bardic literature … It is a great thing, when you find people wanting to learn anything …

It is a moment, too, when we will have to build up again the old form of wild, wasteful historic idealism. The country got into that position, but, like a spendthrift coming into possession of his inheritance, it has wasted that idealism in a year of civil war. We have to build up again in its place an idealism of labour and of thought and it is not asking much that the few hundred a year necessary should be spent to begin what may grow to be a very important work of national scholarship, a work for which all the scholars of the world will be grateful, a work which will enhance the reputation of this country.

Senator Yeats chaired the Irish Coinage Committee and recommended that Irish coinage should bear the images of Irish animals and wild life. *What better symbols could we find for this horse-riding, salmon-fishing, cattle-raising country,* he wrote.

The speech in the Senate, for which he is most remembered, was on the subject of divorce in 1925. By that time, paradoxically, he saw himself as a leader of the Anglo-Irish Ascendancy. This was the very group he had often excoriated in earlier times for its intellectual and political mediocrity. He now decided that this very tradition was necessary to sensitise the majority Catholic population against the vulgarised modernity and restraints on freedom of conscience and individual liberty. He also had no doubt that the same tradition, his tradition, was as much part of the new State as the majority, only more important. Willie, once more, developed his own myth, this time about the great traditions of the Eighteenth Century Anglo-Irish Mind. In the name of an ascendancy pantheon of philosophers and writers, he denounced both the excesses of the Gaelic enthusiasm and the Catholic democracy, he saw about him. The Catholic democracy was, he believed, prepared, at the behest of a majority feeling in the country, to enact legislation forbidding divorce and limiting freedom of expression.

In a passing remark Yeats mentioned some of the Senators by name, including that of Senator Jennie Wyse Power. She interrupted him vehemently, saying that she objected strenuously to having her name raised by him. Many of those present would not have realised, that among the most powerful affidavits John MacBride received in preparation for the Parisian divorce case, was one from Jenny Wyse Power, who had hitherto been an intimate of Maud Gonne's.[12]

Senator Yeats placed the context for his speech within the country as a whole, warning that the non-availability of divorce would demonstrate that Southern Ireland *is going to be governed by Catholic ideas and by Catholic doctrine alone; you will never get the North.* He said that the Committee, which drew up the constitution of the Free State, refused to incorporate the indissolubility of marriage. He went on: *That was the expression of the political mind of Ireland. You are now urged to act on the advice of men who do not express the political mind, but who express the religious mind!* A few interjections occurred with one member remarking, *This is becoming very heated.* Senator Yeats retorted, *I mean it to be heated.*

Senator Yeats then delivered his defiant proclamation on his Protestant people:

I think it tragic that within three years of this country gaining its independence we should be discussing a measure, which a minority of this nation considers to be grossly oppressive. I am proud to consider myself a typical man of that minority. We against whom you have done this thing are no petty people. We are one of the great stocks of Europe. We are the people of Burke; we are the people of Grattan; we are the people of Swift; the people of Emmett, the people of Parnell. We have created most of the modern literature of this country. We have created the best of its political intelligence.

Terence Brown describes the Speech as, *notorious,* adding that Yeats *frankly identified himself with Protestant Ireland, casting his argument against any proscription of divorce in aggressively sectarian terms that caused great offence in the chamber and the country.*[13]

The Senate of the Irish Free State lasted for fifteen years. Donal O'Sullivan wrote its history in 1940. He describes the atmosphere on 11 June surrounding Yeats' contribution thus:

"The Chairman allowed the late Senator William Butler Yeats, the distinguished poet, to open the debate. His speech was nothing less than an envenomed attack on the religion of the majority of his fellow countrymen. He attacked the Catholic Church in general, and in Ireland in particular. He joined issue with Cardinal O'Donnell. He lashed with invective the Protestant Bishop of Meath, who a short time previously had made a striking pronouncement against divorce. He ridiculed the authenticity of the Gospels. And he concluded by bombastic references to the superiority of the Ascendancy class.

This extraordinary speech was happily unique in the history of the Senate. Its author was not provoked into unwisdom by the utterances of previous speakers, for he opened the debate. Nor was he carried away by the self-engendered heat of the moment, since his speech was delivered from a manuscript, which had obviously been carefully prepared. It has been necessary to refer to it because it poisoned the atmosphere that surrounded the question of divorce.[14]

Another issue which caused a fundamental grievance to Senator Yeats was the ongoing attempt to introduce strict censorship, particularly that of publications. Advisory committees were set up to study the matter. The conservative forces, especially those of the Catholic majority, again won the

166

day, as The Censorship of Publications Bill was introduced in 1928. In his usual aggressive style, Yeats railed against it saying:

The zealots have been wise in their generation; they have struck at the moment when the country is unprepared to resist. The old regime left Ireland perhaps the worst educated country in Northern Europe … We were helots, and where you have the helots, there the zealot reigns unchallenged. And our zealots' idea of establishing the Kingdom of God upon earth is to make Ireland as island of moral cowards.[15]

Denis Donoghue has said that Willie felt humiliated by the new law. He felt that all the great epic images that he himself had conjured into being for the benefit of the State, that they were all being spat upon, that the new Ireland was really a wretched petty bourgeois Catholic little shop-keeping country, and he detested that Ireland, he despised it.[16]

Willie did not seek re-election to the Senate in 1928. He had played his part. Conor Cruise O'Brien in *Passion and Cunning,* which is severely critical of Yeat's politics, wrote of Yeats *losing* his seat in 1928, the year after Kevin O'Higgins's death. He says that his term had expired and the Government made no move to renew his nomination. O'Brien felt that in 1922 the Government needed Protestant support, while it required *money and guns from England.* Once firmly established, the Government did not need to show such diffidence to Protestants and *no longer needed British artillery.* O'Brien correctly writes that Yeats was disillusioned by the power of the Catholic Church in the new State.[17] The State had remained true to its majority conservative values. It acted fairly to the defeated Anglo-Irish caste, many of whom continued to play important roles in the new nation-building. Senator Yeats, particularly, had fulfilled that role in a pugnacious fashion. It was in his poetry that he preserved the dignity of his caste, as the old order changed and egalitarianism, which he loathed, became the order of the day.

Nevertheless Yeats did not give up the fight. By 1932 he had established, with the help of other distinguished writers, including George Bernard Shaw, the Irish Academy of Letters. He spoke about the official censorship in Ireland actively using its powers of suppression against Irish writers, causing them to have to depend on British and American sales of their books, and thereby making it impossible for them to live by distinctive Irish literature.[18]

Yeats honoured by Sandymount school children

by Neans McSweeney
Education Correspondent

ONE of the country's greatest literary characters was yesterday remembered in poetry and song by pupils at a school which lies a stone's throw from his birthplace.

Pupils at the Cerebral Palsy Ireland Sandymount School in Dublin abandoned their classrooms for a morning in the sunshine on Sandymount Green, just off Sandymount Avenue, where William Butler Yeats was born 135 years ago.

Principal, Anthony Jordan, has written numerous books about Yeats and continues to read his works to his pupils. "There is little to remind people of this area of the historic links Yeats had with the Sandymount area. Apart from the bust, there is little to mark his association with this region. Sandymount was very important to him. His rich relations lived here. We

just want to remember him on this important day and remind people of his association with the area," said Mr Jordan.

Fifteen pupils at the special school recited poetry and sang songs yesterday as the celebrated Yeats' birthday. One boy with speech difficulties used his voice synthesiser to recite the Lake Isle of Innisfree. Others carried pictures of Yeats while their principal played an old record featuring a reading from Yeats.

The short, moving ceremony ended when one of the 30 pupils who took part in the ceremony placed flowers at Yeats' bust in the glorious sunshine.

"I hope this little ceremony will give our pupils and the people of the general area a greater appreciation of Yeats and will remind them of his deep love for the area. It would be terrible if he were forgotten in this area," the principal said.

CHAPTER 11

A FANATIC HEART

The Ulster poet Louis MacNeice was an admirer of WB Yeats, and reviewed Yeats' *Dramatis Personae* very favourably in *The Criterion* in 1936. He ended that review by writing: *Let us pay homage to Mr. Yeats and his mask. In our world almost the only coherence is that of squads, which march in step; how refreshing to meet someone who is coherent with himself.* In MacNeice's *The Poetry of W. B. Yeats,* in 1940, he was the first person to have raised the uncomfortable question of Yeats' own links with Fascism. He described Willie as having *his own elegant brand of Fascism,* though he later describes him as *the man who nearly became a Fascist.*

George Orwell broached the subject in the London *Horizon* in 1943. Orwell was a fervent advocate of democratic values and an egalitarian society. He found in Yeats a *rather sinister vision of life,* but acknowledged that *by and large the best writers of our time have been reactionary in tendency.* Orwell concluded that Yeats' outlook was that *of those who reach Fascism by the aristocratic route.*[1]

In more recent times, Dr. Conor Cruise O'Brien raised this aspect of WB Yeats again. When I was working on my biography of Dr. Cruise O'Brien more than ten years ago, I was regularly confronted with certain positions my subject had arrived at, with which I did not agree. Yet he was the most rational of men, arguing his case logically. A wise friend advised me to 'check his premises'. In considering O'Brien's famous *Essay on the Politics of WB Yeats,* first published in 1965 for the centenary of Yeats' birth, and expanded in *Passion and Cunning* in 1988, this advice proved salutary.

Patrick Cosgrave, in his 1967 reply to O'Brien's essay wrote:

The triumphal conclusion of Professor O'Brien's essay is that Yeats was a Fascist and that the ingredients of his Fascism were political ambition, cunning, prudence and snobbery. He believes that by the time he has reached 1902, he has established the dominance of the first three of these ingredients in Yeats's character.[1a]

Cosgrave seeks to demolish O'Brien's thesis, and accuses him of an *inadequate approach* to Yeats's *Last Poems* and *A Vision.* Cosgrave continues:

When Professor O'Brien extracts from this and the poetry, a political content hitherto overlooked because, he says, it troubled people 'frightened of Yeats's politics', and then he, with his fine scholastic record, his avowed and high-minded commitments to humane cultural and political values, does great and serious harm and this harm is redoubled because of his reputation. Also because of his reputation and achievement his actions on this occasion remain inexplicable.

Without realising it possibly, it appears to me, that Cosgrave may already have adverted to the explanation for O'Brien's *'inexplicable actions'*. In that same paragraph Cosgrave had already written that Yeats had two fundamental *'political attitudes'*. He was an Irish Nationalist, and he wanted a Government which would provide for artistic institutions, such as the theatre and his proposed Irish Academy of Letters.

This 'explanation' becomes clearer in a short review by Dr. O'Brien of Elizabeth Cullingford's *Yeats, Ireland and Fascism.* He writes that *Yeats was both liberal and a Pro-Fascist at different times, and different moods, and under different circumstances.* O'Brien wrote that Cullingford's book, which was a direct rebuttal of his own essay, had two serious defects. He claimed that she sought to show that Yeats was a far better person than he actually was; he was never a snob, never an elitist, but invariably a thoroughly decent chap. Secondly, and the one point pertinent to my developing argument here, is that O'Brien feels that Cullingford does not have enough 'feel' for Yeats's 'Irish political context'. In particular he is most dismissive of her in writing in defence of Yeats's admiration for poets over parliamentarians. Cullingford wrote *but before dismissing this point of view, one must remember that Irish freedom was not won through parliamentary negotiation, but by the successful poets' rebellion of 1916.* O'Brien retorts, with some emotion, *This particular piece of cant has been current in official Catholic Ireland for sixty years, but that is no reason for accepting it as a truth that ' we must remember'.*[2] O'Brien asserts that the eventual freedom achieved, self-government with partition, was what the 'poets' fought and died to avert. He further argues that by accepting a nomination to the *Senate,* Yeats was turning his back on those poets. O'Brien terms such a decision as brave and sensible. In my view O'Brien is seeking to have it both ways, in describing Yeats's senator-ship, while also claiming in a revisionist way that the new State was a betrayal of the Easter Rising. This is O'Brien's version of history, not one supported by the vast majority of the Irish people, who as Cullingford rightly states, see the 1916 Rising as

170

being the springboard for Irish freedom. This is Yeats's view as an Irish Nationalist. O'Brien is therefore at odds with Yeats's nationalism. He appears to be more understanding, of those who, like the IRA and De Valera, opposed the new State by force of arms. He quotes, though I believe misinterprets, Yeats's lines:

> Maybe a breath of politic words
> Has withered our Rose Tree

He writes, in language laden with emotive terminology, that those who felt in this way tried to reject the Treaty and carry on the *struggle. The majority of the people, tired of war, had voted, in effect, for the acceptance of the Treaty. The Free State Government, with the aid of British artillery and armoured cars, now set about liquidating the Republican forces.*[3] Dr. O'Brien doubts whether that majority favoured such action, but he has no doubt that all the well-off elements did, including WB Yeats. He proceeds to write about the Free State forces 'destroying' the Republican forces, obliged to use some of the same methods of the Black and Tans, though applied with greater efficiency and with proportionally less publicity. He quotes Lady Gregory as writing to Yeats in protest against the Government. Yeats, though, is violently against any protest, saying that it is necessary for the stability of the Government to hold out. O'Brien writes of Gregory and Lennox Robinson composing a letter of protest to the *Irish Independent* and consulting his own father, Francis Cruise O'Brien at the Arts Club.

Dr. O'Brien quotes Yeats as writing in May 1922 that, *out of all this murder and rapine will come not a demagogic but an authoritarian government* and in October, *Everyone notices a drift towards conservatism, perhaps towards Autocracy.* O'Brien adds that Yeats's ideas for Ireland were explicitly linked with the rise of Fascism in Europe, and quotes him as writing in November 1922, the Ireland that reacts from the present disorder is turning its eyes towards individualist [i.e. Fascist] Italy. Mussolin's famous march on Rome and his non-violent acquisition of power had occurred in March of that same year.

It is my contention that Dr. O'Brien's 'inexplicable actions' in attacking Ycats's politics may possibly have been motivated by his own belief that the 1916 Rising was a mistake and unnecessary. He believes that his parliamentarians – the Sheehy side of his family - could have attained as much and peacefully. He sees Yeats as having played a major part in the ethos of the Rising. Declan Kiberd has correctly written: *Easter 1916 is in truth, the foundational poem of the emerging Irish nation-state.*[4] Through

Wedding of Kevin O'Higgins.
Standing De Valera, O'Higgins, Rory O'Connor.

his poetry, Yeats had mythologized, canonised and legitimised the Rising. Then, for Dr. O'Brien, Yeats had the audacity to join with those pro-Treaty forces, which had betrayed the Poets' Rising. Yeats 'cashed in' on the events of 1916-1922 and became as authoritarian as the Government. The Government had to fight for its life, for the life of the new State, against the IRA and De Valera. It won the approval of the people against opponents who refused it any legitimacy. Its members were the 'Founders of the State', which still exists. Yeats supported the Government to the hilt, and was an important sign that the Government was a legitimate heir to the Easter Rising. Rather than Elizabeth Cullingford *not having enough feel for Yeats's Irish political context,*[5] it is in my view, Dr. O'Brien himself, who demonstrates such a characteristic.

In *Passion and Cunning,* Dr. O'Brien goes on seeking to bolster his argument against Yeats by aligning him with the Minister of Justice in the Free State Government, Kevin O'Higgins. O'Higgins was a friend of the poet, and admired him greatly. O'Higgins was the 'strongman' of the government and the bete noir of the IRA and De Valera. O'Brien says that O'Higgins was thought to stand for what was most ruthless and implacable in the party of property. He then purports to quote O'Higgins as saying that, *if necessary seven hundred and seventy seven* executions would be carried out in reference to the seventy-seven executions already carried out by his

172

Government. O'Brien tells us that this was not repugnant to Yeats, as the right of the State to take life in its own defence *became dear to him.*[6] This attempted portrayal of O'Higgins reflects the commonplace of republican propaganda during the 1920's and 1930's. Grattan Freyer writes: *there is no support for it in the carefully documented life of O'Higgins by Terence de Vere White, published in 1948, nor in the Official Reports of O'Higgins's speeches in Dail Eireann.*[6a]

O'Brien then moves to 1932, and suggests that those who, like Yeats, admired in O'Higgins a potential autocrat, might not have expected him to go along with the smooth hand-over of power to De Valera and his party of Fianna Fail, after the *impeccably conducted free election* of that year! The IRA had assassinated O'Higgins in 1927. O'Brien tells his readers of how a police sergeant informed his republican aunt, Mrs Hanna Sheehy Skeffington, *'Ye'll be delighted to hear, Ma'am – Kevin's been shot!'*.[7]

1932 was a turning point in modern Irish history. Those who had opposed the creation of the new State by force of arms in the Civil War won the February General Election, with Labour Party support. The Founders of the State, in the Cumann na nGaedheal party, handed over power to the erstwhile rebels, in a completely peaceful transfer of power and went into Opposition. At fifteen years of age, Conor Cruise O'Brien declared that he was:

Among the people who rejoiced at this victory, since it was nice to be even remotely on the side of someone who was winning. In my own family the State itself was no longer treated dismissively or derisively. It was now a State it would be proper to serve, as our family had believed it would be proper to serve a Home Rule State.[8]

Dr. O'Brien then writes that some of the defeated party began organising a para-military movement, *on the Fascist model,* for the intimidation of their opponents and the recovery of power.[9] Joe Lee, however, says the *Army Comrades Association was founded in February 1932, to protect Cumann na nGaedheal supporters from IRA harassment.*[10] The IRA, which had remained outside Fianna Fáil, but actively supported its electoral bid in 1932, had begun to intimidate the Government election rallies. The IRA naturally expected a *quid pro quo* from their erstwhile allies in the Civil War on assuming power. As public disorder continued during that year between the IRA, supporting De Valera, and the ACA, supporting Cumann na nGaedheal, it provided De Valera with what Joe Lee described *as a chance*

173

to wring the last inch of electoral mileage out of his republican sympathies before turning, if necessary, against the IRA. He called a snap general election in January 1933 and, with IRA support, won an overall majority, and sacked the Garda Commissioner, Eoin O'Duffy. In March the ACA adopted the Blueshirt and a straight-armed salute and renamed itself The National Guard.

Eoin O'Duffy became its leader. The 'shirted' movements were part of a wave of patriotic organisations springing up as far away as Australia, where ex-servicemen from the Great War were uniting against the communistic threat.[11] Great tension developed throughout the country, as some feared the IRA might stage a coup d'etat and impose communism.[12] O'Duffy announced a march on Dublin, ostensibly en route to Glasnevin Cemetery to honour the founders of the State, Collins, Griffith and O'Higgins, for 13 August. This was too reminiscent of Mussolini's March on Rome, and assumption of power, to many. The IRA mobilised to attack the march lest the Government fail to act. During the early hours of 13 August, De Valera declared the march illegal. He also banned The National Guard, using the notorious Section 2A of the Free State Constitution. O'Duffy cancelled the march..[13] He later became leader of the Opposition, which changed its name to Fine Gael, and the Blueshirts therefore returned to mainstream politics. Despite intensive ongoing discussions between De Valera and Sean MacBride for the IRA, relations between the Government and the IRA deteriorated. The IRA, too, was later proscribed by DeValera.

It was into this milieu, with competing forces in frenzy against their opponents, that WB Yeats returned to Ireland from an American tour in early 1933. He was then living outside Dublin in Rathfarnham and not immune to what was happening in the country. He utterly opposed the IRA and the possibility of communism. He admired De Valera as a strong leader who could counter the power of the Catholic Church. He was naturally closer, though, to the old government allies of the Blueshirts. He wrote to Olivia Shakeaspeare that he found himself urging the despotic rule of the educated classes as the only end of the country's troubles. It would, of course, be his kind of people who would be in a majority among that class. He possibly saw himself as being the philosopher to the new movement, just as the Italian Minister of Education, Giovanni Gentile, had been to Mussolini. The founder of the Blueshirts, Captain Dermott MacManus, was a friend of Yeats. MacManus came from an old ascendancy family in Mayo. He had fought in the British army during the First World War. He moved in artistic circles, was a devotee of black magic and shared Yeats' theosophical interests.[13a] Willie found him lively and amusing company, admitting that MacManus probably got his vague Fascism from himself. Yeats wrote marching songs for the Blueshirts and was energised by the excitement. Eoin O'Duffy was taken to meet Yeats at his home. Willie found him autocratic, *not a great man, a plastic man, but one never knows.*[14] In his autobiography, Frank O'Connor wrote;

In his last phase, when I knew him, Yeats was by way of being a Fascist and a supporter of O'Duffy. He wrote unsingable Fascist songs to the tune of 'O'Donnell Abu' and 'The Heather Glen', and caused me acute embarrassment by appearing at dinner in the Kildare Street Club in a blue shirt.[15]

Seamus Heaney displays, not surprisingly, a keen understanding of Yeats, as he acknowledges the challenge, *to the virtue of* Yeats' *commitments*, due *to his espousal of an essentially feudal vision in the realm of politics and culture*, for which the opposition would *disqualify him, because, of his attraction to Italian fascism in the 1930s*. Reminiscent of Auden's criticisms, including that of 'silliness', Heaney identifies the charge of the value of *being influenced by poetry so unready to engage sympathetically with the circumstances of life in a bourgeois democracy, so resolutely opposed to the scientific spirit and so dangerously susceptible to being interpreted as a licence for actions at once violent, romantic and nationalist.* Heaney appears ready to 'explain' and 'defend' Yeats, and it appears to me, to adopt a similar stance for artistic freedom, by stating that:

It is the unconstrained quality of the work that constitutes its majestic as well as its minatory force. Without the danger, we could not have the utterness and daring and our collective and critical life would be less alive to the extreme possibilities, as well as the extreme responsibilities, of those who would 'articulate sweet sound'.[16]

I have no doubt that Yeats himself would agree wholeheartedly with Heaney on, the *extreme possibilities*. I would be less certain that one who wrote, *I hate reasonable people ... I was once afraid of turning out reasonable myself,*[17] would be so cognizant of *the extreme responsibilities*.

As the Blueshirts faded, so did Yeats's flirtation with them wane, and he began to mock them in letters to Olivia Shakeaspeare. Norman A. Jeffares has said *this ironic attitude to the Blueshirts revealed the true Yeats, detached and merely playing with his thoughts, except for intervals.*[18] Dr.

O'Brien counters, finding it less plausible, and argues that the Yeats who was so excited by the thoughts of the Blueshirts winning, is as likely to be 'more real' than the Yeats who sneered at them in decline and defeat. He adds understandably, *It was the same Yeats, strongly drawn to Fascism, but no lover of hopeless causes.*[19] In Seán Ó Mórdha's famous documentary on Yeats for Radio Telefis Eireann, *Cast Cold Eye,* Dr. O'Brien comments:

Reading Yeats is exciting and disturbing because among other things you wonder what is it in me that is responding to this, and that's a bit frightening.

Yeats admired and loved Italy as he made clear in so many of his writings. In his poem, *The People,* he considers his life in Ireland, *in this unmannerly town,* where, *he who has served most is most defamed.* He then says to Maud Gonne how well she knows how he has longed to live in Italy – *in the green shadow of Ferraro Wall-* or climb – *the steep street of Urbino-* where a poet is allowed to choose his company. The poet was a patriot, though, an Irish patriot, fallible and foolish as many are, and did his duty, fulfilled his dream. Elizabeth Cullingford in her detailed rebuttal of Dr. O'Brien's essay concludes that Yeats involvement with the Blueshirts was never formal and existed in his own overheated imagination. He was responding to Irish disorders by envisaging a despotic rule of the educated classes, rather than rule by a Fascist gang.

It may be, as DH Akenson wrote, that O'Brien *had a score to settle with Yeats.*[20] It may well also be that that *score* was fundamentally with Irish Nationalism itself, which O'Brien believed had echoes of Fascism. In attacking the politics of WB Yeats, O'Brien is in reality moving towards an onslaught on Irish Nationalism itself. While a Government Minister himself in 1975, Dr. O'Brien wrote of the blood sacrifice as part of the national movement.

Now this is most essentially a literary invention. Yeats was the great propagandist of this notion …. I have heard Yeats' line, ' A terrible beauty is born' used to glorify or better to bedizen the sordid horrors, which the Provisional IRA and their competitors have brought to the streets of Belfast.[21]

When Liam Cosgrave's Government, of which Dr. O'Brien was a Minister, introduced an Emergency Powers Bill in 1976, the latter hinted that its powers might be used against Irish newspapers. Charlie Haughey retorted, with some irony, ' *There is a militaristic Fascist mentality behind all this.*[22] By 1981 O'Brien was able to articulate: *Those who want to oppose Fascism in Ireland will start opposing it where it is really to be found: at the heart of the Republican Movement.*[23]

An important factor with Yeats is his record of supporting the rights of the 'workingman' against the 'mob'. For him, *the mob* was a certain section of the middle class, which he thought divested the national movement of its idealism. Fascism was for the *State* and against the common mass of people. His letter supporting those on strike in the *Irish Worker,* said:

I do not complain of Dublin's capacity for fanaticism whether in priest or layman, for you cannot have strong feeling without that capacity, but neither those who directed the police, not the editors of our newspapers can plead fanaticism. They are supposed to watch over our civil liberties, and I charge the Dublin Nationalist newspapers with deliberately arousing the religious passion to break up the organisation of the workingman, with appealing to mob law day after day, with publishing the names of workingmen and their wives for purposes of intimidation. And I charge the Unionist Press of Dublin and those who directed the police with conniving at this conspiracy … I want to know who has ordered the abrogation of the most elementary rights of the citizens …

Prime Ministers have fallen, and Ministers of State have been impeached for less than this ... I demand that the coming Police Inquiry shall be so widened that we may get to the bottom of a conspiracy … Intriguers have met together somewhere behind the scenes that they might turn the religion of Him who thought it hard for a rich man to enter into the Kingdom of Heaven into an oppression of the poor.

That letter gladdened the heart of Sean O'Casey, who commented that *Yeats in a strange deep way loved the common people.* Being on the side of Jim Larkin was a natural outcome for a man familiar with John O'Leary, William Morris and Maud Gonne, with their devotion to vulnerable people. Maud Gonne had written to Willie on 29 November 1913, saying: *Thank you for your generous subscription to the children's dinners. It is very kind of you. I hope this will be the last year I shall have to beg for this object.*

Yeats' position is further illuminated by his response to an invitation to a writer's Congress in Madrid, held in 1937 to defend the Spanish Republic. In the first volume of his memoirs, Pablo Neruda, the Chilean poet, wrote of the replies, which:

poured in from all over. One was from Yeats, Ireland's national poet; another from Selma Lagerlof, the notable Swedish writer. They were both too old to travel to a beleaguered city like Madrid, which was steadily being pounded by bombs, but they rallied to the defence of the Spanish Republic.[24]

Yeats's passion for eugenics in the 1930's and his outrageous views in *On the Boiler* on that subject, with his obvious admiration for Hitler's movement are less easy to defend and could be termed, at a minimum, 'loutish'. The Nazis adopted Nietzsche's ideal man for their Aryan superman, emphasising racial superiority, and adding anti-Semitism to fascist militarism and anti communism. *On The Boiler* was to be an occasional publication like Yeats' *Samhain*. He told Maud Gonne that, for the first time in his life, he was saying what he believed about Irish and European politics.[24a] Reading Yeats' distasteful text, there can be little doubt but that he believed that the unintelligent had less rights that the intelligent, and that a compulsory sterilization programme would have his approval.

Had the Nazis come to Ireland, there would have been many who would have collaborated with them, and Irish history may have been more sorrowful than it is. Yeats's feelings can possibly be understood to some extent, however, by his own personal quest for his lost potency, and his belief that old men have a right to be mad, as he wrote: *There is so little in our stocking ... how can we not feel emulous when we see Hitler juggling with his sausage of stocking.* He confessed to Olivia Shakeaspeare that he would remain sinful to the day he died, and would regret all the occasions for sinning that he *wasted in my youth.*

Sir Ian Hamilton, a famous soldier and cousin of Lady Gregory's, later wrote of an encounter with Hitler.

During my two hours talk last year with Adolph *Hitler, as I listened to his eager, nervy voice running up and down the gamut of the emotional scales - laughter, sorrow, pity - the thought kept on rising the back of my head like a question mark, 'wherever have I heard someone speak like this who could it have been?'. Then suddenly as he spoke of his nightingales, the mirror of memory flashed and there I was listening again to Yeats.*[25]

FOOTNOTES

INTRODUCTION

[1] Memory Harbour The Port of Sligo. John McTiernan Arena Publications 1992 p. 40.

[2] The Collected Letters of W.B. Yeats. Volume II 1896-1900. Edited by Warick Gould, John Kelly, and Deirdre Toomey. Oxford University Press 1997, p. 695.

[3] Yeats' Interactions With Tradition; 'Critical Prolegomenon'. Patrick J. Keane. University of Missouri Press 1987. pp. 3-20.

CHAPTER 1

[1] WB Yeats A Life The Apprentice Mage Roy Foster Oxford University Press 1997 p. 568.

[2] A Pilgrimage of Passion The Life of Wilfrid Scawen Blunt. Elizabeth Longford Weidenfeld & Nicholson 1979. pp.191-7.

[3] ibid. p. 349.

[3a] Lady Gregory's Toothbrush Colm Tóibín Liliput 2000. p. 14

[3b] A Servant of the Queen Maud Gonne MacBride Gollancz 1938. p. 332.

[3c] The Woman Behind the Irish Renaissance Mary Lou Kohfeld Andre Deutsch 1985. p. 130.

[4].The Life of WB Yeats Terence Brown Gill and MacMillan 1999 p.134.

[5] Berg Collection New York Public Library (NYPL) letter to Lady Layard 23/12/1898.

[6].Yeats and Women Ed. Deirdre Toomey MacMillan 1997 p.187.

[7] John Quinn Memorial Papers New York Public Library (NYPL) 12/01/1919

[8] Lady Gregory's Toothbrush Colm Tóbín Lilliput 2002 p. 47.

[9] The Gonne Yeats Letters ed. Anna MacBride White & AN Jeffarres Pimlico 1993 p.259

[10] Autobiographies WB Yeats MacMillan 1955 p. 160.

[11] WB Yeats Joseph Hone MacMillan 1942 p. 249.

[12].The Chief Secretary Augustine Birrell Chatto & Windus 1969. p. 159.

[12a] Edmund Gosse A Literary Landscape Ann Thwaite Secker & Warburg 1984.

[13] Yeats And Women ed. Deirdre Toomey MacMillan 1997 pp. 168-204.

[14] Yeats Collection Manuscript 30,688 National Library Ireland [NLI].

[15] Liverpol University Manuscript 8 (3) 9 August 1910.

[16] WB Yeats Joseph Hone MacMillan 1942. 249.

CHAPTER 2

[1] Autobiographies WB Yeats   MacMillan 1955 p. 83.

[2] Yeats Sisters   Joan Harding   Pandora 2000   P. 76

[3] Family Secrets   William Murphy Gill & MacMillan 1995 p. 173.

[4] ibid. p. 277.

[5] Maud Gonne   Margaret Ward   Pandora 1990. p. 25.

[6] The Apprentice Mage   Roy Foster   Oxford University Press 1997 p.64.

[6a] Foster-Murphy Collection. Letters and Documents of Lily and WB Yeats. NLI.

[7] Memoirs   Denis Donoghue   MacMillam 1972 P. 156.

[7a] Foster-Murphy Collection Letters and Documents of Lily and WB Yeats. NLI.

[8] Family Secrets   p. 277.

[9] Berg Papers NYPL 8 January 1906. ref. 342.

[9a] Foster-Murphy Collection Letters and Documents of Lily and WB Yeats. NLI.

[10] Autobiographies p. 167.

[11].The Man From New York BL Reid Oxford University Press 1968.   p. 524.

[12] Willie Yeats and the Gonne MacBrides Anthony Jordan Westport Books 1997 pp. 171-2.

[13] The Man from New York p 425.

[14] Willie Yeats and the Gonne MacBrides p. 17.

[14a] Foster-Murphy Collection Letters and Documents of Lily and WB Yeats. NLI.

[15] Letters to WB Yeats Vol 2. p. .531

[16] My Father's Son Frank O'Connor Gill & MacMillan 1968 p. 196.

[17] Manuscript 5919 NLI.

[17a] Foster Murphy Collection Letters and Documents of Lily and WB Yeats. NLI.

CHAPTER 3

[1] Gonne-Yeats Letters p. 276.

[2] The Man From New York BL Reid Oxford University Press 1968 p.8.

[2a] The Apprentice Mage p. 37.

[3] Yeats and Artistic Power Phillip Marcus Syracuse University Press 2001. p. 20

[4] ibid p.30.

[5] Gonne-Yeats Letters p. 18.

[6] ibid p.50

[7] ibid p.60.

[8] Yeats & Artistic Power pp.33-4.

[9] The Man From New York p. 10.

[1] Collected Letters of WB Yeats Vol III Ed. John Kelly & Ronald Schuchard Oxford University Press 1994. 06/02/03 & 20/03/03 pp. 313 & 335. And Foster-Murphy Collection . Letters and documents of Lily and WB Yeats. NLI.

[11] WB Yeats A Life 1: The Apprentice Mage Roy Foster Oxford University Press 1997. p. 272.

[12] The Life of W. B. Yeats Terence Brown   Gill & MacMillan 2001. p. 159.

[13].William Butler Yeats Denis Donoghue Fontana 1971 p. 53.

[13a]. Yeats and Nietzsche Otto Bohlmann MacMillan 1983 pp. 16-17.

[14] Gonne-yeats Letters op. cit. p. 165.

[15] WB Yeats Joseph Hone 1865-1939 MacMillan 1942. p.97.

[16] Berg NYPL.

[17].The Man From New York op. cit. p. 13.

[18] John Quinn Memorial Papers 06/06/03 NYPL.

[19] Churchill A Founder of Modern Ireland Anthony J. Jordan Westport books 1995. p.16.

[20] John Quinn Memorial Papers NYPL 23/08/1906.

[21] Bodleian Library 24/07/1918.

[22] Gonne-Yeats Letters p. 276.

[23] Berg . 25/12/1911. NYPL.

[24] The Man From New York p. 167..

[25] John Quinn Memorial Papers NYPL.

[26] ibid.

[27] The Man From New York p. 179.

[28] ibid. p. 217.

[29] ibid. p. 307

[30] Berg. 29/11/1917. NYPL.

[31] John Quinn Memorial Papers NYPL.

[32] The Man From New York p. 419

[33] John Quinn Memorial Papers NYPL.

[34] Dear Yeats, Dear Pound, Dear Ford. Jeanne Robert Foster and Her Circle of Friends. Richard Londraville & Janis Londraville Syracuse University Press 2001. p. 87.

[35] The Man From New York p. 526.

[36] Dear Yeats, Dear Pound, Dear Ford p.p. 86-7.

[37] Willie Yeats and The Gonne Macbrides Anthony J. Jordan Westport Books 1997.

[38] The Man From New York p. 527.

[39] Dear Yeats, Dear Pound, Dear Ford. p. 147.

[40] ibid. p. 241.

[41] ibid. p. 238.

CHAPTER 4

[1] The Abbey Hugh Hunt   Gill & Macmillan 1979. p. 113.

[2] United Irishman 11 March 1899.

[3] Manuscript 1,729. NLI.

[4] The Listener 2 March 1939..

[5] Autobiographies WB Yeats MacMillan 1955.

[6] The Listener 3 March 1939.

[7] United Irishman 5 November 1902.

[8] We Two Together James & Gretta Cousins Ganesh Madras 1948.

[9] The Apprentice Mage Roy Foster Oxford 1997 p. 280.

[10] Gonne Yeats Letters pp. 176-7.

[11].Manuscript 13,068 (1). NLI.

[12] George Roberts Collection NLI.

[13] Fool of the Family WJ McCormack Weidenfeld 2000 p. 21.

[14] The Apprentice Mage op. cit. 329.

[15] Berg Papers NYPL

[16] Memoirs   Denis Donoghue (Ed.) MacMillan 1972 p. 203.

[17] The Listener   March 1939.

[18] Manuscript 10,952 NLI.

[19] ibid.

[20] The Abbey Theatre Cradle of Genius   Gerard Fay Dublin 1958. p. 137.

[21] Hail and Farewell: Ave, Salve,Vale. George Moore Appleton 1912-14.

[22] Red Headed Rebel Susan Mitchele Hilary Pyle Woodfield 1998. pp. 130-1.

CHAPTER 5

[1] A Magazine of Verse Horace Gregory p. 153. 3/6/1954.

[2] WB Yeats Terence Brown p. 6.

[3] The Apprentice Mage Roy Foster Oxford University 1997. p. 443.

[4] James Joyce Stan Gebler Davies Granada 1981 pp. 70-71.

[5] Autobiographies WB Yeats MacMillan 1955. p. 402.

[6] Memoirs of Yeats Denis Donoghue (Ed.) MacMillan 1972. p. 100.

[7] ibid p. 270.

[8] ibid. p. 500.

[9] The Apprentice Mage p. 482.

[10] Hail & Farewell p.270.

[11] Autobiographies WB Yeats p. 405

[12] Kilkenny Magazine Spring 1962. pp. 25-28.

[13] The Apprentice Mage op. cit. p. 168.

[14] Brief Mention, Modern Language Notes 52: 12 December 1937. pp. 618—9.

[15] Partisan Review Spring 1939.

[16] Gonne Yeats Letters p. 170.

[17] WB Yeats Terence Brown . p. 141.

[18] Gonne Yeats Letters p. 163.

[19] ibid p. 442.

CHAPTER 6

[1] Yeats & Artistic Power Phillip L. Marcus Syracuse University Press 2001. p. 101.

[1a] WB Yeats Terence Brown p. 29.

[2] John O'Leary A Study in Irish Separatism Marcus Bourke Anvil 1967 p. 182.

[3] Autobiographies WB Yeats p.101.

[4] Yeats & Ireland Scattering Branches ed. Stephen Gwynn MacMillan 1940. pp. 15-34.

[5] John O'Leary A Study in Irish Separatism Marcus Bourke Anvil 1967 . pp. 182-8.

[6] Autobiographies WB Yeats

[7] Passion and Cunning Conor Cruise O'Brien Paladin 1990 p. 22.

[8] The Yeats Gonne MacBride Triangle p. 15.

[9] Autobiographies WB Yeats p. 213.

[10] Prodigal Father   The Life of John Butler Yeats 1839-1922   William Murphy London 1978 p. 144..

[11] Manuscript 5925 NLI.

[12] Pall Mall Gazette   12 July 1899.

[13] A Servant of the Queen   Maud Gonne MacBride   Gollancz 1938 p. 240.

[14] John O'Leary p. 194.

[14a] Memoirs   Ed. Denis Donoghue   MacMillan 1972. p. 60.

[15] Gonne Yeats Letters   p. 113.

[16] Freeman's Journal   20 March 1900.

[17] The Yeats Gonne MacBride Triangle pp.32-41.

[18] ibid p. 50.

[19] ibid. p. 52.

[20] ibid. p. 20.

[21] ibid pp. 84-5.

[22] The Apprentice Mage p. 367.

[23] John O'Leary p. 231.

[24] Yeats & Artistic Power   Phillip Marcus   Syracuse University Press 2001 pp. 101-104.

CHAPTER 7

[1] Willie Yeats and the Gonne MacBrides p. 30.

[2] Gonne-Yeats Letters p. 154.

[3] Vale George Moore Colin Smythe pp. 110, 281.

[4] Gonne Yeats Letters p. 372.

[5] ibid. p. 375.

[5a] Foster-Murphy Collection Letters and Documents of Lily and WB Yeats. NLI.

6 George's Ghosts Brenda Maddox Picador 1999 p. 77

[7] The Man From New York   BL Reid.   p. 306.

[8] Willie Yeats and the Gonne MacBrides. p. 58.

[9] ibid p. 160.

[10] ibid. p. 160.

[10a] Foster-Murphy Collection Letters and Documents of Lily and WB Yeats. NLI.

[11] Gonne Yeats Letters p. 402.

[12] ibid . p. 404.

[13] ibid p. 434.

[14] ibid. p. 439

[15] Scattering Branches p. 23.

[16] Becoming George: The Life of Mrs WB Yeats Ann Saddlemyer Oxford 2002 pp. 604-610.

[17] Willie Yeats and the Gonne MacBrides pp. 194-5.

CHAPTER 8

[1] The Kilkenny Magazine Spring 1962. pp. 25-28.

[1a] "Yeats" Louis Kellner. Die Nation Berlin. 8 August 1903.

[2] The Poetry of WB Yeats Louis MacNiece Faber & Faber 1967   p. 228.

[3] We Two Together James & Margaret Cousins Ganesh Madras India 1950 p. 159.

[4] Manuscript 5919 NLI.

[5] The Partisan Review Spring 1939.

[6] The Freeman's Journal 20 March 1900 & 4 April 1900.

[7] The Abbey   Hugh Hunt Gill & MacMillan 1979. p.76.

[8] The Apprentice Mage   p. 369.

[9] Berg Papers NYPL.

[10] Gonne-Yeats Letters   pp. 384-5.

[11] WB Yeats Terence Brown p. 229.

[12] Gender and History in Yeats's Love Poetry Elizabeth Cullingford Cambridge 1993 p. 121.

[13] The Crane Bag 2 1985   Terry Eagleton.

[14] The Partisan Review   Spring 1939.

[15] Inventing Ireland Declan Kiberd   Jonathan Cape 1995. pp. 114-204.

[16] Terence Brown op. cit. p. 235.

[17] Gonne –Yeats Letters p. 378.

[18] Passion & Cunning Conor Cruise O'Brien   Paladin 1990. p. 240.

[19] Terence Brown op. cit. p. 276.

[20] Gonne-Yeats Letters . p. 425.

[21] Manuscript 5919 NLI.

[22] ibid .

[23] Gonne-Yeats Letters. p. 421

CHAPTER 9

[1] The Kilkenny Magazine   Spring 1962.

[2] The Man From New York   BL Reid   Oxford Uni. 1968. pp. 35-6.

[3] The Yeats Gonne MacBride Triangle   p. 18.

[4] My Life Story   Arthur Lynch   John Long London mcmxxix p. 157.

[5] Young Douglas Hyde   Dominic Daly   Irish University Press 1973.   p. 202.

[6] National Archives Dublin.

[7] ibid 14 Jan 1897.

[8] MacBride's Brigade   Donal P.McCracken   Four Courts Press 2000 p. 21.

[9] ibid p. 23.

[10] ibid. pp. 24-25.

[11] Gonne-Yeats Letters p. 477.

[12] WB Yeats   Terence Brown op. cit. p. 140. O'Donnell had been a journalist and M.P. He was inimical to Maud Gonne and was a controversialist.

[13] Songs of the Irish Rebellion. Irish Political Street Ballads and Rebel Songs. 1780-1900. Denis Zimmermann   Four Courts Press 2002 p. 293.

[14] The Long Gestation Irish Nationalist Life   Patrick Maume   Gill & MacMillan 1999 p. 85.

[15] The Yeats Gonne MacBride Triangle pp. 12-13.

[16] Yeats Gonne Letters p. 122.

[17] MacBride's Brigade p. 136.

[18] A Servant of the Queen op. cit. p. 319.

[19] ibid. p. 321.

[20] Gonne-Yeats Letters. p. 139.

[21] ibid. p. 140.

[22] Maud Gonne   Nancy Cardozo   Gollancz 1979. p. 207.

[23] MacBride's Brigade p. 150.

[24] A Servant of the Queen p. 342.

[25] Gonne-Yeats Letters p. 154.

[26] Yeats Gonne MacBride Triangle p. 30.

[27] A Servant of the Queen p. 344.

[28] Gonne Yeats Letters p. 153.

[29] A Servant of the Queen pp. 155-6.

[30] The Lives and Lies of Maud Gonne   Conrad Balliet   Eire-Ireland 14 1979.

31 ibid..

32 Memoirs   Denis Donoghue   MacMillan 1972. p. 63.

3 Gonne Yeats Letters pp. 157-8.

34 ibid. pp. 164-7.

35 The Cuchulain Plays of William Butler Yeats   Roy Skene   MacMillan 1974. p. 38.

36 Textual Practice   Elizabeth Cullingford Thinking of Her..as.. Ireland : Yeats, Pearse and Heaney Spring 1999. pp. 1-21.

37 A Servant of the Queen. p. 348.

38 The Guardian Review   27 January 1989.

39 A Servant of the Queen   p. 349.

40 Yeats Gonne MacBride Triangle   p. 40.

41 ibid. p. 42.

42 Yeats   Harold Bloom   Oxford 1970   pp. 158 & 243 & 248.

43 Yeats, The Man and the Mask   Richard Ellman   New York 1948. p. 42.

44 Gonne Yeats Letters p. 184.

45 Ibid. p. 183.

46 ibid. p. 184.

47 ibid. p. 232.

48 Family Secrets   William Murphy   Gill & MacMillan 1995. p. 355.

49 Gender & History in Yeats' Love Poetry   Elizabeth Cullingford   Syracuse University 1996. p. 88.

50 ibid. p. 75.

51 The Apprentice Mage p. 331.

52 ibid p. 592. Cf. "John MacBride's Good Name". Tony Jordan   Irish Literary Supplement. Irish Studies Programme of Boston College, Massachusetts Fall 1998.pp. 23-4.

53 Passion & Cunning   Conor Cruise O'Brien   Paladin 1990 p. 43.

54 Maud & Willie   Barry Shorthall   Collins Press 2002.

55 Yeats Gonne MacBride Triangle p. 101.

56 Life & the Dream   Mary Colm   MacMillan 1947. p. 142.

57 Gonne Yeats Letters . p. 272.

58 " How Major John MacBride Became Involved in the Easter Rising" . Anthony Jordan. Cathair na Mart . Journal of the Westport Historical Journal.2001 pp.

45-56.. &   Peadar O'Cearnaigh Story   Trinity College Archives Dublin.

[59] The Crane Bag   2 1985. pp. 138-142. Politics & Sexuality in WB Yeats.

[60] Yeats Gonne MacBride Triabgle p. 60.

[61] Maud Gonne   Margaret Ward   Pandora 1990 p. 97.

[62] Daughters of Erin   Elixabeth Coxhead   Secker 1965. p. 62.

[63] GonneYeats Letters   p. 384.

[64] Ibid pp. 374-5.

[65] The Tradition of Myself Marjorie Perloff. Journal of Modern Literature. Feb. 1975 pp. 529-73.

[66] Gonne Yeats Letters p. 434.

CHAPTER 10

[1] Manuscript 5919 NLI.

[2] Willie Yeats and the Gonne MacBrides p. 172. cf.

[3] Churchill – A Founder of Modern Ireland   Anthony Jordan   Westport Books 1995. pp. 103-4.

[4] ibid. pp.119-120.

[5] Yeats's Worlds; Ireland, England and the Poetic Imagination Pierce Yale 1995.

[6] Gonne Yeats Letters p. 429.

[7] Scattering Branches. Tributes to the Memory of WB Yeats   Ed. Stephen Gwynn MacMillan 1940. p. 25.

[8] Parliamentary Debates Official Reports Vol.1. 11 December 1922-9 August 1923. p. 471.

[9] Journals Lady Gregory Vol. 1. Coole Edition. Colin Smythe 1978   p. 455.

[10] Manuscript 30,168. NLI.

[1] WB Yeats Interviews & Recollections. Ed. EH Mikhail MacMillan 1977. p. 201.

[12] Willie Yeats and the Gonne MacBrides p. 17.

[13] Social and Cultural History 1922-1985   Terence Brown   Fontana 1987 . pp. 130-1.

[14] The Irish Free State and its Senate   Donal O'Sullivan   Faber 1940.

[15] Manchester Guardian   22 September 1928.

[16] Cast A Cold Eye. RTE Documentary Programme by Seán Ó Mórdha.

[17] Passion & Cunning passim.

[18] Irish Literature & Drama   Stephen Gwynn   Thomas Nelson 1936. p. 232

CHAPTER 11

[1] Yeats and the Anti-Democratic Tradition Grattan Freyer Gill & MacMillan 1981. pp. 124-5.

[1a] Yeats, Fascism & Conor O'Brien London Magazine July 1967.

[2] What Rough Beast? The Observer Review 19 July 1981.

[3] Passion and Cunning p. 46.

[4] Inventing Ireland Declan Kiberd Vintage 1996. p. 114.

[5] What Rough Beast? op. cit.

[6] Passion & Cunning . p. 50.

[6a] Yeats and the Anti-democratic Tradition. p. 127.

[7] ibid. p. 51.

[8] To Laugh Or To Weep - A Biography of Conor Cruise O'Brien Anthony J. Jordan Blackwater Press 1994. p. 9.

[9] Passion & Cunning p. 55.

[10] Ireland 1912-1985 Joseph Lee Cambridge University Press 1989. p. 178.

[11] George's Ghosts A New Life of WB Yeats Brenda Maddox Picador 1999. p. 260.

[12] WB Yeats Terence Brown . p. 340.

[13] Sean – A Biography of Sean MacBride Anthony J. Jordan Blackwater Press 1993. pp. 64-5.

[13a] Yeats and the Anti-Democratic Tradition Grattan Freyer Gill & MacMillan 1981. p. 107.

[14] Passion & Cunning p. 57.

[15] My Father's Son Frank O'Connor Gill & MacMillan 1968. p. 109.

[16] A Yeats Symposium The Guardian Review 27 January 1989.

[17] The Apprentice Mage p. 53.

[18] Passion & Cunning p. 59.

[19] Ibid. pp. 58-9.

[20] Conor - A Biography of Conor Cruise O'Brien Donal Harman Akenson McGill-Queens University Press 1994. p. 288.

[21] To Laugh Or To Weep p. 188.

[22] ibid p. 160.

[23] Magill Magazine June 1981

[24] Nationalism, Colonialism & Literature: Yeats & Decolonisation. Edward Said. AField Day Pamphlet 15. Derry 1988.

[24a] Gonne Yeats Letters, Letter dated 16 June 1938. p 451.

[25] Manuscript 5919. NLI.

SELECT BIBLIOGRAPHY

Bohlmann Otto   Yeats and Nietzsche – Macmillan 1983

Bloom Harold   Yeats – Oxford 1970

Bourke Marcus   John O'Leary A Study in Irish Separatism – Anvil 1967

Brown Terence   WB Yeats – Gill & MacMillan 2000

Cousins James & Margaret   We Two Together – Ganesh Madras 1950

Cruise O'Brien Conor   Passion and Cunning – Paladin 1990

Cullingford Elizabeth Butler   Yeats, Ireland and Fascism – MacMillan 1981

Daly Dominic   Young Douglas Hyde – Irish University Press 1973

Foster Roy   WB Yeats, 1. The Apprentice Mage 1865-1914. – Oxford 1997

Freyer Grattan   Yeats and Anti Democratic Tradition – Gill & MacMillan 1981

Gwynn Stephen   Scattering Branches Tributes to the Memory of WB Yeats – MacMillan 1940

Harding Joan   Yeats Sisters – Pandora 2000

Hunt Hugh   The Abbey – Gill & MaMian 1979

Jordan Anthony J.   Major John McBride – Westport 1991

Willie Yeats and the Gonne McBrides – Westport Books 1997

The Yeats Gonne MacBride Triangle – Westport Books 2000

Kiberd Declan   Inventing Ireland – Jonathan Cape 1995

Longford Elizabeth   A Pilgrimage of Passion Life of WS Blunt – Weidendeld 1979

MacBride Maud Gonne   A Servant of the Queen – Gollancz 1938

MacBride White & AN Jeffares   The Gonne Yeats Letters – Pimlico 1993

Marcus Phillip   Yeates and Artistic Power – Syracuse University Press 2001

McCracken Donal   MacBride's Brigade – Four Courts Press 1999

Murphy William   Prodical Father Life of John Butler Yeats – MacMillan 1964

Reid BL   The Man from New York – Oxford 1968

Siubhlaigh Máire Nic   The Splendid Years – Duffy, Dublin 1955

Thwaite Ann   Edmund Gosse A Literary Landscape – Oxford 1985

INDEX

Abbey Theatre: 9, 11-13, 42, 50-4, 68, 72-3, 75, 95, 121-2, 126, 145, 150, 181
Acton Rural Cemetery   31
Adam's Curse   118
Akenson DH   175
Academic Committee of English Letters 19
Adirondacks The   40, 57
'A *Friend's Illness'*   14
Allan Clara   150
Allan Fred   131
Algood Molly   34, 75, 77, 161
Algood Sara   34
America 8, 12, 36, 56, 118, 131, 136,137, 144
American Red Cross   126
An Acre of Grass   47
Anglo-Irish Treaty 112, 153
Anglo-Irish War   126
Aran Islands   70
Argeles   105
Army Comrades Association 172
Arrow The   98
Artistic Vanity   22
Arts & Crafts society   29
Arts Club   43, 158, 170
Asquith Herbert   125
Auden WH   116,119, 120, 124, 174

Balfour Arthur,   19
Balylee   39, 60, 155
Barry Kevin   126
Beautiful Lofty Things 129
Bedford Park   27
Belfast Little   80
Ben Bulben   113
Bertie-Clay May   147
Binyon Laurence   19
Birrell Augustine   21
Bishop of Meath   165
Blake William   30, 47, 48
Black 'n Tans   111, 127, 170
Blake Col.   132
Blenheim Road   25, 98
Blowick Joseph   114
Blueshirts The   173, 174

Bloom Harold   144
Blunt Wilfred Scawen   8, 83
Boer War   85, 102, 120, 131-3
Bohlman Otto   49
Boston Pilot   92
Boulanger Georges   99
Bournville   42
Boyle O'Reilly John   92
Bridges Robert   158
British Museum   115
British Red Cross   126
Broadstone Station   104
Brown Terence 48, 86, 88, 123-5, 165
Bulfin William   66
Burke Edmund   165
Butt Isaac   6

Cadbury   42
Camden St. Theatre   66, 69
Cap Martin   43
Carey Tupper Canon   44
Carnegie Hall   52
Carnegie Lyceum   52
Casadh an tSugain   63
Casement Roger,   58
Castle of Heroes   140
Cathleen ni hUalachain 31, 62, 80, 84-5, 98
Catholic Church   72, 80-82, 84, 86-7, 115, 131, 138, 164, 173
Catholic University of America 53
Celtic Literary Society 93, 131
Censorship of Publications 166
Centenary Committee 92, 96, 132
Chamberlain Joseph   92
Ceylon   12
Chesterton GK   25, 162
Churchill Winston   153, 155
Civil List,   15, 19-24, 124, 161
Civil War,   10   97, 157, 158
Clan na Gael   137
Clarke Kathleen   109
Clarke Tom   109
Clondalkin   26
Closing Rhymes   84, 105
Coates Dorothy   46, 54-6
Cockran Bourke   53, 58
Collins Michael 153, 155-6, 173

Collis John Stewart   127
Mary Colum   149
Colum Padraig   53, 67
Conrad Joseph,   19
Connolly James   100, 115, 123, 126, 151
Contemporary Club   49, 88
Coole Park,   10 13, 16, 18, 390, 42, 141
Corbets   6
Corneille Hotel   70
Cosgrave Liam   175
Cosgrave Patrick   168-9
Cosgrave WT   112, 152, 155-6, 173
Cradle Song   *117*
Cruise O'Brien Conor   90, 125, 148, 166, 168-9, 171, 175
Cruise O'Brien Francis   170
Countess Kathleen   31, 62, 80, 84-5, 98
Court Theatre   14
Cousins James   50, 63, 66, 119
Coxhead Elixabeth   151
Cuala Industries   36-8, 59, 128
Cullingford Elizabeth   124, 140, 148, 169, 171, 175
Cumann na nGael   65-7, 93, 96, 172
Cumann na mBan   153

Daily Mail   151
Daily Telegraph   95
Daly PT   96
Darragh Florence Miss   75
Das H.   154
Davitt Michael   85, 92- 3, 134
Defence of the Realm Act   106, 110
Deirdre   64-5, 143
Desart Countess   158
De Valera Eamon,   7, 10, 114, 153, 155, 170-1
Devon,   30
Devoy John   96, 135, 137
Dial The   125
Dillon Andrew   85
Dillon Myles   85
Divorce Case   95, 102, 146, 148-9
Divorce Speech   164-5
Donegal   99, 126
Donnybrook   39
Donoghue Denis   6, 49, 166

Dowden Edward;
    Row over professorship 37
    Row over poetry   38
Drumcliffe,   6, 45, 113
Dublin   56, 80, 85, 100, 106, 109, 126, 156
Dublin Corporation   151
Dublin University Review   88
Dublin Workers Strike   104
Duffy George Gavan   92
Dun Emer   32-33, 36, 52, 54
Dysalt Chanoine   141

Eadleton Terry   124, 150
Eardley Crescent   26
'Easter 1916'   10, 123-5, 129, 150, 153, 169
Easter Rising   10, 123-5, 129, 150, 153, 170
Egypt   12
Ellis Edwin   47
Ellman Richard   144
Emergency Powers Bill   175
Emmet Robert   165
England   116-7
English Review   104
Enniscrone   25
Erasmus Smith School   4
Everret James   114
Executive Council   157

Farley John Archbishop   52
Farrell Seanin,   12
Fascism   10, 168-177
Fay Frank   63-78
Fay WG   63-78
Fenians   80, 86, 120
Ferguson Samuel Sir   89
Fianna Fail   172
Fine Gael   173
Fisher Unwin   91
Fitzgerald Desmond   126
Fitzwilliam Museum   12
Flat Earth Society   91
Flogging Act   158
Fontenoy   94-5
Foster Jeanne Robert   41, 45, 60-1, 110, 154
Foster Roy   48, 73, 76, 80, 96, 122, 147-8
Four Courts   156
Freeman's Journal   80-1, 120

Freyer Grattan   172
G.A.A.   96, 131
Gael The   92
Gaelic American 96
Galway   109
Gaol Gate   77, 95
Gentile Giovanni   173
George's Villas   6, 7
Glasnevin Cemetery   131
Gleeson Evelyn   31,36
Gillingham Solomon   132
Glasthule   150
Glenavy Baron   158
Glenshesk   131
Godolphin School   8, 25
Gogarty Oliver 41, 61, 84, 111, 125, 158, 162
Golden Dawn   72, 121
Gonne Georges   85, 99, 100, 144
Gonne Iseult   cf. Millevoye
Gonne Kathleen   98, 106, 138, 140, 143
Gonne Maud: praises Gregory's work 16, 17,
    Muse to WBY 16
    Spiritual marriage 18, 102-103,
    Rejects Nietzsche   49-50,
    Advises WBY on Dorothy Coates 55-56,
    Acts in Cathleen ni hUalachain 64,
    Rows with Fays   67,
    Resigns as Vice President of National
    Theatre 67-70,
    Criticises WBY on Playboy Riots 75-76
    Defends conversion to Catholicism 86
    Attitude to O'Leary 94-95
    Meets WBY 98,
    Parisian life 99,
    Meets WBY in Dublin 99,
    Confesses all To WBY 102
    Love letters 103
    Supports Dublin strikers 104
    Moore's relevations 104-105
    Praises Georgie 108,
    Flees to Ireland 108,
    Hollaway Jail 108-109
    Row with WBY at Dublin house 110-111
    Criticised by Lily 111,
    Supports Anglo-Irish Treaty 112
    Inimical to Provisional Government 112
    Old age 113

Chides WBY on Theatre 70-72, 75
Praises his Poetry 16-17, 118
Attitude to Easter Rising   123
Irish Transvaal Committee   133
Meets John MacBride in Paris 135
Joins MacBride on American Tour 136-7
Converts and marries 138- 140
Disastrous marriage 143-145
Birth of Sean MacBride 143
Meets WBY 143
Allegations against husband 145
Reconciliation attempts 145
Divorce Case 143-148
Relies on WBY 146
Verdict disappoints 146-7
Meets WBY in Dublin 149
Continues living in Paris 149
Changed attitude to husband   151
Proposed to again by WBY   150
Excoriates Senator Yeats 158-9
Continues to seek help of WBY 111-2
Gonne Thomas   141
Gosse Edmund   15, 16
Grattan Henry   165
Gregory Augusta Lady;   marriage 12
    Affair with Blunt 12, 14
    Patron of WBY   15
    Writing praised by Gonne   16,17
    Canvasses for Civil Penion for WBY 20
    Row with Gosse   20-21
    Feels betrayed by WBY 21
    Detests Gonne   15
    Affair with Quinn 17, 57
    Tours America with Abbey   57
    Jealous of Horniman 69, 73
    Offended by Fay 77
    Anti Catholic   83
    Encourages WBY to write on
    Easter Rising 123
    Soothes WBY at Coole   141
    Death 10, 42
    Blunts Description 12
    Collaborated with WBY 14, 16
    Illness upsets WBY 19
    Manages Abbey 51, 57
    Angry with WBY 21
    Resents lack of recognition   17

Gregory Robert 13, 16-18, 21, 39, 97
Gregory William 12
Griffith Arthur 53, 62, 81, 85, 120, 126-7
   131-2, 135-6, 140-1, 159-160, 173
Grosvenor Hotel 132
Gurteen Dhas 33-4, 39-40
Gwynn Stephen 88, 90

Hamilton Ian Sir 119, 177
Harold's Cross 119
Harrington Tim 134
Haughey Charlie 175
Headfort Marquis of 158
Heald Misses The 43
Heaney Seamus 174
Heather Field The 62-3
Helen of Troy 151
Henry Augustine 32
Higgins FR 42
Higher Certificate in Education 29
Hitler Adolph 177
Hodgkins Disease 18
Hollaway Joseph 108
Home Office 109
Home Rule 10, 58, 123, 153, 172
Hone Joseph 39
Honeymoon Betrayal 107
Hone Nathaniel 52
Horniman Annie 33, 69, 72, 74, 146, 150-1
   Finances theatre 34
   Bitterness to WBY 51
   Background 121
   Infatuation with WBY refused plays 122
   Arbitration by AC Scott 122
Hour Glass The 65, 69
House of Commons 134, 155
House of Lords 19
Howth 9
Hunger Strike 159
Hyde Douglas 61, 63, 66, 72, 89, 161
Hyde-Lees Georgie: marriage 10, 106
   Honeymoon 107
   Courage 107
   Automatic writing 107
   Buys house in Dublin 154
   Pregnancy 109, 111
   Relationship with Lily & Lollie 39

Reburial of WBY 113
Miscarries 128
Ideal Sejour Hotel 43-44
Infant Death 8
Inghinidhe na hEireann 64-7, 70, 104
In Memory of WB Yeats 120
Irish Academy of Letters 166
Irish Brigade 85, 94, 120, 132-3, 135
Irish Coinage Committee 163
Irish College Paris 137
Irish Examiner Report 167
Irish Fireside 48
Irish Free State 112, 158, 164, 169
Irish Identity 115
Irish Language 163
Irish Independent 95
Irish Literary Society 29, 31, 45, 83, 94
Irish Literary Theatre 62-3, 65, 80
Irish National Alliance 131
Irish National Dramatic Society 64-5
Irish National Theatre Company 78
Irish National Theatre Society 67, 69, 70, 72
Irish Parliamentary Party 96, 134, 153
Irish Race Convention 153
Irish Republican Army (IRA) 170, 172, 175
Irish Republican Brotherhood 131-132
Irish Times 69, 80, 84
Irish Revival 9
Irish Transvaal Society 133
Isle of Man 6
Italy 18, 54

Jacob's Factory 149
James Connolly Pipe Band 113
James Henry 20
Japan 154
Jeffares AN 146, 174
Johannesburg 131
John Augustus 58
John Gwyn 59
Jordan Anthony 167
Joyce James 59

Kavanagh Patrick 84, 115, 117, 129
Kegan Paul 90
Kellner Leon 115-6
Kelly John 81

Kenny PD   51
Kerry Earl of   158
Kiberd Declan   25, 124, 170
Kildare St. Club   174
Kiltartan French   79
Kingstown   110
Kipling Rudyard   19
Kruger President   121

Lagerlof Selma   177
Lake Isle of Innishfree   117
Lane Hugh Sir   36, 54, 59, 83, 104, 106, 125,
Larkin Jim   176
Laval   140
Lecture tours   135-6
Lee Joe   172
Leader The   69
Leinster Literary Society   131
Lenin Peace Prize   143
Library of Ireland   92, 100
Loughrea   32
Logue Cardinal   81-2l
London   7, 19, 94, 105, 117, 121, 143
Longford Elizabeth   9
Loutish Behaviour   21-2, 29, 32-5, 37-8,
    40, 42, 50, 55-6, 66, 73-4, 82, 84-5, 06,
    107, 129, 150, 152, 165, 177
Love Letters   103
Lusitania   59, 106
Lynch Arthur   131

MacBride White Anna   146
MacBride Anthony Dr.   131, 145
MacBride John:
    Family   131
    Member of IRB   131
    Life in Dublin   131
    Visits America   132
    Visits South Africa 132
    Organises Irish Brigade   132
    Mayo bye election 134
    Boer War   132-135
    Meets Gonne in Paris 135
    Tours America with Gonne 135-136
    Advice against marriage 138-139
    Marriage   141
    Birth of son   143

Abandons marriage   144- 145,
Recriminations and divorce case 145-149
Lives in Dublin 149,
Involvement in Easter Rising   150
Admired by Voluntereers &
Mairenic Shiublaigh   150
Traduced by WBY   129, 152

MacBride Joseph   139, 141
MacBride Sean   93, 104,106,110, 114,
    143 147, 158-9
MacDiaramda Sean   149
MacDonagh Thomas   123, 149-150
MacNeice Louis   118, 168
MacKenna Stephen   135, 162
MacLysaght E. Senator   163
MacManus Dermot Cpt.   173-4
MacNeill Eoin   131
Madrid   177
Maloney Helena   108, 110
Manchester   122
Marckievcz Countess   53, 124
Marcus Phillip   88
Martyn Edward   9, 62, 64-5, 79, 83, 94,
    104, 105, 161
Matheson Hilda   43
Mayo   134, 173
McCracken Donal   136
McGinley PT   65
Mechanic's Institute   72
Meditations In Time of Civil War 156
Merrion Sq.   41, 154
Merville   7
Metropolitan School of Art   8, 26
Michigan   136
Middle East   12
Middleton Family 6
Millevoye Iseult (Gonne)   10, 100, 104,
    107, 110-112, 129, 138, 151,159
Millevoye Lucien   99, 100, 102, 106,
    109, 135, 137, 141, 143
Milligan Alice   64, 96
Mitchell Susan   31, 33 79, 104
Monte Carlo   44
Moore George   46, 62, 65, 79, 83, 94,
    104-5, 121
Morris Embroideries   28

195

Morris May   28, 29
Morris William   28, 176
Mountjoy Jail   111, 126
Mussoline Benito 170, 173
Murphy William   147

Nassau Hotel   37, 68
Nation The   115
National Gallery of Art   158
National Guard   173
National Library   158
National Literary Society   62
National Museum   158
National Theatre Company   54, 66-7, 71
National Theatre Society   13, 3-4, 122
Nazis   10, 177
Neruda Pablo 176
Nevinson Henry   102, 138
New *Statesman* 125
New York, 10, 35-7, 40, 46, 52, 59, 60, 136
New York Daily Tribune 72
Nice   44
Nietzsche Friedrich 10, 46,48-50, 58
Nobel Literature Prize 7, 10, 41, 161
Nobel Peace Prize 143
Nobel Speech 82, 161
No Second Troy   143
Normandy   106, 119
Nineteen sixteen Widows Association 108

O'Brien Dermod   43-4
O'Brien Mabel   43-4
O'Brien Richard Barry 31-2, 83, 92, 94, 145
O'Casey Sean   176
O'Connor Frank   43
O'Connor James   96
Ode   48
O'Dempsey Brigit 75, 78
O'Donnell Cardinal   165
O'Donnell Frank Hugh 62, 81
O'Donnell Peadar   162
O'Duffy Eoin   173
O'Grady Standish   53, 89, 129
O'Hanlon John   96
O'Higgins Kevin 112, 152, 157, 162, 166, 17-3
Ohio   46
Oireachtas   119. 157

Old Age   112
Oldham Charles   8
O'Leary Ellen   88, 91, 98
O'Leary John: 26, 28, 80, 85, 88-97, 115
                117, 135, 145, 176
O'Mordha Sean   175
O'Neill Maire   161
On the Boiler   177
Ormonde Dukes of   80
Ormonde Dramatic Company   63, 65
Orwell George   168
O'Shaughnessy Arthur   48
O'Sullivan Donal 165
Oxford   117, 125
Oxford Book of Modern Verse   84
Oxford Union Speech   127
Owen Aherne and his Dancers 107

Palestrina Choir   84
Parnell   100, 131
Parnell Split   134
Paris 55, 85, 135-7, 144, 146
Parry Margaret   13
Paymaster's Office   23
Payne Ben   76, 122
Pearse Patrick 58, 115, 123, 126, 157
Persse Family   12
Playboy of the Western World The 11, 51,
                53, 57, 75, 96, 122
Philadelphia   57
Poets Rising   171
Pollexfen curse   37
Pollexfen George 6
Pollexfen Susan   6
Pollexfen William 6
Pound Ezra   38-9, 59-60, 106-7, 110
Praetoria   132
Proselytisers   10, 83
Protestants   9, 80, 82, 164
Pot of Broth   54
Prayer for my Daughter   11, 151
Providence Sunday Journal   92
Provisional Government 153, 155
Punch   120
Purser Louis   28, 30-1, 34, 39, 42
Purser Sarah   26, 28, 32

Queen's Shilling   20
Queen's University 157
Quarrel in Old Age 112
Quinn John: 9, 16, 29-30, 34-6, 40, 42, 46,
    52, 54-9, 65, 79, 107, 129, 154, 158
    Admires Lollie & Lily 35
    news of death of John Yeats 40, 60
    Death 12
    Visits Ireland 46, 52-3
    promotes WBY 53
    row with WBY 55-6
    affair with Gregory 57

Rathfarnham 173
Reading Committee 68, 70, 73
Reconciliation   102
Red Cross 110, 126
Redmond John   58
Reitz State Sec. 135
Rhys Ernest   115
Rhys Grace   115
Riders to the Sea 70, 76
Rising of 1798 131
Riversdale   113
Robinson Lennox 170
Rolleston TW   88
Rooney William   131, 136, 159
Roosvelt Theodore 53-4
Roquebrune   44, 113
Rose Tree The, 10, 126, 153
Rothenstein William Sir 123
Royal Dublin Society   42
Royal Hospital Kilmainham 162
Royal Irish Academy   163
Roxborough 8
Russell George 8, 35-6, 62-4, 66, 70, 72-4,
    79-80, 104, 145
    Family friend   34
    Bitter at WBY   51
    Meets Fays via Cousins 63
    Honest broker   67
    Defers to WBY   68
    Rows with WBY 73
    Criticises WBY   74
    Mocks WBY 80
Ryan Fred   65, 68
Ryan Mark 92, 131, 135

Sandymount   6, 39
Sandymount Castle 6
Sandymount School Commemoration 167
Saint The   126
Saor Eire   162
Saranac   57
Savoy   47
Saxon Shilling The 67, 69
Scott CP   122
Scottish Tour   74
'Secret Memories' 8
Sectarianism   10, 86
Senate The 10, 61, 86, 157, 159, 162, 169
Shadow of the Glen In 70
Shakespeare Olivia 30, 159, 173-4, 177
Shaw Bernard 109, 166
Sheehy Skeffington Francis   81
Sheehy Skeffington Hanna   172
Shelley Percy Bysshe   8, 161
Sherman John 8
Shiubhlaigh Maire nic   33-34, 36, 50,
    74, 79, 150
Short Edward   109-110
Shorthall Barry   148
Sigerson George 88, 100
Sinn Fein 79, 84, 108, 126, 153
'Sixteen Dead Men' 126, 153
Skene Roy   140
Sligo   6, 31, 80, 113, 117
Smylie Bertie   161
Sold   69
Souls for Gold   81
South Africa   131
Southampton   106
Spanish Republic 177
Spiritual Marriage 86, 149
Stuart Francis   111, 113, 141
St. Malachy's College   131
St. Nahi's Church   45
St. Patrick's Cathedral 113
St. Stephen's Green   108, 150
St. Teresa's Hall   64
Synge JM 9, 34, 36, 49, 51, 69, 76, 122, 161

Taylor John F.   88, 100
Tetuan Duke of 153
Terenure   8, 26, 88

Theatre of Ireland 35, 74
Thomastown 80, 98
Thoor Ballylee 39, 125
Times The 126
Trinity College 6, 157, 163
Tulira Castle 14
Tynan Katherine 8, 26-7, 35, 48, 89-90

Urbino 18, 97,175
Unionism 10
United Irishman 12, 62, 69, 80,
            132, 135, 137, 159

Vegetarian The 28
Vanderbilt Hotel 135
Victoria Queen 93, 100, 120
Vision A 107, 144, 168

Wanderings of Oisin 90
Ward Margaret 151
Warren County 41
War of Independence 111, 125
Wellesley Lady 43
Westminister Abbey 120
Westchester 41, 46
Westport 104, 129, 140, 144, 146
Where there is Nothing 46
White Birds The 99
White Cockade 11
White Cottenham Mary 30
White Cross 126
Wicklow Earl of 158
Wilde Oscar 90
Wilson Eileen 145
Woburn Buildings 17, 30, 108-110, 143
Women's Education 28
Women's Political Defence League 159
Women's Role 159
World War One 105, 124
Wyndham George 9
Wyse Power Jenny 148, 164

Yeats Anne 39, 42,44
Yeats Elizabeth "Lolly"
    Constant rows with WBY 25-4
    Ambitious 26
    Home maker 27

Metropolitan School of Art 26
Early poverty 26
Meets K. Tynan 26
"The Pleiades" 26
Painter 26
Writer 28
Teacher 28
Mother's illness 31
Family accountant 28
Hopes of marrying Louis Purser 31, 34
Dislike of Gonne and Gregory 31
Offered secretaryship
    of Irish Literary Society 32
Studies printing 32
Returns to Dublin 32
Dun Emer Industries 33
Row with Gleeson 33
Criticises WBY 34-35
Wooed by J. Quinn 35
Rows over Cuala business 35-38, 42, 43
Likes Georgie Hyde Lees 39
Praised by Frank O'Connor 43
Death 45
Yeats Jack 8, 25, 27, 29, 39, 31, 33, 46, 154
Yeats Jane 25
Yeats John Butler 6, 8
    Meets George Pollexfen 6
    Marries 7
    Moves family to London 8
    Anti-religious 6
    Bohemian lifestyle 7
    Cultivates WBY 7
    Anti Pollexfen 25
    loutish behaviour 26, 36
    Refuses to return home 10, 26
    Dublin exhibition 32
    Artistic integrity 55
    Letters published 59
    Death 60
    Daughters maligned 40
    Accident 58
    Kept by Quinn 60
    Death in America 40, 60
Yeats Lady 14
Yeats Michael 49, 44, 61, 153
Yeats Robert 7, 25
Yeats Susan 6, 7, 25, 27

198

Yeats Susan "Lily" childhood 25
   Friendship with WBY   25
   Metropolitan School of Art 26
   Meets K. Tynan 26
   Illnesses   31
   Works at Morris Embroideries 28-29
   Mother's illness 31
   Dislikes Gonne and Gregory 31
   Returns to Dublin 32
   Dun Emer Industries 33
   Row with E. Gleeson 33
   Wooed by J. Quinn   35
   Father refuses to return from America 36
   Friendship with JM Synge   37
   Comforts WBY on death of Synge 37
   Dislikes Lollie   41-42
   Confidant of WBY 38, 44-45
   Corresponds with Mrs Foster 41
   Critical of Maud Gonne, Iseult and Sean 111
   Death,   45
Yeats William Butler;
   Childhood   25
   Coole Park   15
   Authorial primacy 46
   First tour of America 53
   Civil Pension   20-24
   Family dynamics   25
   Poverty   19
   Leaves home 30
   Mother's death 31
   Hostile to Lollie 25-45
   Loutish behaviour 21-2, 29, 33-42
   50, 55-6, 66, 73-4, 82, 84-5, 90, 96
   107, 129, 152, 165, 177
   Synge's death   37
   Rows over Cuala 35-38
   Poetic influences, 46-48
   Nietzsche,   46, 48-49
   Gonne, Horniman, John Yeats reject
   Nietzsche 49-50
   Playboy Riots   51, 75
   Rows with Quinn over Coates 55-57
   Makes up with Quinn 58
   Sells manuscripts to Quinn 58
   Collaborates with Fays 65
   Rows with Nationalists 69
   Uses Annie Horniman   72-76

   First season at Abbey   73
   Marginalizes Fays 74-78
   Takes over Abbey   73
   Countess Cathleen row 80-83
   Criticises Irish Catholics 82
   Rows with Moore 83-84
   Car from Gogarty 84-85
   Oxford Book of Modern Verse 84
   Meets O'Leary 88
   Assisted by O'Leary 88-92
   Distraught at Gonne's
   conversion & marriage 102, 139-140
   Refuses to attend O'Leary's funeral
   96 Spiritual marriage 102-103
   Proposes to Maud and Iseult 106
   Marries 106
   Automatic writing 107
   Assists Gonne in Hollaway Jail 108-110
   Rows with Gonne in Dublin   110
   Birth of daughter 111
   Supports Iseult   111
   Supports Sean MacBride 112
   Death   113, 144-145
   Burial at Drumcliffe   114
   Description of in 1899   116
   Writing poetry   26, 119, 162
   Criticism by Auden 119-120
   Objects to Queen Victoria's visit 121
   Refuses to give plays to Horniman 76
   Reaction to 1916 Rising 123-126
   Oxford Union speech   127
   Meets Gonne after her marriage 141, 143
   Assists Gonne in divorce case   146
   Hatred of John MacBride 112, 129
   Returns to Ireland   125, 153
   Receives Honours 157
   Made Senator   58
   Supports Government 158
   Griffith Settlement Bill 159-160
   Nobel Prize   161-162
   Subsidy for Abbey   162
   Speeches in Senate   162-165
   Irish Academy of Letters   166
   Fascism ; Criticised by Orwell,
   McNeice, Cruise O'Brien,
   Defended by Cosgrave, Cullingford.
       168-177

Yeats William Butler:
  Assists Blueshirts   173-174
  Outrageous views in "*On the Boiler*" 177
  Voice like Hitler's   177
  Patriotism 76, 121, 127, 158, 162-165
  Elitist   73, 86
  Life's work clear   115-117
  Disillusioned with State 166
Ye Pleiades   26
Young Ella   65, 145
Young Ireland Society 8, 62, 95, 131